Live well —

In Vino Veritas

WINE FOR INTELLECTUALS

Other works by John J. Mahoney

The Year

Summer Tides & Cinnamon Thyme

Symphony of Seasons

Wine of the Muse

Every Bottle has a Story

Mystic Isle

WINE FOR INTELLECTUALS

A Coarse Guide into the World of Wine for Intelligent People

JOHN J. MAHONEY

DUBLIN NEW YORK MILMAY

John J. Mahoney can be reached through e-mail at j.mahoney@juno.com

ISBN: 978-153944673-6

3 5 7 9 8 6 4 2

To fellow wine drinkers who endlessly continue to learn and to future wine drinkers like Cameron A. Mahoney and Liam M. Ortiz who will, I hope, learn about civilization through a knowledge of wine. Everything in moderation.

CONTENTS

ACKNOWLEDGMENTS

This *Coarse Guide* into an intellectual's study of wine is possible because of all the people who have shared their wines and their wine knowledge with me over the past four decades. Only by sharing both wine and knowledge, are we able to teach or learn anything about either of them. Even those people who have shared wines with me, and I've somehow neglected to record them, should consider this work an extension of themselves. I've learned from scholars, the misfortunate, saints, and sinners; remember, we are all a product of everything we've ever seen, heard, smelled, tasted or touched.

Jacqueline Apgar, Frank and Elizabeth Aquilino, Joe Ardito, JB Borreggine, Sharon Byrne, Carl Brandhorst, Sherman Bruchansky, Joe Broski who never misses a chance to study wine, Frank Calderaro, Vince Casbarro, Robert Casella, Tom Castronovo, Tula Christopoulos, Joe Courter, Andrea Daniel, Robin Daplyn, Frank DeCicco, David DeMeo, Jack Egan, Bill Fennen, Anthony and Arlene Fisher, Marc Franken, Tom Galbiati, John Gartland, Richard Gerber, Cosmo Giovinazzi, Donald Graham, Karen Goetz, Marion and Henry Gorelick, Glenn Gorman, Jerry Gorman, Mike Grass, Jim Hemesath, Alan Hess, Mark and Marianne Imbesi, Joe Ingemi, a long time Dionysian, Barbara Johnston-Yellowlees, Maynard Johnston who has Sabered more bottles of Champagne than anyone, Sharyn Kervyn and her husband Emmanuel who know and love every aspect of wine.

Author and grape-grower Barry Lawrence, Murk Lels, Joe Lertch who loves being a wine educator, Larry and Sharon Levine, Diana Liberto, Susan Luckan, Alana Coburn-Medeiros and Dannie Medeiros, Peter Mariotti, Sharron McCarthy of *Banfi*, who is one of the world's great wine educators, Shelia McHenry, Mary Millar, Arthur Miller, Greg Mills, Janet Mitrocsak, Valerie Mollick, Anthony Monfredo, and Tad Naprava who never stops learning.

Al Natali, winemaker and scholar, Carolyn and Jay Nemia, Roger and Semerita Oliva, Gary Pavlis, one of the world's top educators of wine and blueberries, Gary Pulz, Winemaker Jim Quarella and his wife Nancy, Bob and Diane Rone, Patrick and Jane Ruster, Walt Salvadore who ties wine to culture, Armand Savino, Frank Scarpa, Mike Schaefer, Chuck Schaffer, Barbara Latina and Michael Segarra, Christine Skandis, Pete Steenland, Zebulon Smith, Charlie and Jack Tomasello, Adrienne and Bob Turner whose lives are filled with sharing wine, George Ushkowitz, Anne Vercelli who pairs wine and food like no one else, Bob and Cynthia Walker, Frank Wander, Vince and Susie Winterling who appreciate everything, Ben Yang, Nick Yankanich, and every Dionysian who never stops learning and sharing their wine knowledge.

Others who have contributed to my appreciation and thinking about wine are, Austin Hudson, Kym Antonelli, Owen Altbaum, Bill and Gail Boyan, Peter Benziger and Doug Jones who both love to discuss wine, Jason Banks, Barbara Headley, Russell Baruffi, Ruth Ann Bishop-Sotak, and of course, Ed Blake and his wife, who love to share wines, Alain Blachon an expert on Bordeaux, Lena Brattsten, Bob Bucknam, Mark and Lisa Cantrell, Nick and Linda Cashan, Paula Cella, Mark Ciotoli, Delmo Cifaloglio, Clemence Lelarge-Pugeot of the eponymous Champagne House, Dean and Dom Cordivari, Chris Creasey of the Las Vegas AWS, wine experts Dave and Michael Craig from Cape May, Adriana DaSilva, Ron Dandrea, Steve Dandrea, Peter Dandrea and Frank Dandrea, all of *Vinedrea Wines*. Joe Dautlick, David DiCaprio, Fran Docherty, Mark Ehienfeldt, Monika Elling, Cecilia Enriquez and her father Dr. Edward Enriquez. Andy Fruzzetti, Joseph A. Fiola, Willie Glückstern wine consultant and author, Carmen Genaro, Lenny Gagliardi and Gino, Tom Gildea, John Hames, and Mario Plazio, Italy's finest wine taster, and Keith Bader who shares, sells and teaches about wine.

Rick Hardin who has similar tastes, Steve Hendricks, Michael Huber, Mike and Sofia Hayner future Dionysians, Anne Izzillo, Danny Klein, Kristin Colasurdo-Keating and her father Rocky Colasurdo, Bill & Harriet Lembeck, Michael Matilla with whom I've traveled and learned so much, Biliana Marinova, Corinna McNally, Vince Minutillo, Jack Morey, Sam Niglio another food expert, Antoinette, Archie and Diane Mazzoli, Tom Moleski a wine glass expert, Michael Antolini, Jennifer Negro, Marsha Palanci, Chris Pells, Paul Tonacci, Robert Polillo, and with no hesitation at all, Lorraine Raguseo, who loves to share her wine knowledge. Also, Rob Lawson, Bob and Therese Maher, Tony Russo & Andrea Kish from decades ago, Paul Sandler of the Palm, Coach Paul Rodio, Larry Sharrott, Jeff & Karen Seibert, Jim Sorebo, Steve Piccirillo, Paul and Fran Rixon, George M. Taber who recorded wine history, Peter Tampellini, Tim Ensmenger, Lizanne Tracy, and Paul Wagner who always ties wine to the culture surrounding it. Lisa Weidlich, Khadija Woods, Ed Wolkowicz, Dawn Yorke, and David Zappariello; they're all wine lovers; all civilized intelligent people.

Also, to everyone else who has added to my wine knowledge, be it volumes of data, or just a small wine reference that was new and interesting. Thank you. Also, to Joanne, Sean and Erin Mahoney, wife, son and daughter, who have never failed to let me study, explore, or talk about wine, and a "special thank you" to June Kim, who married Sean, and Jeff Ortiz, Erin's husband; both have joined in on the adventures of my many wine endeavors.

Any intellectual who wants to expand their appreciation of the finer things in life will, of course, start and continue on that quest by learning, and understanding, all they can about wine. It is the symbol of all the civilized arts. *In vino veritas.*

INTRODUCTION

Let's taste some wine!

There are books and programs designed to be helpful that openly insult you. If you're really bromidic, you won't learn anything no matter how many books you review. If you're not totally inept, wouldn't you rather be seen, while reading on the beach, during a lunch break, or sitting on the subway or a bus, with something in your hands directed toward *Intellectuals,* instead of something for the dull vapid clusters of humanity? You will attract brighter, more interesting and better-looking strangers of both sexes when people see you reading a book with this title. They may start conversations and you'll make new friends who, like you, want to better themselves and enjoy more in life. The journey starts with some basic, but key wine knowledge. One of my favorite writers Thoreau said, "Simplify," so I deleted nearly as many pages as this final draft contains. I kept only the specifics that bright people want, not loads of general information.

Wine is food; it's the liquid part of every meal, and its history runs parallel to that of the growth of civilization. This *Guide* is called "coarse" because it is simplistic, *rough,* and easy to follow, but designed to increase your appreciation of wine on a higher intellectual level. That will, in turn, open the doors to art, music, literature, history, geography, psychology, and in general, a deeper intellectual self-review on how to better enjoy life as you journey through it. It's not a picture book, nor an Atlas; no index, it's meant to be an enjoyable read. Chapter Fourteen is best read in the bathroom, or before going to sleep while resting in your bed. Other parts should be read in public. When people ask what you're reading, and they will, tell them it's up for discussion at your next Mensa meeting.

Ideally, this book will open some doors into further studies of wine covering more specific locations, and a deeper analysis of how wine is made. It may also lead you into archeological and historical studies about the cultures that preceded us, and left us so much to build upon, places where wine was held in very high esteem.

Geography seems to be defunct in our American education systems, but it is absolutely necessary for a deeper level of wine appreciation. Start looking at maps, as Chapter Five will suggest.

Your self-confidence will increase by simply carrying this *Coarse Guide*. Hopefully, you'll find it easy to read, help you recall what's really important in the world of wine, and lastly, give you a source where you can borrow from to exhibit the necessary skills used in the wine and food trades. Remember what the old lady told the judge when she was arrested for shoplifting; "Yes, your honor, I do steal, but only from the very best stores."

Lastly, as you acquire more knowledge about viticulture and oenology, and are able to better pair wines and foods, your friends will expect you to take the lead with regards to selecting wines in restaurants, opening and serving wines at parties, and even to make suggestions about what wines to add to their cellars. After this happens, never forget what Michael Broadbent, a wine scholar, once said: "The aristocrat of the table, the nature's gentleman of the cellar, the true *amateur*, the deeply knowledgeable, is rarely, if ever, a wine snob." Put no one down regarding their wine opinions, just help to raise them up and use the following information to do so.

WHERE TO BEGIN
Necessary fundamentals

Learning to enjoy wine means following simple, basic techniques designed to focus the senses. It's best to experience at least two different wines simultaneously. It is easier to quickly note the differences, see variations in color, and smell different aromas. All wine-lovers use the Five–S Technique to target these differences. The top fifty percent of the world's wine drinkers call this *"The Five-S's"* technique. They all use it. So you're already among the top 50% of the world's wine drinkers as soon as you repeat these steps, and begin a better understanding and enjoyment of wine.

Sight: checking for clarity and the many different shades of each wine's color. You can guess the age of a wine by its color.

Swirling: spinning the wine in the glass to expose it to more oxygen and to help lift the aromas above the liquid so you can more easily smell them.

Smell: relearning to use our most powerful sense. We can differentiate over 12,000 different aromas, but only taste four basic concepts. (Sweet, sour, salt and bitter) I know, some say that umami is a fifth taste; it's a combination of salt and sour.

Sip: learning to take a small amount of wine into your mouth, move it all around your palate and suck some air through it; the aromas will go up the back of your nose. The front tip of your tongue will tell if it's sweet or dry. (The term, *dry*, with regards to alcoholic beverages, means *not sweet*.) It does *not* mean "without moisture."

Spit or **swallow**: Either way, you can **savor** the wine. Both work just as well to assess the mouth feel; is it light or heavy? After you spit, you measure the length of time that the fruit lasts before it dries out, and sometimes turns bitter highlighting only the tannic acids. That time-period is what we call the *aftertaste*. You swallow with meals, and spit at wine tastings to stay sober and rational, and be able to experience many more examples of interesting wines. The **5-S's**: without learning this, you will never learn much more about the world of wine, so practice these steps with every wine you taste no matter where you are.

Remember, there are no taste buds past the back of your tongue, so by swallowing, all you do is add alcohol to your blood stream and decrease your ability to properly judge the quality and value of the wine. If you've been to a really big tasting, one with dozens or even hundreds of wines, swallowing will prevent you from remembering anything you might have learned, and it will also make the drive home a dangerous adventure, more precarious to your health than the alcohol consumed.

Note: This is a good time to point out that the sickly-hangover-feeling people experience after a full night of drinking is basically dehydration. Swallow the wine only if you're enjoying it with a meal. Food in your stomach will slow down the rate of the alcohol's absorption into the blood stream, but mostly, drink some water with each glass of wine to avoid the dehydration caused by the alcohol. When you fully understand that wine is indeed food, and that it's the liquid part of a meal, you'll know to drink water when you're thirsty, not a mouthful of wine. The gift of Dionysus is used to cleanse your palate, and to help enhance the flavor of the food. Of course it works both ways; certain foods will completely change some wines.

Lastly, ideal "food wines" are lower in alcohol than most made in the modern western style of big jammy high alcohol wines. These wines taste good enough, but they do nothing to enhance food. Use them for party sipping where the food doesn't really matter, and when you have someone to drive you home. If you host a party like this, be sure to offer lots of water to your guests and explain why they should drink lots of water to avoid feeling hungover the next day!

If you've read this far without some wine to drink, you're missing the point. Call two friends. Ask one to bring a Pinot Grigio, another to bring a Chardonnay, and you open a bottle of Pinot Noir. Have three glasses for each person. Open and pour about two ounces of each wine so you have all three samples in front of you and your friends. You always remember more when you talk about what you're trying to learn, so tell your friends you're practicing,

"The Forty-Five Minute Wine Expert." It's demonstrated and covered more in Chapter Two.

Look at the color of each wine. Discuss which has more depth of color. Then, swirl and smell each wine. The Chardonnay has more depth of color than the Pinot Grigio and also a bigger aroma. The Pinot Noir has the most color, and also the most fruit aromas. Taste all three from the Pinot Grigio, then the Chardonnay, and lastly, the Pinot Noir. The last wine should wash away all the flavors from the second wine as the second wine did to the first wine.

The top 30% of the world's wine drinkers understand that more shades and depth of color tell you that there will be a bigger aroma, and the stronger the aroma, the more flavor you can expect from its taste. You can now make predictions about any wine you drink by ranking it among all the past wines you've tried.

You, and your friends, should leave this simple tasting experiment feeling a greater intellectual awareness about the qualities of different wines. After all, this is a *Wine Study for Smart People*. If you noticed the increasing development of aroma and taste, you belong in at least the top 40 percent, or even the higher top 30 percent of the world's wine drinkers. Lastly, if you remembered the 5-S's final instruction, and spit each sample while doing this experiment, you stayed fresh and alert while learning. Then you can finish (swallow) a little wine with your friends as you discuss the vinous epiphany you just had.

Pedagogical studies of "how" something works are far easier than philosophical reviews of "why" things happen, and especially difficult when contemplating the "what" that is experienced when we debate the impression of the senses. (Borrow and use this sentence with your wine-snobby friends)

Learning to love wine demands the ability to analyze your own assessment of the impressions your senses make upon you. As you learn more about wine, you will learn more about yourself. It's a Zen-like journey, but filled with fun and adventure. You'll soon want to collect some wines to have quickly available to share with friends. Get or build some wine racks; block off part of a closet, or build a small wine cellar to allow a few of your better wines time to mature.

You should visit a few local wineries, taste a barrel sample, and absorb and try to remember the aroma of the barrel room. Then, plan a vacation to wine country, any wine region, the Outer Coastal Plain of New Jersey, or maybe Mendocino or Sonoma counties in California, the Bordeaux region of France, or Rioja in Spain. New York's Finger Lakes, Long Island, or any of the Virginia wine regions will do. Since all 50 states now produce some wine, you can, at least, make a Saturday driving tour to a few of the closest wineries near your home. From that point on, there's no going back. Family vacations will soon involve touring wine districts in Tuscany, Napa or Burgundy. Enjoy. Learn. Your life will never be the same.

WINE FOR INTELLECTUALS

1 BASICS
What it is & how it's made

Gallop polls have recently shown that wine, not beer nor cocktails, has become the primary beverage of choice for most Americans. This is a drastic change from the "moonshine" 1920s, or the "beer chugging" 1970s, or even the "martini craze" of the 1990s that ran well into the early 2000s. Wine is food. As people have learned that wine has superior health benefits, tastes good and complements nearly every type of food, they have begun drinking more wine with meals, as well as in other social situations.

According to a recent Beverage Media article, it seems that the largest group of wine drinkers, the 51 to 70 year-olds, or Baby Boomers, has dropped to second place behind the Millennials, age 21 to 39 when talking about "occasional" wine drinking. However, the Baby Boomers still consume and enjoy wine the most as the group who savors wine at least once a week by 38% to just 30% for the Millennials. Of course this will quickly change as younger wine drinkers learn more about wine, and share it more often by adding it to their educated life-style activities.

Wine consumption, I am certain, will continue to expand throughout this decade and well into the next one. There will be more wine snobs, but even more basic wine lovers. You can easily be among the world's top ten per cent of knowledgeable wine drinkers who have learned to increase their dining pleasure because of wine, and even increase your own hedonistic pleasure by coarsely becoming aware of a few basic concepts about this most ancient and revered liquid food.

Most people who are just starting to enjoy this *beverage of the gods*, are intimidated by all the pomp and circumstance associated with wine. Great sommeliers help you match wine and food together without being insulting or intimidating. The rituals, opening a bottle, deciphering a wine label and even the simple act of pouring wine into a glass can be frustrating. However, if you learn to ignore most of the superficial antics of some poorly trained professional sommeliers, you can quickly find yourself among the most knowledgeable and highly respected appreciators of wine.

Let's roughly review how it all starts.

All alcohol is made when yeasts eat sugar and give off carbon dioxide and alcohol. The CO_2 goes into the air, unless you're making *sparkling wines* like Champagne, German Sket, Italian Spumante or Spanish CAVA. In those examples, the bottle is capped to keep the CO_2 in the wine. However, there are cheaper ways to make sparkling wines. You can simply inject CO_2 into the juice just like they do to make soft drinks. Or, make it in a large sealed tank, and then transfer it into the thicker sparkling wine bottles. *Still-wines* are what you call wines without bubbles. All table wine should be still wines.

The yeasts will keep eating the sugar and turning it into alcohol until the higher alcohol kills them, or they run out of sugar and die.

If they convert all the sugar into alcohol, you're left with a dry wine; if not, the wine will be slightly sweet. In the world of wine, the antonym for "dry" is not *wet*, it's "sweet." Over the years, yeasts living in individual vineyards will develop special characteristics unique to those vineyards. They can easily be used to ferment grape juice into wine. However, all yeast exhibit special characteristics so a winemaker might want to kill off the local indigenous yeast with sulfur, and then add selected yeast from elsewhere hoping to add a special aroma or flavor to his or her wine.

Simply then, grapes are crushed; the clear juice is kept away from the skins for white wines, and then permitted to ferment. For red wines, the juice and skins are mixed together so the juice can absorb the color from the skins. Tannins are also absorbed giving the red wine a necessary acid needed to help the wine age.

Another method for reds is called "Carbonic Maceration." With this process, the grapes are put into a tank without being crushed and then the grapes are covered with carbon dioxide. Fermentation takes place inside each grape where color is extracted, but not much tannin. It's sometimes called, "Whole Berry Fermentation," and this process makes wines that are light, fruity and meant to be drunk very quickly like *Beaujolais Nouveau*.

Wine Developed As Civilization Developed

Many wine books still say that wine was first made just 4,000 years ago, but contemporary research shows that wine making has been around for twice as long. Humans made wine around the Black Sea about 8,000 years ago in the Caucasus Mountains and near the Black Sea. The climate and soils were ideal for grape growing in Georgia where about 500 indigenous varieties of grapes still thrive. Ancient *Qvevri* techniques of winemaking still linger in the Georgian wine districts where grapes like *Chinuri, Rkatsiteli, Mtsvane, Kisi, Tsolikouri* and *Tsitska* still make unique white wines. Georgian red wines were, and are still, made from grapes like the *Ojaleshi, Mujuretuli, Aleksandrouli, Shavkapito, Tavkveri* and *Saperavi*. For you students, there are no test questions on any of these grapes. Read on.

Historians say that Egypt procured its first wines and vines from Assyria or maybe Canaan. Well before that, as mankind changed from being nomads into a rural farm culture, and formed early clusters of tiny cities, the first pottery was made, most likely around the Caspian Sea. Clay jars called *kwevri,* dated to nearly 6,000 BC, have been found with grape residue in them in what's now Georgia. It may well have been the Persians who spread grapes and wine around their known world more recently, but late Stone Age men seem to have stumbled onto wine. This discovery, I think, may possibly have been the cause of an ever-faster rate of civilization developing, and not long after the last Ice Age, mankind began its love affair with the fruit of the vine.

China was quite advanced during the Bronze Age. However, even though they made some wine, no *Vitis vinifera* grapes grew there so they never achieved any high quality examples. It's well known that they received this quality species in 128 BC when a Chinese expedition took the seeds they found in Persia, back to China.

Still, the very early winemaking areas extended from south of Russia to just north of Turkey. Georgia today, using mostly modern French winemaking methods, is the area considered one of a few places where early humans began making wine. Only an intellectual wine lover would be interested in knowing this type of wine data. Knowing just this limited history of wine puts you in the top half of all the world's wine drinkers. Now, let's contemplate grape types, vineyard development, harvesting, and making wine.

As the winemaking got better, so did the societies that consumed it. For centuries, people have known that wine is food; it's the liquid part of a meal.

We'll discuss vineyard location in more detail in Chapter 10, so aside from where we grow our grapes, we next have to choose what yeast to use, in what type of containers we'll make and store it, and decide if we should blend different grapes together hoping that the end product will be greater than the sum of its parts, or make a 100% varietal. Then we decide what style to make, and what to ship it in, and lastly, how long to age it before we release it to be consumed.

Grape Species

The best species of grapes for making wine is *Vitis vinifera*. Chardonnay, Cabernet Sauvignon, and Merlot are well known examples. *Vitis labrusca* include the Native American grapes that evolved separately over the pre-explored centuries. Catawba, Niagara and Concord dominate this collection along with Delaware, Isabella and Dutchess. They were grapes that Thomas Jefferson first used to make wine, but found that they all tasted "foxy" having an animal musk scent. They all have the smell from the *labrusca* ester. Concord is great for jam but offers little in the way of quality wines. Because these native grapes had adapted to local soils and weather, they became the basis for another category of wine grapes, the French-American Hybrids. Crossing the two species gave a grape vine that has some of the *vinifera* fruit and taste flavors with a plant that could withstand freezing temperatures and different rain patterns. Chancellor, Seyval Blanc, Vignoles and Chambourcin are well known examples of these type of wine grapes. Even though they produce a lesser quality wine, they are easier to grow, so many Eastern American states started out with these grapes for making their wines.

The late Dr. Konstantin Frank, who started Vinifera Wine Cellars in New York, proved to most Americans that, when treated properly, *vinifera*-based wines where what the world liked best and could be grown in states other than California. Frank grafted the European vines onto American rootstocks at the start of the 1950's and was successful with Johannisberg Riesling, Chardonnay, Gewurztraminer, and the Rkatsiteli from his native Russia. He found it also worked for Pinot Noir. Today, the entire East Coast makes their best wines from either French Hybrids, or the classic *Vitis vinifera* grapes.

Stolen Names of Wines

Nearly everything we do regarding wine growing, production and drinking today is based on what was copied from Germany and France. Even our early "jug" wines were named for French or German wine areas. Rhine and Burgundy are two easy examples. The Old World had centuries to experiment with different varieties and locations to determine what grew best in each location. Europeans named their wines by telling where they came from. Bordeaux is a blend of up to six possible grapes, but it simply says "Bordeaux" on the label. The same goes for Burgundy, Rhine, Mosel, etc., while we in the New World called our wines by the name of the grape that made them like Chardonnay or Riesling instead of Burgundy or Mosel. This started before today's "blends" became so popular, and blends are simply a winemaking strategy to copy an Old World style of wine. Blending helps to balance a wine's aroma and taste.

Viticulture

Ideally, each type of grape grows best in a soil to which it's suited, i.e., the correct pH, sandy, gravel, or clay, the direction of the sunlight, and the possible total hours of sunlight each vine can get so the right grape planted in the right place can make the best possible wine. For example, Chardonnay grows better over limestone than it does over granite. Wind speeds, winter temperature and average rainfall must all be considered before planting a vineyard. Heavy, dark rich soils promote veggie flavors while lean less fertile soils promote fruity flavors. If the canopy of the vines is dense and thick, you get grassy flavors. If it's pruned and open to the sun more, you get fruity-flowery notes. Too much fruit results in watery thin wines. When vineyard production is limited, by cutting off extra grape clusters, called a "green harvest," to one or one and a half tons of grapes per acre, the resulting wines have deeper, darker concentration of flavors. Pinot Grigio used to have beautiful lime and mineral flavors when it came from vineyards producing at two to three tons per acre, but as it became more and more popular, and producers needed more juice, they let the vineyards explode to five, six, even seven or more tons per acre resulting is a thin watery wine with a slight hint of lemon.

Remember, if you raise just two children, you may be able to send them both to the Ivy League, or if just one child, possibly the University of Chicago, but with seven children, you'll be stressed to get them all through the local community college. It's the same with the mother vine; she can only properly develop a limited number of grape clusters with Ivy League, or top-shelf potential.

For decades, growers were paid for the volume of grapes they produced. They were paid by the tonnage. Most of today's better wineries pay their growers prices set according to the final *brix* (sugar count), acidity levels, and especially the ripeness of the tannins in a specific limited tonnage.

Quality grapes are achieved by performing a "green harvest" which means cutting off or dropping some green grape clusters before they change into their final color. This color change is called *véraison*. Grape berries are green because of the chlorophyll before this change, and due to *carotenoids* in white grapes and *anthocyanin* in red grapes. Since this read is for intellectuals, not geniuses like the *Big Bang* Sheldon Coopers of the world, let's not go any further into microbiology…for now.

White wines are best fermented in steel and left to rest and settle in steel tanks to preserve more of the grape's distinct fruit qualities. If stored in a barrel for a bit, oxygen will add some complex levels of flavor to the wine. It all depends on what goal the winemaker has in mind. Also, the colder and slower the wine ferments, the more fruit esters remain in the finished product. If you use a balloon press to squeeze out the grape juice, you break fewer grape seeds, which can release tannins into the wine. They will also add some bitterness, so you can avoid this happening by using the proper press to crush the grapes.

If the white wine producer wants to add a subtle creaminess without using new oak barrels, he or she can let the wine rest a while on the dead yeast cells. That is called *sur lie* (pronounced *sir - lee)* or letting it age on the lees to pick up additional flavors before it is racked (syphoned off into a clean container) and filtered before bottling.

Most red wines, on the other hand, need some tannin to help preserve them as they age. It can come from the seeds, skins, or from the wooden barrels where the wine is fermented and aged. American oak, which cost one-third the price of French oak, is a different species. It has a wider grain. It adds more vanilla compounds to the wine.

For example, Cognac and Armagnac style brandies could use American oak instead of the French wood they now use from the *Limousin Forest* to get more vanillin, ($C_8H_8O_3$) the phenolic aldehyde substitute for pure vanilla. Wine makers who want to highlight the original flavor of Spanish grapes use it instead of the French oak. French oak, with its tighter grain, adds a sort of milk chocolate flavor to the wine, making them taste sweeter. This always works quite well with Cabernet Sauvignon, but not with the Tempranillo grape. I feel that the best Spanish Tempranillo wines are made and aged in American oak. They cost less money while maintaining, in the finished wine, its original characteristics. When done in French oak, they smell and taste fine, but they no longer depict their original Spanish highlights making them, I think, more common, as well as more costly.

Rosé wines were made by leaving the grape juice and the skins together just long enough to absorb a pinkish blush. Many modern Rosé wines are made by adding a splash of red wine to a white wine base to obtain the salmon or copper-pink color that is desired. Ideally, a blush color should come from slight skin contact with the clear grape juice and grape skins that provide the coloring pigments.

Each forest also has its own *terroir*. The French forests of *Allier*, *Nevers*, *Tronçais*, *Limousin* and *Vosges*, are all used in winemaking, and each oak forest inflicts a subtle, but different, flavor note. The standard 59-gallon (225 liter) barrel is called a *barrique* and its small size provides a lot of wood contact with the wine. Large casks, holding up to and over 250 gallons permit a wine to get some air and help aging, but they do not add a lot of oaky flavors to the wines. Many of the best Italian wines are made using very large casks. Young modern Italian, Spanish and American winemakers feel that the smaller *barriques* add additional spice and round out a wine faster. As a wine lover, you should try both styles and decide for yourself which style you prefer.

The final percentage of alcohol in the wine is determined by how much sugar the yeast have to convert. It was one of Napoleon's ministers, Chaptal, who promoted the idea of adding sugar during fermentation when the growing season had fewer sunny days and not enough natural sugar developed in the grapes. It is called *Chaptalization*. The wine laws for Italy and California do not permit Chaptalization, but it happens almost everywhere else. California may add acids to their wines, tartaric or citric, for example, but no sugar.

"Contains Sulfites" is printed on all American wine labels by law. Because you don't see it on many European wine labels while visiting the Old World, you should know that the wine is exactly the same. They just know it's there and don't have to label it. Natural fermentation creates some sulfur compounds and additional sulfites are added to wine to preserve them. Federal regulations permit 350 parts per million (ppm) of sulfites in wine. In actual practice, most wineries only use 40 to 60 ppm to help preserve them. White wines will always have far more sulfur in them than red wines, because they need more SO_2 to preserve them; red wines have more natural preservatives.

Drinking Wine and a Three-part Rule

All wines taste better with food as most foods taste better with wine. Wine is best savored during meals or after dinner during a cheese course. Dessert wines are designed to complement sweeter dishes served at the very end of a meal, and *before* any coffee or tea is served. Coffee sedates your taste buds and should only be served at the conclusion of any meal, and not as a companion to dessert, which should ideally be enjoyed with a dessert wine, or all by itself. Restaurants have conditioned most Americans to this unnatural pairing to help move you more quickly away from the table so they can fit in another seating. The table is yours for the night in most European places.

The most knowledgeable wine drinkers know one simple **Three-part Rule:** drink lighter wines before heavier wines, drink younger wines before older wines, and drink drier wines before sweeter examples. This Three-part Rule alone will forever enhance your pleasures in drinking wine. This knowledge, and very little else, puts you in the top half of all American wine drinkers.

2 WHAT PRECOCIOUS PEOPLE NEED TO KNOW

You may be out of college, or nearly so, but college may not be out of you. How do you know? Well, if you still binge drink, if beer chugging is still fun, if you still put your vodka in Jell-O to make it more palatable, or if you have to mix all of your alcohol choices with some type of juice or soft drink, well then, college is still in you. Learning to enjoy what you drink, and how it matches with food is a pleasure in itself. If it's the inebriated effect you still desire, then you need a book on psychological self-help, not a guide into the intellectual pleasures of wine.

It can be a post high school effect, or even the "experimentation of youth" that's still fluttering about you. If however, you are tired of hangovers, have begun enjoying many foods you'd never have eaten when younger, or if you are trying to get back your youthful healthy shape, wine is about to become your regular drink, and you'll want to know all you can about it. Precocious men and women like to be articulate about things they enjoy and want to share their knowledge with other curious humans.

Like anything else in life, the more you know about something, the more you can enjoy it. Whether it's fishing, musical comedy, impressionistic art or wine, you'll experience more pleasure from it when you more fully understand it.

The more you like something, the longer you look at it. I doubt you ever sat and stared at that beer you chugged. As you begin your journey into the pleasures of wine, you hear over and over again about the five S's. We've already described this in the opening Introduction, but you can never do this too many times, so let's review what we learned in the Introduction.

The 5 S's

Sight is the first "S", followed by *swirl, smell, sip, spit* or *swallow* as you *savor* and think about what you just experienced while tasting a wine. At tastings with a dozen or more wines, you always *spit*, or more properly, you *expectorate*, the wine and stay mentally alert. With food, and at meals, you can usually swallow the wine if it's limited to half a dozen samples. If we used the mannerly term expectorate instead of spit, we'd have to change the professional tasting procedure to *4S's and an E*; not quite as catchy.

You can learn a lot about a wine by looking at it properly. The top thirty-five percent of all wine drinkers in the world begin by looking closely at their wine.

Your wine glass must be clear glass. A long stem is nice because it keeps your hand away from the subject matter, and the thinner the glass, the better it feels on your lip. Wine is not made to be drunk from colored glasses; it is easier to see the many shades of color and different hues without any distortions when using clear glass. Pay attention to the shades of color; the deeper, darker color near the stem, the main hue throughout the liquid, and the perfectly clear and colorless top edge in every white, pink and red wine.

Wine is sipped, not chugged. To easily know and remember a wine, you have to spend a long time smelling it before you put any of it in your mouth. Let your brain record the memory of its aromas. Describe it to yourself or to friends. Your sense of smell is located very near to memory sections of your brain. Whenever you smell a familiar scent, you quickly recall where and when you first recorded it. The smell of your grandmother baking an apple pie or sun tan lotion on a high school date: your brain associates and records aromas far better than your tongue can register the flavors of taste.

After discussing what fruits, flowers, oaks, tars, grasses, or nuts you seem to pick out of a wine, taste it slowly. As kids in America, we weren't trained to do this like many European children often are, so remember, it will take a while before you can quickly identify certain aromas. After all these mental exercises, enjoy it with your meal, and notice how it changes as it airs longer, or what happens to it when you have different foods in your mouth. Ask yourself if it's as dry or bitter with some cheese or as tart with some salty food?

So few people pay any attention to what they're drinking, you can easily be among the top 35 or even the top 30 per cent of knowledgeable wine people anywhere by simply paying a little more attention to what you're drinking. Always smell it before sipping it.

Know that white wines turn darker as they age, and red wines lose their darker colors with time, and get lighter in color. White wine's watery, pale straw shades of color turn to yellowish shades and then to golden amber colors after years of cellaring. Brilliant golden Sauternes when young change into sherry-colored browns after three or four decades.

Purple red wines will change to garnet, and drink best when they're ruby colored. The edge will show orange-brownish shades first, and as the color gets lighter and thinner, it will fade to a schoolhouse brick, you know, that classic reddish-brown color. Thirty-year-old Bordeaux drinks best after its color fades, and its aromas pick up leather and tobacco notes that marry so well with big meat dishes.

Also, the more color, usually, the stronger the aroma. A deeper yellow or golden wine will have heavier aromas than watery pale straw colored wines. Rosé will have more of a nose than most whites will, and deeper inky-red wines will show deeper dark fruit notes than lighter garnet-colored red wines. The color helps predict the aroma and the wine's nose will help predict its taste. Wine experts know this. Just knowing that puts you among the top 30 per cent of all wine drinkers.

Once you make a habit of using the 5-S's, you will easily understand the basic fundamentals pointed out in my "45 Minute Wine Expert" exercise about color forecasting aromas, and the smells forecasting the flavors. Then learning that tasting more than one wine at a time, greatly helps you to notice the differences in each, and quickly helps you to come to know the style of different wines. You'll easily notice the difference in each grape's basic aroma, taste, and even the finish and aftertaste of many types of wine.

Decant young wines to help them quickly open up and show off their fruity aromas. The oxygen will also soften some of the bite that many young wines tend to have.

Older wines need to be decanted into a carafe slowly through cheesecloth, or a screened wine filter to prevent the sediments from making the wine cloudy and bitter. The sediments are mostly bigger molecules of tannic acid, and some other compounds that have bonded together and dropped out of the wine. It takes almost no practice to decant properly. Just pour the wine slowly from the bottle into a carafe. I shine a tiny flashlight under the neck of the bottle to see when the sediment starts to come up, and then stop before any of it pours into the clear wine in the carafe.

Air helps young wines open up and permits them to exhibit their fruity aromas. Air can quickly break down wines that are many decades old, so they are best consumed right after decanting to experience them at their best.

If you have to decant an old wine before traveling to a friend's house, or restaurant, where driving is necessary, do it just before you leave. Rinse the bottle and decant the clear wine back into the bottle and seal it with a vacuum pump and rubber stopper that is made for just this necessity.

If you travel and shake up a non-decanted wine, the fine sediments will make the entire bottle cloudy, and more bitter, than if it were decanted prior to any shaking.

Drink with friends. Never drink alone. This work assumes you have a high IQ so remember that only dull people drink alone, or people with serious psychological troubles.

Talk about the color, the smells that you notice and discuss if you think it's dry, a little sweet or very sweet. Discussion reinforces the skills that you'll develop and help you enjoy wine even more. Time how long the aftertaste lasts. You can watch seconds click off your watch or phone. If the fruitiness fades in a few seconds, leaving an acetic or bitterness on your tongue or gums, it has a short aftertaste. If some fruit flavor lingers for 20, 30 or even 45 seconds, the wine is said to have a long aftertaste. The best food-wines have a medium or long aftertaste to help highlight the next forkful of food. Again, wine is food; it's the liquid part of every meal.

Tongues vs. Noses

The human tongue is an evolutionary masterpiece. The different taste buds evolved to focus upon sweetness at the front tip of the tongue. Sour notes from the acids in foods like lemon juice lie along the topsides of the tongue. Bitterness is picked up by the buds at the rear of the tongue and evolved as a safeguard against poisons; nearly all poisons are bitter. Another ability that taste bud evolution developed was sensing saltiness, but you should never find any salt flavors in any wine except cooking sherry, so we can ignore that ability.

When someone says, "That smells sweet," what they mean is that their sense of smell is noting fruitiness and they call it sweet. Only the tongue can determine sweetness, not the nose. So putting the ability to taste together with skillful smelling will provide you with a lifetime of sensory pleasures.

Drink half a glass of water with each glass of wine and prevent the hangover that is caused by dehydration. Drink water when thirsty and wine as a food enhancer. Intelligent people learn this truth about all alcohol consumption very quickly. Only an idiot goes through life and continues to drink to levels of intoxication. Be smart. Be an intellectual when it comes to wine knowledge and its enjoyment.

3 TASTING

How to taste

Wine is made from grapes grown in many different types of soil. As you learn to pay attention to what you're tasting, you'll soon be able to distinguish the different grapes as well as where the wine came from. Talking dirty with regards to wine really means discussing the same variety or same grape, like a Chardonnay for example, but grown in different types of soils around the world, and pointing out how the different types of soil affects the grapes. When I do corporate wine seminars on this topic, I call it, Let's Talk Dirty.

French Chardonnay (white Burgundy) grown above layers of limestone tastes different and has a different mouth feel than Chardonnay grown in the iron rich soils of Australia, or the sandy loam in parts of California. It's the *terroir* that makes the difference. (See Chapter Fourteen about *terroir*)

Tasting wine is more than just drinking wine. Being able to separate smell and taste will put you in the top 30 percent of the world's wine drinkers. Be specific. Things don't smell sweet; they taste sweet. Your nose has no taste buds. You've heard people say, "This tastes like apricot," when what they should say is that it smells like apricot.

Our vocabulary distorts our ability to pay attention to the

aromas. We say things like, "It tastes like cherry," while sipping a Pinot Noir, or, "This tastes like grapefruit," while drinking a Sauvignon Blanc. What is really happening is that we smell the aromas of cherries or grapefruit rising up through the back of our nasal passage.

All we can taste is sweet, sour, salt and bitter. (Some foodies believe there is a fifth taste called umami, but that's up for debate. I haven't seen any taste bud research proving it.) So, when we refer to the plum and black pepper taste of Syrah or Zinfandel, the real Zinfandel, the red wine, what we're really doing is picking up the esters and phenols that have developed in the skins of the respective grapes. They are the same chemical components that developed in cherries, blueberries, or grapefruit. In fact, they are the dominant compounds in those fruits, so we have come to associate each fruit with its single dominant aroma.

Smell More – Swallow Less

In other words, we should do more smelling than sipping and swallowing to really get more pleasure out of wine. Understanding where a grape is grown will change its aroma, and its flavor drastically, and will help you understand what the French call *terroir*.

You swirl the wine to help the esters rise and mix with the air. Don't be afraid to bury your nose into a wine glass. Try to associate what you smell with some fruit, a flower, your spice cabinet, or anything from your aroma-recorded-memory. "It smells like cherry candy," you might say. The chemical compounds that make a strawberry smell like strawberries are also found in grapes. There are just fewer of these compounds in a grape than in a strawberry. However, the Grenache grape does have more of them, and many times people will pick out hints of wild strawberry in a wine made with Grenache, especially if it's a Rosé wine made from all, or predominately Grenache.

Merlot will have blueberry scents; Cabernet Sauvignon will show black cherry; Sauvignon Blanc always delivers some white or pink grapefruit aromas; Pinot Noir will present the most cherry; Viognier reflects honeysuckle flowers and peach; Chardonnay, unoaked, sends out apple aromas, and with lots of oak aging and malolactic fermentation, it shows buttery vanilla and tropical fruits; Cabernet Franc's dominant ester leans toward rose petals. Beaujolais, made from the Gamay grape, when really ripe at harvest, will offer hints of banana over red fruits. No kidding, banana.

The container in which the wine was made affects the final aroma; the terroir also plays a major part, and even what surrounds a vineyard can add to its aroma. Eucalyptus trees nearby or around a vineyard will deposit some of their oils on the grapes and the grape leaves that will infiltrate the wine during fermentation leaving the finished wine with hints of mint.

Grapes have many of the cherry, lemon, peach, strawberry, apple, rose petal, and acacia flower esters. These are just some examples of the esters that all fruits and flowers have; the dominant one will become the aroma that we associate with any wine. I always look for hints of over-ripe tomatoes in wines made from all or mostly Sangiovese grapes.

Clifton Fadiman said that to take wine into our mouths is to savor a droplet of the river of human history. It's true. Each wine has a history that was affected by current and past human beings.

To easily learn to smell better, just pay attention to and record what aromas you denote after swirling the wine. This process demands a large clear wine glass. Any glass smaller than 12 or 14 ounces is worthless. Since the most pleasure comes from the smell of a wine, you're cheating yourself and taking away the pleasure you should derive when wine is served in a tiny glass. I've see people use tiny shot-like-glasses for their dessert wines because they'll taste the sweetness, but they will also miss out on sensing the aromas, the category where most of the pleasure is found. The ideal wineglass needs taller sides to create a chimney effect to funnel the aromas up to your olfactory nerves.

The secret here is to know that we smell aromas, and not to confuse it with what we taste.

Take Notes

At professional wine tastings, a booklet of all the wines presented is provided with space to record your thoughts about the wine. I jot down its depth of color, any or all the aromas I can perceive, any RS (residual sugar) or how dry or sweet it is, and its body or weight. I, when possible, record a note about what food I'd serve with it, and if I liked and enjoyed it. I guess how it will change as it ages, and also guess as to how long it will take to fully develop, or make a note that it's meant to drink upon release, like most Beaujolais wines. The actual process of making notes, even short hand, helps you to recall what you've had. Without some record, the memory will fade faster than the sensation of a quick kiss.

Dionysian Society Members use a modification of the 20-point Cal-Davis scale. The American Wine Society also uses a similar scale of 20 with fewer points for aroma and taste. It has 2 points for clarity and 2 points for color; even today's home wine makers should be able to obtain proper color and then filter to produce a clear wine. The Dionysian Scale lets you use your ability to smell and taste to judge the highest number of points. The overall Impression Category is for you to judge what you're sampling compared to all the similar styled wines you've enjoyed in the past. It requires a good memory. A Total Score of 19 says it's very special, and a 20 means that it could not get any better; it's the perfect example of what the wine should be.

The Heading on the Dionysian Society's Wine Judging Score Sheet

Appearance	Aroma Bouquet	Taste Texture	Balance Aftertaste	Overall Impression	Total Score
Max-2	*Max-7*	*Max-5*	*Max-3*	*Max-3*	*Max-20*

Any wine scoring under 11 points should have some technical fault. (See Chapter Twelve to know about faulty wines) A score of 20 is that rare heavenly treat, one of the best you've ever had in your entire lifetime. Scores of 11 to 13 are basic wines showing little character but are quite drinkable; 14 to 15.5 scores win Bronze medals; 16 to 17.5 get Silver, and 18 to 20 scores are Gold medal wines.

Tasting Types

A **Vertical Tasting** compares the same wine, i.e., the same producer, all from different vintages. No other tasting teaches you as quickly the value of aging wines. For example, I recently hosted a Vertical of Chateau Pichon-Comtesse de Lalande starting with the 1994, then, 1990, 1988, 1985, 1982, 1978, 1975, 1970, 1952, and the 1940. All the wines where pre-poured before people sat. Guests reviewed the colors to see how the very oldest had lost their ruby red hues and turned brick with a brown edge. The aromas were very complex adding more leather and tobacco from older vintages. The taste also got softer with age; all had to be decanted to remove the sediments leaving a clear wine sans much of its tannin. Discussions covered how they were cellared, temperature, humidity and darkness, how much longer some might last, and what foods would now pair well with them. It's a highly intellectual discussion and usually lots of fun.

You can host a Vertical tasting with as few as three bottles of the same wine and producer, from just three different years. Being able to do Vertical Tastings is another reason to cellar some wines.

Horizontal Tasting is easier to do. It's comparing different producers, usually of the same type of wine, and all from the same vintage.

You can compare Chateaus Pontet-Canet, Dauzac, Belgrave, Clerc-Milon and Cantemerle, all Bordeaux, all classified Fifth Growths, and all from the same vintage. Maybe it's easier to find five or six Napa Valley Cabernet Sauvignon wines all from the most current release year and do a Horizontal Tasting with wine friends to see which one stands out and might be a good purchase to add to your cellar.

Horizontals Tastings can have enormous ranges; maybe Sauvignon Blanc from five different countries, but all from the same vintage. This type of tasting can easily be the basis for a very social wine party and bright people will easily learn things to add to their mental wine bank.

Triangular Tastings can be very easy and help reinforce your wine judging abilities, or be quite difficult when the wines show only slight differences. Like a triangle with three sides, you set up wines in rows of three, where two wines are exactly the same and one is different. Row A might have Sauvignon Blanc in glasses one and two, but glass three is an unoaked Chardonnay. Row B might have Zinfandel in glasses one and three, but the middle glass is an Australian Shiraz. Two of the three wines are always the same wine and one is different.

The most difficult examples might be all three glasses having the same Sonoma County Russian River Pinot Noir in them, but one glass has a different vintage. This type of tasting teaches you more about your own abilities and awareness than it does about the wines. However, it can be quite entertaining.

Comparative Tastings are reviewing similar types of wines from different places. You might ask your friends what wine goes best with lobster, and have each bring a bottle to sample with some lobster. The vintage should be within a year or two of each other and the body or weight of the wine should be similar such as having Chablis, Meursault, Sonoma un-oaked Chardonnay, and a South American white. It is important that this tasting be a **Blind Tasting**. No one knows what's in each glass until all your scores, rankings or comments are completed. Double Blind is when the host may remove all the corks and bag the bottles. Then, someone else numbers the concealed bottles in any order they want so even the host doesn't know what wine is in any bag.

Ideal wine tastings are always done with a separate glass for each wine, pre-poured before sitting, set on a white or very light colored table cloth or background. A spit cup and a water glass are necessary. A spill-out bucket should be set for every four people. Salt-less crackers are best for clearing the palate. (If you use cheese or lean meats, that will affect the scores of wines tasted right after eating either one) Of course, you'll need a tasting sheet and a pen to record notes at each setting. Lastly, never be embarrassed to notify your guests ahead of time that no perfumes, colognes or after-shaving lotions should be worn at a wine tasting. God forbid someone comes in reeking of cigarette smoke. It will absolutely prevent you from being able to smell anything in the wine, and limit your memory from recording it. Smart people want to learn and be able to recall the things that enhanced their pleasure.

Before starting, explain the 5-S's to anyone new to proper wine tasting. Remind them, it's not snobbish to hold a wine glass by the stem; it prevents your hand from over-warming the wine. Tell them it's a procedure to help ascertain the most pleasure from drinking.

Old world families teach their children how to drink and to savor the aromas. New World families eat too fast, serve sugared drinks to children and never discuss the wonderful world of aromas. All your senses should be used to better enjoy wine. *Sight* will help you know the age of the wine and if it's the right shade of color for each wine. *Smell* will tell you the most. It can detect a faulty wine, dominant fruit aromas and help guess what grapes made the wine. *Taste* will help you decide if the wine should go with certain appetizers, entrées, or served with dessert, and if the wine is too young or well past its peak. Let it *Touch* your inner cheeks and roll it all over your tongue. If your *Hearing* didn't enjoy the sound of a popping sparkling wine being opened, make a toast and clink your glasses. Every sense should be put to use.

The hardest thing I've found for Americans to do is identify the aromas. We simply do not grow up discussing smells. With a little practice and selecting wines with very noticeable scents, like Sauvignon Blanc's grapefruit scents, you'll quickly learn how to look for obvious aromas and even the more subtle ones. Just practice and know that you have to spend a long time smelling a wine before you sip it. Once it's in your mouth, it is harder to distinguish the components.

It is said that even the early Greeks, centuries before Christ, had professional tasters help select wines for their nobility. They were called *oinogeustes*. If you really want to get more pleasure out of wine, you should arrange a small tasting party as soon as you've finished this chapter. Host any style of tasting. The important thing is to start paying attention to what you're drinking, try to guess what components you notice, and record some notes to help you recall it. After just one tasting using what's written here, you'll be on your way to being intellectually among the top 25% of all wine drinkers. The nose knows.

Wine Glasses

Smart people always use a clear wine glass, *with a stem*, and never fill the glass more than one-third of its volume. That way, you can swirl the wine, tilt the glass, and see the legs form and slowly slide downward. *Riedel* glassware is very good. Austrian glassmaker, Georg Riedel, convinced many wine lovers that you needed a different wine glass for each type of grape used to make wine. No so, but what a great way to sell more glasses. I've used only two of all their designs.

Really smart people know that a taller glass with a wider mouth works for red and white Burgundies, so it's fine with *all* Pinot Noir and Chardonnay wines, and a taller glass, with more chimney height, is needed to permit the complex aromas of Cabernet-based wines to rise and make them easier to smell. Two basic shapes are all that's needed.

I am the Ambassador for the *Chef & Sommelier Grand Vin* wine glass series, which I think are among the best. Their five and a quarter ounce Champagne Flute is an ideal size. Bigger glasses permit the sparkling wine to get too warm. From their *Grand Vin* line, the 20.25 oz. Tulip is perfect for every red wine and may be the strongest crystal glass made. Its smaller sister, the 16.5 oz. Tulip enhances every white wine and together they make the ideal team of glasses to cover every wine drinking experience you could have. They ring musically when you clink to toast, and the pulled-glass stem, unlike any others, is perfectly round for your fingers to fondle.

Of course, you need perfectly clean Champagne flutes for all your sparkling wines, even though many Champagne specialists now say a wider, shorter glass, close to the shape of many white wine glasses, will help you perceive the subtle aromas of sparkling wines. Champagne served in an old-fashioned coupe saucer-like glass, permits the wine to go flat much too quickly. If someone is still using them, try your best to break as many as possible, all accidently of course.

Another very important item regarding wine glasses is to serve your Porto and other dessert wines in the same large glass you'd use for a white wine. Serving Ports, Madeira, Cream Sherries, or Sauternes in a tiny cordial glass is uncouth. You want to enjoy the bouquet from these wines just as much as you would any other wine during the meal.

Lastly, remember that the easiest way to learn the differences between wines is to taste them together. Sometimes it means using a lot of glasses, but it's the only way. Serve a glass from last night's bottle, with another glass of this night's new bottle every time you have wine at home. Comparing the two wines will teach you very quickly how different two Chardonnay wines can be or how different the same grape from two different locations are and it's easier to see the difference in color and flavor between wines of different ages. You should enjoy wine more every time you drink it by knowing it's always a learning experience.

Helixophiles

Many dedicated wine lovers, besides collecting wines for their cellars, also collect wine books, wine-related artworks, songs with wine mentioned in them, and corkscrews. People with large collections of corkscrews are called **Helixophiles**. The former Christian Brothers Winery, now the Culinary Institute of America's west coast campus, keeps and maintains Brother Timothy's famous corkscrew collection. It consists of between 400 to 500 corkscrews from 17 different countries.

Another famous corkscrew collection is at *Domaine de la Citadel* in Mènerbes, France. Their Corkscrew Museum has well over 1,500 different corkscrews covering key developments over the centuries.

The corkscrew was first used in the 1700's and today there are hundreds of different styles. As long as your have a Teflon-coated helix, it's easy to extract a cork. Opening very old bottles, with corks that often break apart, requires more skill and practice. Pulling out modern plastic corks is easy enough, but getting the cork off the corkscrew is the hardest part. Remember to always cut the capsule at least one-half inch below the top, not just the very top edges like some foil cutters do. Wipe the bottle top before extracting the cork to remove any bacteria. The intellectual wine drinker would *never* pull the cork out right through the foil covering.

4 WINES TO CELLAR

What to cellar and age for future drinking

Your partner wants to take a $9 bottle of Australian Shiraz to a party with you, but you think it's about time you both became leaders instead of followers. You briefly talk about it, and decide to take that bottle of Spanish Rioja you won as a prize at the holiday office party for telling the best joke.

If you want to be in the top 30% of skilled and knowledgeable wine drinkers, you have to be aware of the trendy wines, but seek out unique lesser-known wines with higher quality. You also have to have the confidence to share your special finds with your wine-loving family members, and especially with your wine-loving friends.

Italy is presently the hot spot, however, far too many Italian wines have become over-priced. That simply means that they cost more than they are really worth. For example, when producers of Pinot Grigio made this favorite Italian white wine from vineyards where they produced three or four tons of grapes per acre, there was a concentration of lemon and lime aromas, and sharply acidic food-friendly flavors. Pinot Grigio used to be worth the money.

As people learned about the wine and learned how to pronounce the grape, it grew in popularity. Producers increased their production to six, seven, and even more than eight tons of grapes per acre to meet demand, but that decreased the concentration and quality. However, they did increase the price. It may be popular to take a Pinot Grigio to a party, but modern wine lovers are looking for new and unique wines. They're not hard to find because there are hundreds, even thousands of excellent inexpensive wines now available. Wines from Spain, Greece and Portugal offer countless opportunities for new wine adventures.

The less expensive Spanish whites are a good place to start, and, of course, red wines made from Pinot Noir that are grown in Oregon, New Zealand, Bulgaria and South America.

A Wine Cellar

Aging your own wines: Roughly, 85 percent of the world's wines are made to consume as soon as you buy them. If you get a case of Chardonnay in the $15 range and consume half the case at a party you hosted the same evening you bought the case, and then you don't touch the remaining bottles until later that year, you'll notice a more than subtle difference in the wine. The $15 Chardonnay will be smoother, have some additional aromas, and taste a bit more complex. Its color may even be a bit deeper yellow, and the cork will be easier to pull out than it was when you first bought it.

Note: White wine corks are harder to withdraw because you drink them younger than most red wines. This is because the sides of the white wine corks are rougher than the sides of longer-aged red wine corks that have smoothed out from being crushed against the sides of the bottle for a longer time. That smoothness helps the corks slide out easier. Any waiter who does this over and over again can tell you when they first noticed the difference in extraction between corks from young white or older red wines.

The 15 percent of wine lovers who buy by the case, and build wine cellars for their collections, can again be divided into two parts. About 75 percent will age their wines for a relatively short period, and drink their wines within five to ten years. The remaining 25 percent of all collectors will buy wines to keep for at least a decade or more, and then sell, or drink them. Only one-third of these long-term collectors or wine investors as they should be called, buy only to re-sell. They know that during many periods of economic trends, auction wines have gone up in price faster than gold; they have made some very good profits. This *coarse guide* is primarily interested in those people who see wine as a life-enhancer, and will cellar some wines planning to open, drink, and enjoy them in the distant future.

Many wine collectors spend tens of thousands of dollars to have a showcase wine cellar built. They have special lighting, a tasting table, usually a glass door to view it from another room and will even heat it a bit while hosting a wine tasting with friends. None of this is good for the wine but it probably helps the ego.

You need to store your wine in a cool, dark location with no vibration near by. Never use neon lighting; it quickly affects the color and aromas of wine. All light affects the flavor components.

Heat ages a wine too quickly, and it will brown and even cook the wine long before it has a chance to slowly develop those great mature flavors and aromas. Bottles stored near a washer or dryer get too much vibration. The molecules move too much for proper bonding and softening of the wine. This prevents proper aging.

If you live in a house with a cellar, frame in a space along the northern wall because that area stays the coolest the longest, and put your money into racks. Insulate it from the rest of your basement. I've always said that you can do most, if not all of this yourself, and use your savings to buy more wine.

Figure the space needed for the number of cases you'd really like to store and then double it. Yes, double it. Once you start collecting, you'll quickly fill your cellar. Everyone I know who cellars some wine had to add an extension to his or her storage space. I did too. Twice.

Once you have just 18 bottles of wine waiting to drink, that's just a case and a half, you can call yourself a collector. If you don't have a basement that stays in the low 60's or even lower, you can store your wines on the floor of your coolest room. Ideal cellars are a constant 55 degrees Fahrenheit or 12.8 degrees Celsius, but it's rapid temperature change that hurts wines more than being stored at slightly higher temperatures. Heat rises so it's always much warmer half way up your closet than on the floor. You can easily make space for six cases under a staircase or by using the lower part of a closet. That's 72 bottles of wine, enough to save and age a few years without much worry. Wines stored at or above your head in wine shops are breaking down faster than the ones resting near your feet.

I never drink wine in my cellar. It's much nicer sitting in the kitchen with a white tablecloth and proper lighting so you can examine the shades of color, enjoy the aromas, and not need a jacket to avoid the chill of a proper wine cellar.

What you put into your wine cellar is just as important as the storage area itself.

Whites vs. Reds

Even if you currently love white wine more than red ones, you'll eventually come to love and drink much more red wine than white wine.

Only a few dessert whites and some top-end white Burgundies will age well. You should start with 60% red wine and 40% white wine. You'll be using the whites quickly, so your wine cellar will be more of a storage area for them rather than an aging center. Your collection will quickly change about 10% each year until it has 85% red wine aging, and only 15% white wine sleeping with them.

If you're keeping some sparkling wines like most people do, you can count them as whites and thus have a larger percentage of this category.

Rosé wines don't count toward either white or red and you'll buy them, like most people do, to quickly consume during spring, summer and fall meals on your deck, or with light foods indoors. Rosé is great party wine when it's dry and fresh, so keep some Italian, French and Spanish examples on hand.

Starting your cellar

Reds:

3 Merlot (2 Washington State, 1 from California)

3 Zinfandel (from Renwood, Rosenblum, or Ridge)

3 Chianti Classico (from Monsanto, Nozzole, or Piccini)

3 Brunello di Montalcino (from Banfi)

2 Barolo

1 Barbaresco

3 Nero d'Avola (from Sicily)

3 Amarone

6 Rioja (two bottles from three different producers)

2 LBV Porto (Late Bottled Vintage)

1 Vintage Porto

3 Châteauneuf-du-Pape

3 Burgundy (from Gevrey-Chambertin)

3 Burgundy (from Beaune)

3 Bordeaux (2 Medoc – 1 Graves)

1 Pomerol

1 Saint-Emilion (get one that says Grand Cru)

1 Second Growth Grand Cru (any of the 14 options)

3 Napa Cabernet Sauvignon (that say "Grown, Produced and Bottled by")

48 total bottles = four cases of red wine

Whites:

2 Mosel Riesling (A Piesport Spätlese)

1 Rhine Riesling (A Rheingau Auslese)

3 Gavi (northern Italy)

3 Chassagne-Montrachet

3 Puligny-Montrachet

3 Sancerre

3 White Bordeaux

2 Alsace (Pinot Gris & Pinot Blanc)

3 Chardonnay (one Napa, two Sonoma)

1 Sauvignon Blanc

24 total bottles = two cases of white wine

With this simple collection, you will now have an ideal six-case wine cellar. Try not to drink them all during the first year or so. Once you start adding to it, saving a few bottles gets easier, and in just 36 months, you'll be able to serve a big red that's at least five or more years old depending on its release date. Remember, the vintage date on the bottle is always the year the grapes were harvested and made into wine. The best wines for aging come from years that had ideal weather conditions during the growing season.

Buy your Spanish Rosé by the case for summer drinking. You'll have a bottle on hand for a house gift when visiting, and you'll keep at least three of them in a refrigerator and ready to open on a moments notice. Twelve bottles will not last long. Before you finish your Rosé wine, you'll, most likely, have tried a few of your cellared whites and have started to add a few new bottles too. Wine cellars grow fast. Remember, a "wine cellar" can be as simple as a few cardboard cases lying on their sides in the coolest, darkest spot in your house, apartment or campsite.

As we've said, light and especially heat hurt wine the most. It's a food item, and should be treated as a food. Vibration prevents proper aging. So even if stored at 55 degrees, out of direct light, and on their sides, vibrations will break down the wine much too soon. Bottles lying on their sides keep the corks wet and swollen preventing air from getting in and turning the wine into vinegar.

Note: I like to buy wines from shops that have their selections lying down. You never know if the standing bottle was recently placed there, or has been standing all year and now has a dried-out cork. If the fill level in the neck is a little low, the wine is evaporating out and air is getting in. Check all the neck levels. A reputable wine merchant is the best friend you can have.

Note: Storing wine for just 15 years at a steady 73 degrees Fahrenheit or 22.8 Celsius, is equivalent to storing it for 120 years at 55 degrees Fahrenheit or 12.8 Celsius. Heat destroys wine faster than anything! Never have a wine rack in your kitchen, or God forbid, over your stove.

Only about 20% of the world's dedicated wine drinkers build and keep a wine collection. Most people simply buy a bottle or two just prior to needing it for a meal or as a house gift when visiting. So, this easily stored, small collection puts you among the top 25% of intellectual wine lovers. You should feel good about yourself, and your status among the world's wine drinkers.

5 READING WINE LABELS

We need more Geography education

This is really simple but few people understand it. A rough knowledge of wine grapes and some geography is all you need. Enjoying wine starts with being able to read a wine label.

Note: Most of the Old World wines are named after the towns, areas or even the houses that produce them. The majority of New World wines are named after the grapes that the wine was made from along with the producer's name.

It gets a little tricky here, but bright people will quickly learn a few simple rules to follow in order to determine if the bottle came from a real winery, or was just a producer's extra wine that was bottled or blended, and sold by someone else.

Since we've already learned how to taste wine by keying on its smell, and seeking out the varied tastes extracted from the soils in different wines, we can now easily tell from a wine label a lot about the wine inside.

Oporto is a city in Portugal, Bordeaux is a city in France, Chablis is an area northwest of the major Burgundy region of France, and the Mosel is a river along with its nearby areas of Germany. Wines with those names all come from those places.

Merlot, Pinot Grigio and Cabernet Sauvignon are grapes. Wines with those names on the label are made entirely, or with at least 75%, of that grape.

When most new wine drinkers begin learning about wines as opposed to just drinking them, they wish that they'd studied more geography in high school or college. It's America's biggest failure. Most Canadians can name all of our states and many of their Capitals too, but Americans know few, if any, of the Canadian provinces.

Because wine, good and great wines, reflect their *terroir*, the place they came from, we need to know those places so we can expand our selections and styles of wine to increase our enjoyment of these vinous treasures. Start by getting a shower curtain with a world map on it. Use a new Atlas, or Google maps of wine-growing areas. This book is not an Atlas, so I've decided to not include maps. We think with words. That's all bright people need for now. However, as soon as possible, learn more geography.

Hungary has a *Kadarka* grape used to make *Egri Bikaver*, meaning Bull's Blood. It's a dark red full-bodied wine with a lot of history. You don't need to know the Hungarian wine regions, or where they make their *Tokaj* dessert wines, but you should be able to point out Hungary on a map.

Bulgaria, on the Black Sea, has a semi-dry *Misket* white wine. They are also now competing with great examples of Pinot Noir, Chardonnay and Merlot. All their wines reflect the soil and weather of Bulgaria, and you should look up its location.

Greece's Peloponnese, and the Greek islands of Crete and Santorini all make distinctive excellent wines reflecting their climates and soil. Being able to picture where these spots are located helps us better enjoy their wines.

England made the wines from Cyprus famous during the reign of Queen Elizabeth I, and Sir Walter Raleigh had the importing monopoly for all the Cyprus wines. They use *Mavron* grapes for their red *Othello* wine. The white *Aphrodite* from Cyprus is made near Aphrodite's birthplace.

Measuring degrees of intellectual pleasure is hard to do, but we all comprehend that the more you know about something, the greater you understand it, and with greater understanding comes more knowledge and pleasure. Don't be afraid to be a hedonist. Knowing more geography will add to your intellectual curiosity about wines.

Let's discuss maps and learn to better read and understand wine labels. Bottles from France's Bordeaux region will name the house or Chateau that made the wine. The vintage date is the year the grapes were harvested. The top Bordeaux wines are released about two and a half years after the grapes were picked and the wine was made. *Mis en Bouteilles au Chateau* means the wine was bottled where it was made, at the Chateau. The alcohol will be shown as a percentage of the volume, which is marked in milliliters (750ml is standard). A 1.5L (liter) is called a magnum and is equal to two standard bottles. The more specific the noted location, the better the quality of the wine.

A label saying just "Bordeaux" can have its grapes come from anywhere in the entire district. Medoc and Haut Medoc are more specific because they are sub-sections of Bordeaux. Within Bordeaux there are even more specific villages like Margaux, Saint-Julien, Saint-Estèphe or Pauillac. This is where knowing the geography, or map study, comes in handy.

Note: Specific is terrific when it comes to telling where the wine is from; that is, the more specific the location printed on the label, the more distinct the wine should be. Medoc should be better than simply Bordeaux, or Napa wines will have more character than ones just labeled California.

Burgundy will name a village. If the wine comes from a **Premier Cru**, that name will be under the village name. Morey-Saint-Denis is a village, and one of its Premier Cru vineyards is *Clos Bussière*. If the Burgundy comes from a **Grand Cru**, like the vineyard of *Clos de Tart*, which is also in Morey-Saint-Denis, the law says that only the Grand Cru name is necessary on the label.

You simply have to know that red Burgundy is made with Pinot Noir and that white Burgundies come from Chardonnay. Most of France follows similar rules so expect the same in the Loire Valley or the Rhone wine areas. Only wine labels from Alsace will note the grape used in the wine.

Note: In years past, French vintners followed a proverb, "*Le dessin revele le raisin*" or "the label betrays the grape." It was their way of secretly conveying quality information. Among the most basic information of producer, vintage, region and classification where hidden bits of information. For example, on a label with no

Chateau named, if the vintage date was above center, the wines were of poor quality.

If there was a picture of a Chateau, you had to count the windows; an even number of windows was noting good wine and an odd number noted a rotten year.

If the metrication was in milliliters, *(ml)* they were saying it *might last*, but if printed in centiliters *(cl)*, it meant the wine *can't last*.

Horizontal rectangle labels were for French consumption and vertical rectangle labels were for export. A horizontal label with the four corners cut making it an eight-sided label was wine for large parties or maybe a gift. This inside coding has mostly faded in modern times.

Do look for the French words, *Appellation d'Origine Contrôlée*. Meaning the controlled name of the place it was made. All of their rules and laws can be studied in detail, but knowing that their government regulates what grapes can be grown where, and what size the harvest can be, helps maintain quality.

Italy has twenty regions; all making wine and all following similar rules for items placed on their labels. Knowing the geography of Italy can pretty much predict the grapes used to make the wine. The Italian label will have an ITG printed on it for basic table wines, and like the better French AOC wines, Italy uses DOC, or *Denominazone de Origine Controllata*, the controlled name of origin. They also have a higher status notation, DOCG. This one means it is a controlled name of origin, but it is also guaranteed.

All Italian wines with DOCG on them, since 1992, have to pass an analysis and a review by a tasting panel.

Denominação de Origem Controlada is what you'll see on a Portuguese wine label, which has very similar regulations to Italy and France, as well as Spain.

Spain's wine labels will have *Denominación de Origen* printed on them standing for "name of the origin," and also specific regions like *Rueda, Ribera del Duero* or *Rioja* as examples of the 66 wine regions with this status.

Nowadays, most wine producing countries will have some sort of notation showing the location of where the grapes were grown. The United States uses AVA or *American Viticultural Area* to inform you about the area for the source of the grapes in the bottle. It does not have to put the words or letters AVA on or next to the name. Simply put, if it says American, the grapes or juice can come from anywhere in the USA. If it says California, the grapes had to be grown somewhere in the state. If it says Sonoma, the grapes must have been grown within that county, and even more specific, for example, is the Russian River, found within Sonoma County within California.

Note: Remember to check the back label. Look for the words, "Grown, Produced and Bottled by…" as the best possible quality. If it says "Vinted" or Cellared by," the wine could have come from anywhere within the noted AVA. It doesn't mean it will be bad; it just won't have a specific *terroir* to analyze.

Also, in America, we have to put "Contains Sulfites" on the label. The rest of the world has the same sulphur preservative, but they don't have to label it as such unless it's coming into the USA. It only affects people allergic to sulphur. If you can eat a raisin or a dried apricot with 600 times more sulphur in it, the wine will never hurt you.

Lastly, the USA, South Africa, Australia, South America and New Zealand will also name the grape that made the wine unless it's a blend of a number of grapes. These blends will have some cute or personal made up name. In most of the USA, whatever grape name, Merlot, for example, need only be 75% of what's in the bottle. Nearly every Merlot has some Cabernet Sauvignon in it to add body, and most wines labeled Cabernet Sauvignon have some Merlot added to soften it. Many have a subtle blend of grapes in them. If no grape name is mentioned, that means none of the blending grapes came to 75 % of the total. A few places, like Oregon, require 85% by volume to name it after the dominant grape.

Simply put, the more geography you know, the easier it is for you to select a wine of distinct characteristics because it came from a more specific and unique area, and usually, with a *terroir* better suited to growing that specific grape.

New Jersey, for example, has three AVA's with its *Outer Coastal Plain* showing the most promise. They'll soon have a fourth AVA within the Outer Coastal Plain. Missouri, if you're interested, had the first AVA in America. In the 1860's, Missouri produced 40% of all American wines. Now California produces about 90% of the total national production.

Germany gives you nearly everything you need to know on their wine labels. It will give the location of the winery, where the grapes were grown, and a region like the Rheingau or Mosel-Saar-Ruwer. German labels will give the vintage, many times with an "er" attached, for example, 1999er or 2015er. It will give the village with an "er" attached like a person from New York is called a New Yorker. Example: *Graacher Himmelreich* from the village of *Graach.* The second word, *Himmelreich*, is the vineyard name in the village of *Graach.* A Mosel-Saar-Ruwer 2014er *Reiler Sorentberg* is another example. It will then tell you the grape used if simply a *Qualitätswein* wine, and a classification if it is a *Qualitätswein mit Prädikat.* If indeed it is the higher quality *QmP* classification, it will add words like *Kabinett, Spätlese, Auslese, Beerenauslese* or *Trockenbeerenauslese,* all going up in their residual sugars and also in their prices.

Rare German examples may say it's an "Ice Wine," found only in 375ml size bottles, and made from frozen grapes, are very sweet and very expensive wines. We'll discuss these dessert wines more in Chapter Thirteen.

German wine labels will also show the volume in milliliters (ml) and in smaller print give the A.P.Nr., such as 2707401313. The last two digits tell you the year that the wine was evaluated by the governing body to confirm its authenticity. On a 2016 vintage, the last two digits should be 17 or even 18, a year or two after harvest. The other numbers note the region, and the local area of the vineyard and the judging location.

If the name of the producer is extremely famous, like *Schloss Vollrads,* that name may be all they will print, and they print it at the top of their label. Another famous name like *Rudolf Muller*, also quite well known, prints their name at the bottom of the label. Both positions are legal.

Studying maps, taking wine tours, and learning geography is a big factor in your future wine enjoyment. Don't miss out on any of it. Start today. Learn that Napa and Sonoma are north of San Francisco, and Mendocino and Lake counties are above both of them. Learn that Santa Barbara is north of LA and also where the Chilean and Argentinian vineyards are located. The more geography you know, the easier it is to learn and enjoy the distinct style of wines from many more places.

6 STYLES
Old World vs. New World

Style means many things. There are earthy, fruity wines made to age, and big jammy wines designed to consume the same day you buy them. Great Old World wines need time to mature, round out, and develop complexities. Many have to be decanted before serving. Quite a few New World wines seem to have the motto, "It's ready to sip when it hits your lip!"

Decanting Note: You can decant a young wine to add air quickly and help soften a powerful, young wine, but mostly, you'll need to decant your older wines. These are bottles that have developed sediment in them from the tannins bonding together, and then dropping out to settle along the bottom edge of your horizontally stored bottle. This sediment is bitter and will make a glass of wine cloudy, unpleasant to look at, and hard to judge its color. Decanting is simple, and even adds to the romance of a wine's presentation.

First: Remove the entire capsule hiding the neck of the bottle.

Second: Since most red wines are in green or brown glass, you'll need some light shining up through the bottle to see the wine moving out. Romantically use a candle, or like me, a small flashlight placed on the table below the bottle you'll be decanting.

Third: If you're right-handed, hold the decanter, glass pitcher, or any carafe in your left hand. Reverse this if left-handed.

Fourth: With the bottle uncorked and neck naked, use your right hand to slowly pour the wine into the decanter while holding it above the light so you can see through the bottle's neck and watch the clear wine pouring out.

Fifth: Don't stop pouring or shake the bottle until you see sludgy sediment coming through the neck.

Sixth: Stop decanting. Set the bottle down which will probably still have half an ounce in it, and pour the clear wine from the decanter into your glasses.

Seventh: Use the 5-S's to enjoy the wine.

Now, let's do a coarse review of all the basic styles you'll need to be aware of if you really want to be among the top 25 per cent of the wine drinkers in the world.

As stated in Chapter Five, Old World wines are those wines that are made in places that have been making wine for centuries like France, Italy or Greece. Basically, we're talking about traditional European wines. New World wines come from North America, Australia, New Zealand, Chile, Argentina, and South Africa. These are usually dry earthy reds that can be laid down to rest for five or more years before you consume them. The term used most often for this style is "food wines."

New World wines are made to satisfy the tastes of younger people, or those who are newly introduced to wine. They reflect the same sweeter or fruitier taste that most people became used to while growing up with soft drinks and fruit juice. It's neither good nor bad; it's just what we're used to, and we have to learn that excessive fruit, or too much sugar, deadens the tastes buds and distracts from the greater enjoyment of wine and food being paired and enjoyed together. These wines, all too often, taste like a spread of fruity jam on your tongue and dominate your palate; they don't marry as well as Old World wines do with most foods, but they're very nice as "social drinking wines."

This New World style is now being made everywhere, and in Europe they are simply called "modern." These wines are very likeable even when you open them quite young. Sadly, after their charming youth fades away, they dry out leaving only the heat of the higher alcohols. They don't usually age well.

Note: Calling China "New World" might be ridiculous, but it will soon be competing with all New World wines. France's Moët-Hennessy is selling a $300 bottle of *Ao Yun* in New York, a Cabernet blend, from the *Yunnan Province* in China where the vineyards are 8,000 feet high. Also, excellent sparkling wine will be coming from *Ningxia* in China.

Oak. The type of wood used in barrel fermentation, or barrel aging, can greatly change the nature of a wine. Old World Spain uses American oak on its Tempranillo wines because American oak highlights the grapes' natural aromas and permits the wine to show its place of origin. However, French oak works more like salt and pepper on a food. It is overused as a flavor ingredient because so many New World wine drinkers want a sweeter, chocolate flavor. Like the soft drinks so many Americans grew up with, they are easy to satisfy the human desire for sweetness. When paired with refined dishes, however, they clash and make the food taste dull.

The smaller the barrel, the more contact the wine has with the wood. The large old Slovenian oak barrels used by the Italians who continue to make Old World food wines, use their barrels to round out a young wine, but don't want to add additional flavor ingredients to their grapes' natural taste and aromas. The use of smaller French *barriques* adds loads of additional flavors to the wine, and sometimes it over-powers the grape's original smells and tastes. Both styles have their purpose. I enjoy both, but skilled tasters and intelligent wine lovers tend to like picking out the *terrior* of a wine, and usually drink their wines with meals, so the Old World style best suits their needs.

Big jammy fruity wines are easy to please and win awards more easily. The worldwide trend is toward winning medals to help their advertising, and to please modern drinkers, both young and old, who have grown up with sugary soft drinks in their diets.

Old World and New World wines are becoming harder to separate and determine a location or source of the wine, because universal winemaking techniques, and similar oak aging are making all Cabernets, Merlots, Chardonnays, or Chenin Blancs smell and taste the same. However, not all is lost. Both styles are still prolifically produced and since French oak barrels cost much more than other oak barrels, lots of Old World style wines will usually be a better buy.

This Coarse Guide, being read by bright people, will quickly come to understand that the smart thing to do would be to host some comparative wine tastings between Old World selections and New World examples of similar types and styles to learn the difference, and see which you enjoy more at this present stage of growth in your wine appreciation.

Host a wine party with Pacific Northwest wines made with Pinot Gris, Dry Riesling, Pinot Blanc and Gewurztraminer vs. similar examples from Alsace, France. Sip each pair first to see which excites your palate more. Then match the same finger-food to each, and see if your winner in the first round changed or stayed the same.

Pair California and Australian whites made with Marsanne, Roussanne and Viognier to the white wines of Cotes-du Rhône and Condrieu.

Compare and contrast a few Sauvignon Blancs from New Zealand to wines from Sancerre, France. Be sure to include a Pouilly-Fumé.

Try an Italian Spanna (made with Nebbiolo grapes) a Barbera, and maybe an Amarone with your favorite American and South American reds like Merlot, Syrah and Cabernet Sauvignon with a beef or pasta dish. Add a drop of truffle oil on either to increase the complexity and make the wines work harder to marry well with the foods.

Host a light luncheon or picnic style event, and do a comparison with Italian Valpolicella, French Beaujolais, and maybe an Austrian Muller-Thurgau to a New World Sauvignon Blanc and any two light red wines costing under $15. The first thing you'll notice is the higher sugar levels of the New World wines, and a lack of refreshing acids. Only you can decide which type of wines fit into your lifestyle at present, keeping an open mind that as you grow and change, so will your appreciation of more refined qualities in both wines and foods. I never tire of trying a wine made from a grape I'm not familiar with, and then pairing these newly found wines with a very familiar and favorite dish.

Old World wines come from Europe; France, Germany, Italy Spain, Greece, Portugal, Austria, and now more often, the Eastern block of Europe like Bulgaria, Romania, Georgia, Croatia, Turkey, and Israel.

New World wines are from Australia and New Zealand, South America, South Africa (even though wines were made there since the 1600's) and, of course, the USA.

New World wines usually have more alcohol, lower acids, and are sweeter; all too easy to quickly like.

Old World wines are usually drier, have lower alcohol, need more years to age and round out, and can be harder on your palate when very young, but will marry with foods much easier making a meal more enjoyable.

Please don't hold me to this for every wine you try. These general statements are extremely basic and are guides to use when playing wine guessing games involving what is the grape, and where does it come from? Dedicated wine enthusiasts never reject any wine. They want to experience everything, and add wines to their cellars that they think will develop and be even better in ten years when they are no longer available. Always recall that wine is food; it's the liquid part of every meal, and the more styles you compare, the greater your final dining pleasures will be.

Both Old World and New World wines have a place in an intelligent wine drinker's home. If the occasion is more social and less intense, simple easier wines that don't demand analysis are better suited. There's nothing wrong with party wines. Old World wines that have outlived wars and political upheavals need quieter, meditative moments to fully enjoy them.

Enclosures: There was a time when bulk New World wines used a Twist Off Cap to seal them. Corks were thought to be for higher priced Old World wines. Today, New Zealand seals about 90% of all its wines with Twist Off Caps, but many Old World wineries also use them. Because the quality of corks had gotten so poor during the fifteen-year span from 1990 to 2005, many fine quality wines turned to plastic corks, or Twist Offs to protect them from cork taint. Unless you want to age a wine for decades, there is nothing wrong with Twist Off Caps.

Most of the world's better dry Rosé wines come sealed with Twist Off caps, as do many good quality white wines. Having an old fashion cork is no sign of quality.

As the wine world homogenizes, it will be harder and harder to tell the difference between the two contrasting styles. Sadly, I think, the Old World is moving too quickly toward New World styles, but as the new generation of wine lovers become more educated and sophisticated in their wine and food pairing, the trend may reverse. In the mean time, try to enjoy both.

7 SPARKLING WINES
Party with the Stars

Champagne is a sparkling wine. Not all sparkling wines are Champagne. Some sparkling wines just happen to come from a French region known as Champagne. It can be made using three grapes according to the French AOC laws: Chardonnay, Pinot Noir, and Pinot Meunier, and four others consisting of less than 0.3%, are Arbane, Petit Meslier, Pinot Blanc and Pinto Gris. There are only two and a half acres of Arbane growing in all of France; just remember the main three grapes. Since the French label their wines with the name of the place they come from, that Chardonnay, Pinot Noir, and Pinot Meunier-based sparkling wine is called Champagne. Champagne is planted with 38% Pinot Noir, 32% Pinot Meunier, and 30 % Chardonnay. Americans used this name as a style of wine, and until very recently, stole the word and put it on many sparkling wines that were made in the USA. Too many people, especially in America, call every bottle of wine with bubbles in it, Champagne.

Note: The Champagne producer *Moutard-Dilignet* makes *Vielles Vignes* Champagne, which is a blend of six of the seven legal grapes. It excludes Pinot Gris. Few, if any, intelligent wine drinkers will ever need this data. Ignore it and read on.

Every region of France makes a sparkling wine and they are called simply, ***mousseux***, a wine that foams with bubbles. They have sparkling Vouvray, Saumur, Touraine, and Anjou all from the Loire region. There's sparkling Burgundy, and also sparkling Bordeaux.

Back in Chapter One, quite early in the chapter, we learned that carbon dioxide is a byproduct of fermentation. When the yeast converts the grape sugar into alcohol, carbon dioxide rises into the air and dissipates. When fermentation is completed, the wine will no longer expel any carbon dioxide. This was never much of a problem during the centuries when winemakers stored their end product in clay amphora or goatskins, but when producers began to bottle wine in glass to ship or store it, they had to learn that once the bottle was sealed, the remaining CO_2 pressure could build up if the fermentation wasn't fully completed, and cause the bottle to explode.

Many times, winemakers thought the fermentation was completed because the post-harvest colder weather stopped the yeast from doing their job on all the grapes' sugars. Later in spring, when it warmed again, more CO_2 was created and, if lucky, just the cork was blown out. If not so lucky, the bottle exploded. It wasn't until the British glassmakers were able to create the first thin but stronger bottles, that the refreshing bubbles could be safely kept in the wine.

The average automobile tire is inflated with 29 to 32 pounds of air pressure. The average bottle of champagne can have up to 90 pounds of pressure, and a cork can fly out at up to 40 miles per hour. No wonder there are so many eye injuries in restaurants where wait staff is untrained. However, let's not get ahead of ourselves.

The name Champagne comes from Latin for a slightly hilly open countryside or *Campania*. The hilly Italian region, Campania, is just south of Rome. In the Middle Ages, the name was also applied to the area of France around the towns of Ay, Rheims and Epernay. Light salmon-colored still wines were made there for centuries, but nothing like the Champagne, as we know it today.

All the early Champagne samples were cloudy and sweet. The Russians loved it and bought most of it. The British were the ones who demanded drier sparkling wines, and their vast thirst for the product, passing Russian consumption, forced the French to make it the way the British liked it -- dry.

After the widow Clicquot, of the Veuve Clicquot-Ponsardin Champagne House, figured out a way to get the sediments from the dead yeast to coagulate in the neck of the bottle, Champagne stopped being cloudy. She froze it, and removed the cap to permit the pressure to blow out the dead yeast, leaving a clear liquid filled with CO_2 gas. She topped off the bottle with clear wine, called adding the *dosage*, inserted a new cork, and tied it down with straw strings. Today, metal wire, called a *Muselet*, an *Agraffe*, or a *Cage*, is used to secure the sparkling wine cork. There's always six half-turns to loosen this cage when opening a bottle of sparkling wine. Be sure to keep your thumb on the cork after you've made four or five half-turns.

Legend has it that the Benedictine Monk, Dom Pérignon, discovered that corking the bottle near the conclusion of the fermentation, kept some bubbles in the wine, and said when he opened it, "I'm drinking the stars." Like most legends, there is no record of this event. I do repeat it though, whenever I open and share a bottle of Dom Pérignon.

The ***Champagne Method***, also called the ***Traditional Method***, as noted on many wine labels outside the Champagne region of France, means that the sparkling wine was made inside the bottle itself. The first fermentation was in a vat, and the wines were blended with 30 to 60 different *cuvées* to have the taste and style of the House producing it. Then, more yeast is added when it's bottled. They ferment the remaining sugars, and create the carbon dioxide gas that dissolves in the wine. When it is poured into a Champagne flute, the bubbles will escape and rise to the top of the glass. If the glass has residual soap, or a rinsing solution still in it, you will not get many, if any, bubbles escaping to rise toward the sky. Sparkling wine glasses should only be washed with hot water and white vinegar, never with soap and then thoroughly rinsed a number of times. This process will make a world of difference!

When you have a sparkling wine in a restaurant, and there are almost no bubbles rising in your glass, remember, there are 60 to 80 million bubbles available to rise, the problem is usually the wine glass itself, and not the bottle of sparkling wine.

Riddling, invented by the widow Clicquot, is when each bottle's bottom is lifted up a little each day from its horizontal position, and is slightly rotated to help work the dead yeast cells down into the neck so it can be frozen and expelled from the bottle. This starts only after a time period long enough to have the dead yeast add a toasty flavor to the wine. The minimum amount of time is at least one year for non-vintage Champagnes. Most Houses wait much longer; some cellar them up to five or six years before *riddling*. It takes many days of lifting and turning to get the bottle upside down with the dead yeast all in the neck near the opening. It's called *sur pointe* when the *riddling* is finished. Then *dégorgement*, or disgorging the sediment takes place. That's expelling the dead yeasts, which are now frozen in an ice plug near the opening. Good *riddlers* can turn over 25,000 bottles a day. Most modern facilities have machines to do this work.

Vin Nature is drier than *Brut*, which is drier than *Extra Dry*, which is drier than *Sec*, and a bottle labeled *Demi-Sec* is the sweetest Champagne.

Note: It's strange to think something called "Extra Dry" really means a little sweeter than Brut. I've seen staff in wine stores sell the Extra Dry to people who ask for the driest sparkling wine. Knowledgeable people don't make that mistake.

The bubbles in sparkling wines cleanse your palate and prepare it for the food to come. Sparkling wines are a great way to start any meal or celebration. It's expected at all Dionysian Society dining events. I know some organizations serve vodka or cocktails prior to dinner, a culinary *faux pas*! High alcohol does nothing but deaden your taste buds for at least half an hour. The only way to start an evening meal is with bubbles!

The **Charmat** process: besides the Champagne Method, the *Charmat* process is also used to make many sparkling wines. Base wines are blended, just as in the traditional method, but then the sugar and yeast are added, and all the wine is put into a large pressurized tank for its secondary fermentation. The finished sparkling wine is then bottled. It's less costly to do it this way, however, the wine doesn't age on its own dead yeast cells as long, which adds the toasty complex flavors, and there is no riddling of each bottle as in the Champagne Method.

The **Continuous Method**, developed in Russia, has the wine run through four or five tanks all under pressure. It's a cheap way of clearing them, adding bubbles, and basically, it's only used for poor quality sweet wines. They're rarely seen outside of Eastern Europe.

The **Transfer Method** also keeps the base wine under pressure in large tanks until it is transferred into separate bottles.

What smart wine drinkers need to know is that the Charmat method sparklers are fine as party wines. The highest quality bubbles come from sparkling wines made by the Champagne Method, or as it's called outside the Champagne region, the Traditional Method. If you know that the Charmat method is for bulk production of cheaper sparkling wines, that "Traditional

Method" means the "Champagne Method," and also that Champagne only comes from a single French wine region about 60 miles northeast of Paris, then you are among the top 25% of wine scholars, sommeliers and wine educators.

Bubbly Names

The United States calls wines with bubbles in them, simply **Sparkling Wine,** as does New Zealand and Australia. Spain refers to them as **Cava** because they're made in caves. Cava is mostly made with three local Spanish grapes: *Macabeo, Xarello* and *Parellada,* and recent laws permit some Chardonnay to be put in them to help them lean toward American taste, but the ones made with the classic Spanish grapes prove the most interesting for intelligent drinkers.

Portugal calls their sparkling wines, **Espumante.**

The Italian **Franciacorta** area uses the Traditional method as well as the traditional Chardonnay and Pinot Noir grapes to make very high quality sparkling wines.

In Italy, the word for wine with CO_2 remaining is **Spumante.** The Italian word, *Frizzante*, means "with a little fizz," or slightly bubbly. Many wine makers know that CO_2 can refresh the tongue, so they'll try to leave a tiny amount of carbonation in the wine to make it more refreshing. As an example, most of the Portuguese *Vinho Verde* wines have a little spritz in them.

Many Americans think *Spumante* means "sweet" because of the Asti Spumante wine that was, and still is, a popular after dinner wine. Since it is made with Muscat grapes, and has low alcohol with a lot of residual sugar, it does taste quite sweet. Since they are usually very low in alcohol, 5.5% to only 9% alcohol, they are a safe way to end a meal before driving home. The truth is the name simply states that it is a wine from the city of Asti and it has bubbles in it.

Italy also makes **Prosecco**; sparkling wines made from the Charmat method. They traditionally use the Glara grape. Recent Italian wine laws permit the addition of some other grapes to be added to the Glara to increase production.

Germany and Austria call their sparkling wines **Sekt**. The best ones are made with Riesling, and are delightful on hot summer days.

The Traditional Method does the secondary fermentation in the bottle from which you are drinking. It is made in the 750 ml size bottles, and also in Magnums, or the 1.5-liter size bottle. It is usually poured off from these two sizes into other size bottles and re-corked. Big bottles are festive, they age longer, and usually, they taste creamier.

Intelligent wine drinkers like sparkling wines best when poured from Magnums. Listed below are all the sparkling wine bottle sizes, but simply remember that a Jeroboam is the same as four regular sparkling wine bottles and the Nebuchadnezzar is the largest and equal to 20 regular bottles of sparkling wine. Nebuchadnezzars are more trouble than they're worth.

A Magnum, which is equal to two regular bottles, cost more than two separate bottles because the bottle has to have thicker glass, which costs more. Smart people can stretch basic information a very long way. Be selective in what you study to remember.

Champagne (sparkling wine) Names and Bottle Sizes

Name	Size	Equivalent
Split	187 ML	One glass
Half-Bottle	375 ML	Half Bottle
Bottle	750 ML	1 Bottle
Magnum	1.5 L	2 Bottles
Jeroboam	3 L	4 Bottles
Methuselah	6 L	8 Bottles
Salmanazar	9 L	12 Bottles (One case)
Balthazar	12 L	16 Bottles
Nebuchadnezzar	15 L	20 Bottles

The last five sizes, starting from a Jeroboam, are usually special order bottles, but many fine wine shops can procure one for you if you want to host a special tribute with all, or lots of sparkling wine. Opening and serving sparkling wine from a Methuselah during a winter holiday party for forty or fifty people makes for a very festive event.

A Luxury Item

Veblen commodities are items like rare wines that have a demand proportional to their high prices. Luxury cars, some jewelry and wines that cost hundreds of dollars are symbols of conspicuous consumption. Intelligent wine drinkers ignore the Veblen effect.

Serving sparkling wines from extra large bottles makes it a luxury item, and you'll pay much more for the privilege of showing off. Standard bottles of Dom Pérignon don't really cost any more to make than Moet & Chandon's other Champagnes, and with about five million bottles available, it doesn't have to be so expensive. However, its image as a luxury item adds to the mystique, and the mind plays a major part with regards to enjoying things.

As an intellectual wine lover, you'll soon notice that there are many "label drinkers" out there. They haven't read this, or any books about what sincere intelligent lovers of wine, culture, art, music and civilization want to know about their passion. They use famous expensive bottles to impress and try to create self-worth. You can help them by sharing this book after you've finished it. Wine books make great gifts.

Some cars, certain clothing lines, and even candy are sold as luxury items. It's all in the packaging. Canadian Ice Wine is sold in a gift box; one of the few wines to do that. So are certain Champagnes and some of the most expensive Cognacs. Smart people only have to remember that you taste and drink what's inside the bottle, not the label or packaging. The Chinese have a long history of "gift-giving," and their newly found love of wine, will force all producers to expand their packaging appearances, and put prices up. Sparkling wines have led the way.

Interesting to know, but not necessary for enjoying Champagne

On every real Champagne label, not on all the other sparkling wines, in tiny print at the bottom, are two letters and a series of numbers. It's like an address code. They are:

NM Négociant Manipulant: meaning some of the wine was grown elsewhere but made and bottled here. All the large houses have this one.

RM Récoltant Manipulant: meaning the Champagne in the bottle was grown, produced and bottled by the name on the label.

And less frequently seen are:

CM Cooperative Manipulant: meaning the growers were not involved in the wine production.

RC Récoltant Co-opérateur: meaning the liquid inside was owned by a single grower, but the wine was made at a cooperative.

SR Societe de Récoltants: meaning two or more growers share a winery, and label the Champagne under the organization's name.

NM Champagne Houses are well known. Bollinger, Veuve Clicquot-Ponsardin, Deutz, Gosset, Charles Heidsieck, Krug, Lanson, Möet & Chandon, Mumm, Perrier-Jouët, Pol Roger, Pommery, Ruinart, and Taittinger are all examples.

Many of these Houses make a *special cuvée* and sell it as their top brand. Möet & Chandon's Dom Pérignon, Taittinger's Comte de Champagne, Perrier-Jouët's Fleur de Champagne, which is know as Belle Époque, are just a few examples.

RM Champagne Houses are not as familiar to many people. They are smaller, produce fewer bottles, and are available only in larger cities. LeLarge-Pugeot, one of the best I think, Ployez-Jacquemart who leaves their Champagne on the lees for up to 12 years before being disgorged, Pierre Paillard who makes only 8,000 cases, Jean-Marc Sélèque is a one-man show, and Lilbert-Fils, who makes one of the best *Blanc de Blancs* I know are examples.

The RM Champagnes are many times higher in acid, more refreshing and they all have unique flavors.

Some top **Spanish Cava** producers are: Vallformosa, Segura Viudas, Juvé & Camps, Freixenet, Codorníu, Raventós, and the smaller Mestres Cava, that made its first bottle in 1925, and opened it to celebrate Christmas in 1928.

These sparkling wines come from Penedès in the Catalonian region of Spain.

Because Cava is made almost entirely with mechanical riddling, it is priced way below Champagnes. Cava can be found from under $10 up to $40 and above. That is their paradox; they want it to be more of a luxury item. Currently, almost a dozen Cava Houses have withdrawn from the DO appellation, even the historic *Raventós i Blanc*. They want the more specific designation *Conca del Riu Anoia* on their labels. The success of Cava has been in its volume, more so than in its quality.

A specific classification called *Cava de Paraje Calificado,* or qualified single estate Cava, which will require 36 months of aging on the lees, not the basic 10 months of regular Cava, became available for Christmas, 2016. This new class is a bit less than 2% of Cava's total production.

The difference between a $15 bottle of Cava, and one that cost $30 is a 100% increase. Few educated wine lovers and critics will see a hundred percent increase in its quality. Use your wine knowledge to buy wisely.

Most Cava producers, however, see Italian *Prosecco* as their key competitor and don't want to try to raise quality or prices. The high quality *Vallformosa Brut Clasic,* at around $16, is always on my Best Buy List. No need to change anything.

Italy's Spumante is the term used for wines with bubbles. The highest rated Italian sparkling wines are from, and are called *Franciacorta* sparkling wines. The area has its own DOC and is east of Milan in Lombardy. Producers I've enjoyed and shared are *Bellavista, Berlucchi, Ca'del Bosco* and the *Ca' d'Or Noble Rosé* as a special evening treat or with a sparkling brunch. **Prosecco**, made mostly from the *Glara* grape, is Italy's largest selling sparkling wine. *Mionetto, Villa Sandi*, and *Zardetto* are always pleasant.

A few of **California's Sparkling Wines**: Roderer Estate, Domaine Chandon, Schramsberg, Mumm Napa, Gloria Ferrer, Domaine Carneros, and Iron Horse are all made with the traditional method.

Many of the California sparkling wine houses are owned by the Big French Houses like Roderer, Moet & Chandon, Mumm, or Taittinger and they have their French specialists help make the Californian sparkling wines. The major difference is that Californian examples always show bigger fruit flavors because of the riper grapes due to the extra sunshine and heat, while the French Champagnes are more austere with what taste like higher, cleaner and more refreshing acids. Both styles have a place at my table.

Start every special meal with bubbles. Sparkling wines match with nearly every type of food and can be drunk throughout the entire meal. Keep you personal sparkling wine glasses perfectly clean and experiment with sparkling wines from all over the world. Taste as many as possible and consider it homework for your on going study into the world of wine.

Erudite wine drinkers all know that Champagne is a sparkling wine, but not all sparkling wines are Champagne. To quote the real estate business, it's location, location, location. Being aware of, and understanding the data in just this chapter, definitely puts you among the top 25% of all wine drinkers; maybe the top 20%.

8 BODIES AND LEGS
Matching wine with food

Wine **is** food; it's the liquid part of the meal. I voiced this concept decades ago, and have repeated it ever since I confirmed its truth.

If you've ever really enjoyed a great meal at a fine restaurant where the sommelier recommended a wine you've never seen or heard of, but quickly realized that the flavors of the dish and the wine blended into each other, or contrasted with each other, you can be sure that the sommelier knew the trick to matching wines with foods.

If you're aware of the concept of a wine's Body and Legs, you are on your way to greater enjoyment of wine as a food. I teach a wine and food-pairing seminar called, "Bodies & Legs," and for years it has caught the attention of many young men.

White wine with fish, red wine with meat really works, but the top 20 percent of the most knowledgeable wine drinkers know a very simple fact about wine. All you have to do is match the weight of the wine, or the "body," with the weight, or heaviness, of the food.

Let's get right to the analogy. Think of wine in the same way you have come to think about milk: skim milk, whole milk, and heavy cream.

Light wines, ideal for grilled fish, vegetable dishes, and so forth, are like skim milk. They have little weight in them.

Whole milk is what you think about when drinking white Chardonnays, or red Pinot Noir. There are lots of wines that have these medium weights. Wines like these, to pair well, need medium weight foods, which are heavier. I use Rosé wines to pair with shrimp because it always works; they both have the same medium body, and also, because the colors match. Color matching works more often than you'd ever think. Remember, sight is the first sense used to appreciate food. Meals have to look good as well as taste good.

Full-bodied wines are bigger and rounder and lie more heavily in your mouth. The flavors linger longer too. So they demand heavier foods with which to pair them properly.

Heavy cream has the most weight in our milk analogy, and it coats your palate and lingers the longest on your tongue. Cream Sherries, big Ports or Madeira fit into that category, but so do massive Cabernets Sauvignons, higher alcohol Zinfandels and Syrahs. If you think of a wine's weight, you can easily learn to put the wines you drink into one of these three groups. Then, you match the weight of the wine to the weight of the major food item on the dish you're pairing it with. That's it. Simple.

We tend to dumb-things-down like, "white wine with fish; red wine with meat." That will work many times. But salmon or tuna have much more body or weight and fat content than a lighter fish or shellfish would have, so a medium-bodied red like a Dolcetto or a French or Oregon Pinot Noir match it perfectly. Yes, red wines with fish. Too many Californian Pinot Noirs are too jammy with much higher alcohol, so they would overwhelm the salmon. Forget that old quote we all once learned, "white with fish and…" and simply match the weight of any food (consider its category like we did with milk) to the same weight of a wine.

The best food-wines have higher acids, to refresh your palate, and lower sugars that won't sedate your hunger.

Because we are born with an inclination toward sweeter things, we all tend to like sugar. Desserts are filled with sugar. The sweetness of desserts deadens out taste buds and we leave the dinner table feeling satisfied. So if you drink sweet wine with your main course, you miss how the flavors should marry together. The sweetness distracts from the quality of the food. White Zinfandel is high in residual sugar, that's why so many people like it. It can be enjoyable if you've just come out of the ocean or a pool on a hot day, and need a glass of liquid to eradicate your thirst, White Zin can qualify. If, however, you want to enjoy any wine with your meal, save the sweeter ones to pair *with* desserts, or even *after* the meal.

Legs Determine the Body

Legs are the droplets of wine that run down the inside of a wineglass after you've swirled it. Lighter wines produce few or almost no legs at all. Medium weight wines have larger droplets that move slowly down the glass while the wines with the most Body, have large thick legs that may even form a wide sheet, and slide slowly down the glass.

The smaller the droplet, the less Body a wine has and it will marry best with similar, light-weight foods that taste delicate in your mouth. Sugar adds a lot of Body to a wine, so high-acid wines like Sauvignon Blanc, Albarino, or Pinot Grigio, wines without any sugar, will enhance foods with a similar weight the best.

Veal, salmon, tuna, roasted chicken, pasta with just butter or oil, all jump into that medium weight class, and they pair best with medium-weight wines like Chardonnay, Viognier, Burgundies both white and red, Barbera, Beaujolais from the red Gamay grape, Loire Valley Cabernet Franc, white or red Cote du Rhone wines, and a hundred other medium-weight selections from all over the world. Wines were developed ages ago to pair with local cuisines, so matching any dish with any wine from the same region will almost always complement each other. Seafood and Albarino from Spain's Atlantic northwest coast or Malbec with Argentina's beef are obvious examples.

Wild boar, pasta with a cream sauce, heavy meat or cheese dishes are full-bodied foods and they call for the whole-milk type of selections that are full-bodied wines like big Napa Cabernet Sauvignon, Bordeaux, Syrah, Sonoma Zinfandel, Brunello or Chianti and Barolo.

The heavier the food feels in your mouth, the heavier the wine selection should be so that the weight or mouth feel of one guides you directly into tasting the other.

Blue cheese, chocolates, and cheesecakes all scream out for the heaviest of wines like Porto, Sauternes, or Cream Sherries; use any sweeter wine with legs that take forever, after swirling, to slide back down the insides of the wine glass. The Legs of high alcohol and high glycol wines will sometimes bond together and form a wide sheet that slithers down the glass.

Remember, every food will alter the taste of a wine! A smart rule to follow is that it's better to have a wine too light for the food, than to select a wine that has too much Body to dance with the dish. It will stamp out every delicate flavor.

You'll never hear an astute wine drinker say, "I just love Sauvignon Blanc so I drink it with everything." All across America, beautifully crafted meals have their flavors choked out with overly oaked Chardonnays, or excessively high-alcohol New World whites and reds. Eschew high alcohol and excessive sugar, and your dining experiences will explode with newly found levels of enjoyment.

Tannic Acid

Tannins are the compounds that add to the Body and help a wine to age, but they also dry out your mouth. Young short-chain molecules of tannin leave a bitter taste in your mouth. That's why so many youthful drinkers and even older ladies find big red wines somewhat offensive. The lactic acids in cheeses and the protein compounds found in lean means, will counteract the tannins' effect and make then taste far less bitter and smoother in your mouth. Once the dry tannic finish is eliminated, you can concentrate on the aromas and mouth-cleansing aspect of the wine, and then enjoy the meal much more.

These tannins come from grape skins, the pits, and also from the oak. Try to think of oak as a spice that adds a flavor to wines. It gives an impression of sweetness, something we're born to like, and distracts from the natural flavor of the wine so they can easily deaden the flavors of food.

I have actually drunk with people who can ascertain the source of the French oak forest, like *Bercé* in the Loire, *Jupilles*, (pronounced *joo pee*), *Nevers*, *Tronçais*, *Allier* or *Limousin* simply by smelling and tasting the wine. These are the names of the forests where the oak was harvested and used to make wine barrels. When it happens that you notice mostly the wood flavor in a wine, you can be sure the wine is over-oaked and without a doubt, it will destroy the meal.

Serving Temperatures

White, pink and red wines all have different amounts of natural acids in them, and temperature can greatly affect how they will taste and marry with foods.

Most white wines have lots of refreshing acids and they work the same way as putting some lemon juice on a piece of fish to enliven it.

So, white wine, which is meant to be drunk younger while it's fresher, should always be consumed at a cooler temperature than a pink or a red wine. Colder temperatures highlight acids. Many American refrigerators are set to the upper 30's F or low 40's and that is excessive for most white wines. When a wine is too cold, it prevents you from reflecting upon its aromas and even stops your ability to properly taste.

Hint: Serve the cheapest wine you can buy to your non-wine-drinking friends, but be sure to serve it near freezing. It will be wet and cold, have little aroma, and no taste. That's enough to know.

Simple everyday whites can be served at 55 to 60 degrees F, but great white Burgundy and white Rhone wines should be served less chilled, and be thought of and treated as you would a light red wine.

Rosé wine - pink, blush, copper, or salmon, all have a bit of skin contact to extract the color, or have some red wine added, so they'll all reflect higher tannic acid than pure white wines.

Hint: As you lower the temperature of tannic acids, they become much more pronounced and bitter. That's why red wine is served at what we call room temperature so the fruit will show easier, but mostly so there'll be less bitterness.

No matter how slight the color, pinkish wines should be served cool, but not as cold as white wines. The mid-60's F is fine; about 15 minutes in an ice bucket properly filled with one-third ice and another third water, will quickly do the trick. If an ice bucket doesn't have water in it, you cannot push a bottle down to its neck. Icy water chills a bottle much faster than simply having ice around it.

Wines listed as full or round, have medium-weight bodies, like Chardonnay and Pinot Noir. So even though one is white and the other is red, they can be drunk at the same temperature, ideally at 68 to 72 degrees F. The red Beaujolais is best enjoyed slightly cool; white Viognier tastes best when it's just below room temperature.

People, who fill their wine glass to the top instead of just one-third full, and sip at it slowly for far too long, will see its taste and temperature go through many changes. Pouring small, but chilled amounts at regular intervals, will provide a wine with the ideal drinking temperature. It always amuses me that people will pay a lot of money for some bottles of great wine, and then abuse it in a stem-less glass. They never swirl it; they fill it too high; they drink it ice cold, or their hand around the glass makes it way too hot. Again, a little intellectual pursuit can greatly increase all of life's pleasures especially with regards to wine.

Apples & Cheese

There's an ancient quote told by wine merchants: "Buy with apples, and sell with cheese." The malic acid in apples (*malum* was the word for apple in Latin) can make new wines taste more thin and metallic than they really are. If that taste is excessive, the wine may never develop well. The apple helps you notice faults. Cheese, on the other hand, makes wines taste bigger and softer in your mouth, making them an easier sell. That's why people have wine and cheese parties instead of wine and tree-fruit parties.

Being aware of this apple and cheese fact should make you understand the following simplistic rules that will help you when matching wines with foods.

Fourteen Classic Pairing Rules

1. Salt makes sweet wines taste even sweeter.

2. All dry wines taste bad with sweeter foods.

3. High tannic red wines taste less bitter when served with rare meats or soft cheeses.

4. Very acidic foods, like salad with vinegar, will make wines more astringent; use lemon juice with oil on a salad if you want to pair it with a nice light wine.

5. Both artichokes and asparagus are not wine-friendly.

6. Choose a wine to match the meat being served with asparagus and artichokes, and then hope for the best.

7. Hard cheeses make most red wines taste softer and fruitier.

8. Contrary to many promotions, Cabernet Sauvignon does not go well with chocolate. In fact, some chocolates are so sweet that only young Porto can pair with it.

9. Riesling goes with smoked fish and meat beautifully.

10. Game birds are best with red Burgundy or Oregon Pinot Noir.

11. Oysters demand Chablis.

12. Lamb chops and red Bordeaux were made for each other.

13. Crème brulée needs Sauternes.

14. Any wine is better than no wine with food.

The *Mediterranean Diet* has taught us that people who eat well and drink wine moderately live longer and healthier. Certain chemical concentrations in wine have been shown to help the heart and slow dementia. Wine is a healthy food when consumed in moderation and paired correctly. Enjoy.

Leftover wine

If it ever happens that you have wine leftover, here's what to do with it.

Seven uses for nearly empty bottles of wine:

Let it sour, and then use in salads

Red: put in Bolognese Sauce to add complexity

Mull it with spices, warm it, and sip it at the first snow

Red: add to all chocolate recipes

Put it in your compost pile to help the bacteria, or use to fertilize large plants

Make wine jelly

Sweeten it, and add to syrup for Waffles

Note: An opened bottle, red or white, will last *10 times longer* in a refrigerator than the same opened wine stored at room temperature.

If you've learned to match the weight of the food to a similarly weighted wine, you'll seldom, if ever, have a need to deal with leftover wine. The most intelligent gourmets in the world have known for centuries that wine will always enhance a meal, and make dining a civilized event. It permits eating for pleasure and not just for survival.

9 THE TOP VARIETALS

The history of vines and grapes and their fermented end product is a time line of civilization. (Review Chapter One) The making of wine, with all its advances, runs parallel to the study of the development of mankind.

All grape varieties are really *cultivars*. The best single species of grapes for making wine are all found among the *Vitis vinifera* species. *Vitis labrusca*, known for the "foxy" aroma they produce in wines, is better used for jams and jellies as is best done with the Concord grape. The *Vitis riparia* species is found growing wild along streams and wooded areas and produce very poor quality wines. The southern *Vitis rotundifolia* produces a line of mediocre sweet wines, and it too, is best left alone.

There are thousands of different indigenous grapes, but the following white grapes, listed in order from driest to the sweetest styles, are all you really need to know as an intelligent knowledgeable wine person who is just starting to enjoy the gift of Dionysus. So let's learn a little bit about the following.

White grapes you need to know well, and the order in which to taste them:

1. Sauvignon Blanc   2. Chardonnay

3. Chenin Blanc   4. Riesling

Viognier could possible be in the "need to know" list, but you can be very smart about wine without it. Other interesting white grapes could include Gewürztraminer, Gruner Veltliner, Moscato, Sémillon, and Pinot Grigio. Airén, the most widely planted white grape in Spain, Albano of Northern Italy, Albariño from Spain, Italy's Arneis, Greece's Assyrtiko and Moschofilero, and Muscadet from the Loire. Marsanne and Roussanne from France's Rhone area, Spanish Pedro Ximénez, Italian Picolit, and of course, Pinot Gris and Pinot Blanc for nearly everywhere.

You'll eventually learn about the Glera grape that makes Prosecco, Rkatsiteli from Georgia and Russia, Sylvaner and Friulano. The Torrontés grape is from Spain and now it's doing very well in Argentina. Italy's Trebbiano called Ugni Blanc in France, Verdejo, Verdicchio, Vermentino, Vernaccia, and Verduzzo, my list of excellent "V" wines, are all very enjoyable food-wines, and are perfect wines to pair with fish. Xarello is used in Spain's CAVA, and it's also made as a still white called Viura in the Rioja region.

This list could go on for pages, but it's not at all necessary for a really smart wine lover to know them all. Become an expert with the top four white grapes and you'll be among the top 20% of knowledgeable wine drinkers. Taste and review all six of the following red wines too.

The red grapes, you need to know and be familiar with in order of importance:

1. Cabernet Sauvignon   2. Merlot

3. Pinot Noir   4. Syrah

5. Sangiovese   6. Zinfandel

Other important red grapes include Barbera, Grenache, Malbec, Cabernet Franc, Pinotage, Carmenère, and Agiorgitiko from Greece. Nebbiolo could be added to the above list. The grape of Barolo, the name of a place in Italy, is made with Nebbiolo, but just knowing about and enjoying Barolo is enough for most bright people. Gamay, the grape that makes Beaujolais, might be considered for the top list, but it was expelled from Burgundy two centuries ago for making good, not great wine, so you don't have to be a Gamay scholar to be among the brightest wine people. Barbera could also be listed above and Grenache too, but this is a *coarse* guide, not an encyclopedia.

You should sample as many of these grapes you can find, made by as many different producers as possible, if you want to consider yourself proficient in wine and be among the top 19% of knowledgeable wine drinkers. Of course, your highly developed intellectual curiosity will sooner or later drive you to sample grapes like Turkey's Öküzgözü, Verona, Italy's Oseleta, Puglia, Italy's Negroamaro, Bulgaria's Pamid, Burgundy, France's Pinot Meunier, South Africa's Pinotage, and Croatia's Plavac Mali grape, the source of Zinfandel. (Zinfandel was thought to be Italy's Primitivo for decades, but at the start of the 21st Century, DNA testing showed that it first came from Croatia) You'll surely taste and enjoy Italy's Friuli grape, Refosco, and Rondinella from Veneto, as well as the Sagrantino wine from Umbria.

The northern Italian grape Teroldego, Tannat from South West France, and now also doing well in Uruguay, as well as Touriga Nacional from Portugal, are also special grapes that make interesting wines. But, if you study just the six major red grape examples I've suggested, you'll have decades of enjoying great red wines as you become a member of the top 19% of the world's wine scholars.

The Whites and Reds You Must Know

Four White Grapes

Let's review the four white and six red grapes that will be enough to satisfy all your wine and dining needs.

All **Sauvignon Blanc** wine has some hint of grapefruit on its nose, either white or pink grapefruit. After that essence, the *terroir* will add other nuisances. Sauvignon Blanc makes the world's best dry white wines, and this grape is the basis for Loire Valley whites like Pouilly-Fumé and Sancerre. They are crisp and racy wines ideal for shellfish and most seafood. *Menetou-Salon*, *Quincy* and *Reuilly* are each distinct and reflect the Loire styles for Sauvignon Blanc.

By 1990, Sauvignon Blanc surpassed plantings of Ungi Blanc (which is called Trebbiano in Italy) throughout Bordeaux, and with Sémillon, makes the great food-worthy White Bordeaux. It's at the core of French white wines from *Entre-Deux-Mers* and throughout the *Graves* and *Pessac-Léognan* Districts. The Sauternes district too, uses this grape in its blends for their rich sweet wines.

New Zealand's Marlborough region built its wine industry on Sauvignon Blanc. It is a grassy-veggie style with gooseberry aromas and even some hints of asparagus. This style works with salads.

Australia also produces some Sauvignon Blanc, but most are quite basic and not yet worthy of an intellectual's study of the grape.

The Maule Valley in Chile produces very nice, easy-drinking whites made with Sauvignon Blanc, and another grape called, *Sanvignonasse* also called *Sauvignon Vert*. It is still over-cropped, producing too many tons per acre, but it doesn't cost much. Excellent examples come from Colchagua in Chile.

The Sauvignon Blancs I've had from Brazil are dull wines and taste, to me, just like the hybrid grape, *Seyval Blanc*, that is planted all over the American East Coast.

The South African Sauvignon Blanc wines lean more toward the white Bordeaux or Loire Valley style, and not the New Zealand style.

The California and Pacific Northwest Sauvignon Blancs are all pleasant wines. It was the late Robert Mondavi who named his style *Fumé Blanc* to help show the grape's connection to Pouilly-Fumé in France. He did not trademark the name so anyone could produce the grape and sell it with this easy to pronounce name. The word *Fumé* refers to what looks like smoke rising above the Loire River in the mornings, and not to the smoke of a fire even though many superficial wine critics say they smell smoke as one of the wine's aromas.

Our next grape is **Chardonnay**. It's the only grape used to make white Burgundy and the rest of the world tries to imitate the Burgundian style. Blanc de Blanc Champagne is made only from Chardonnay. It means, "white from white." The Chablis area uses a higher acid style to make its wines entirely from Chardonnay. The lower region of Burgundy, where Chardonnay grows over limestone, produces a rich, creamier style.

When Chardonnay is barrel-fermented, softened with malolactic fermentation, and aged for a while on its lees, it is the creamiest, richest, and most buttery of all the white wines. It should never be drunk too chilled, and it can replace many light reds to match with foods. Pork and veal are two examples when this white beats a red wine.

It is grown in every wine-producing country in the world, and most are quite enjoyable. It is the most widely planted white grape except for Spain's *Airân*, Italy's *Trebbiano* and Russia's *Rkatsiteli*. You have to go out of your way to make a bad Chardonnay. However, only from the best *terroir* come the greatest Chardonnays. The origin of the grape was, for decades, thought to be a mutation of Pinot Noir, and it was actually called Pinot Chardonnay for years. However, now it seems that it is its own variety. It's been growing in the Burgundy region of France for centuries and in the Mâconnais, there is a small village called Chardonnay. The grape probably spread from that area as the Roman Empire began to decline.

Its popularity is so great that even Greece, Israel, Moldova, Georgia, Hungary, Romania, and China have it planted and are producing both oaked and the newest trend, the un-oaked styles. Napa and Sonoma lead the USA in Chardonnay production, but fine examples can be found in over a dozen states including New Jersey, Virginia, New York, Ohio and North Carolina. However, the greatest Chardonnay is still made with lower alcohols, minimum use of French oak, and come from the *Côte de Beaune* in France's southern Burgundy region.

Le Montrachet, may be the very best Chardonnay produced. It is a Grand Cru French Burgundy, and the vineyard overlaps the villages of both *Puligny* and *Chassagne*.

I believe that *Corton-Charlemagne* is a close second. It is made in the village of Aloxe-Corton. It's said that King Charlemagne, while riding through the area, saw lighter snow on one of the hillsides, so he planted the first Chardonnay there proving that location makes all the difference for fine wines.

Bâtard-Montrachet also tastes and costs almost the same as the first two wines mentioned above.

In the village of Meursault, the vineyards of *Charmes, Santenots* and *Les Perrières* all make excellent white Burgundies with their distinctive Chardonnays. Besides these top-classified wines, I think you'll also greatly enjoy the white Burgundy from Rully, Givry, and

Montagny. Seek them out; they cost much less and are what I call, "Good Buys."

Beware the food pairing problem many New World Chardonnays have when they are so over oaked that the natural fruits and acids become subdued by the wood, leaving overly cloying flavors in your mouth. Low alcohol Chardonnays with less wood are always the best wines to serve with meals. Indisputable.

Chenin Blanc has nowhere near the popularity of Chardonnay, but it should. It is known as *Pineau de la Loire* in its home section of France. It's called *Steen* in South Africa, and it helped build South Africa's excellent wine reputation. Modern producers there are now using the name Chenin Blanc because so few people are academically enthusiastic enough to research the name Steen, as you would have done. That's why intelligent wine drinkers get to appreciate so much more. Every academic effort pays off.

California has more Chenin Blanc planted than France does, and even though much of it is used in box wines, excellent quality examples can be found in both a dry and a slightly sweet style. France, however, made Chenin Blanc famous with wines from *Anjou-Touraine;* with great examples found in *Montlouis, Saumur, Quarts de Chaume,* and the best-known one, *Vouvray.* The finest examples are soft and refreshing whites with just a hint of sugar on the finish. The sweeter ones age very well. I've enjoyed 35 and even 45 year-old examples of *Vouvray.* Look for word *Moelleux* on the label if you plan to age it.

In Argentina, Uruguay, Brazil and Mexico, it is many times called *Pinot Blanco*, confusing it with the Pinto Blanc grape of Europe. This is starting to be corrected.

In America, Chenin Blanc is way underrated. It makes a fine food wine because it has good acids just as Riesling does. It's never exceptionally high in alcohol, is medium-bodied, and when permitted to be affected with Botry*tis cinerea,* the noble rot, it can produce marvelous dessert wines that have been known to age at least half a century. Few wines can compare when matching it with peach-glazed pork dishes. Whenever you're making a cream sauce, add some Chenin Blanc. Stick to the French or South African selections. Too many Chenin Blancs from California have lower acids and higher sugars. If you want it for a dessert wine, seek out a *Bonnezeaux* or *Coteaux* wine from the Loire Valley.

Because of its high natural acids, Chenin Blanc makes charming sparkling wines especially the *Crámant de Loire* and *Saumur Mousseux*. Understanding the qualities of this lesser known, but great grape, puts you among the top 19% of America's wine drinkers, if not higher. Share this knowledge. It will help you remember it.

Riesling, although less popular in America over the past 25 years, may be the queen of all the white wines. It was the most popular grape for wine during the 1800's and early 1900's, before Chardonnay's simplicity pushed it out of first place. Because it's made in so many different styles (as Chapter Thirteen explains) the uneducated become confused and have spent decades missing out on enjoying a great wine.

When it's labeled as *Trocken*, it's "dry" and very food friendly. Riesling is pleasantly low in alcohol and high in natural acids, ideal for many types of food, and especially for Asian cuisine. It's planted throughout the world, but it matures to perfection in cooler regions like Germany's Rhine and Mosel areas, New York's Finger Lakes, Michigan, and Washington State. Also, the French region of Alsace produces some of the best Rieslings in the world. Start your tasting studies with Riesling samples from the Alsace.

Documentations noting the Riesling grape go back to the 1500's, and a few from the 1400's. I suspect that it was growing locally when the Romans settled in Trier, Germany.

Riesling is absolutely a grape you must know and should enjoy because it always has low alcohol, high refreshing natural acids, and costs way below other world famous wines made from other grapes. It always reflects the place (its *terroir*) where it was grown, and Riesling pairs with more foods than any other grape.

Riesling is Germany's best and most famous grape. The Mosel Rieslings, bottled in green glass, are more delicate and flavorful with mineral and citrus notes. A sub-region of the Mosel, the Saar, produces wines with the highest acids, and they seem to age forever. The Ruwer, another Mosel sub-region, are the smoothest with very subtle flavors.

The Rhine Rieslings, bottled in brown glass, make fuller-rounder wines with a pronounced petrol nose, that's considered a positive aroma, mixed with a scent of flowers. I like Mosel wines with appetizers, and use the Rhine wines with white meats or a cheese entrée. Rieslings from the Rheinpfalz are less complex, but they also cost less than wines from the other regions making them great party wines.

The best French Alsace Riesling examples are dry. Also, there is no doubt that Riesling makes the best white wine in the New York's Finger Lakes wine producing region. The Austrian examples usually cost less than the German ones, and are made in the same styles from bone dry to completely sweet so they too will marry with many desserts.

Six Red Grapes

Cabernet Sauvignon is the king of all grapes, not only the red ones. It is the heart of Bordeaux and the basis of all of the most expensive New World red wines. Its black cherry, chocolate and cassis aromas, braced with strong tannins, provide a classic red meat food wine. It is usually full bodied, and should always have a long aftertaste. With age, it develops a pleasant tobacco aroma laced with subtle leather notes, aromas that blend very well with meat dishes. It is traditionally paired with lamb chops; try it. I suggest never drinking any classified red Bordeaux until it's at least ten years old, and Cabernet Sauvignon from other places in the world, at least eight years old. Most high quality Cab-based wines need 15 years to peak. Lay some big Cabernets down today.

In 1997, the DNA procedure of fingerprinting proved that Cabernet Sauvignon evolved from the crossing of Cabernet Franc and the white Sauvignon Blanc grape.

The blue thick-skinned grape is small; this gives it a high ratio of juice-to-skin contact that results in powerful age-worthy wines with lots of tannic acid. It needs years to soften and develop complex aromas. Cabernet Sauvignon is excellent as a base wine; then blending it with some Merlot to soften it, Cabernet Franc to add fragrance to its nose, Malbec and Petit Verdot to deepen its color and to increase its backbone for aging.

Besides in Bordeaux, Cabernet Sauvignon is planted in the south of France, and is revered in many other European countries as well as throughout South America, and in Australia and New Zealand. It is also a major force in South Africa.

In America, it is the heart and soul of the great Napa and Sonoma red wines. It also does very well in Washington State, and with Merlot, is making Washington State's red wines noticed throughout the world.

Both Italy and Spain have built a super class of red wines by adding Cabernet Sauvignon to their native grapes. While they are quite nice to drink, I fear that they distract from the local *terrior* and homogenize the taste for the world's wine drinkers, especially the American desire for big fruity wines with excessive oak.

Aside from the fact that Cabernet Sauvignon dominates whatever grape it's added to, it remains the king of red wines, and once your acquire a taste for it, most other wines seem to line up in its shadow.

Merlot, the prince of Bordeaux's Right Bank, is always easy to enjoy and makes the perfect red wine for pairing with so many different types of meals. It's what makes *Chateau Petrus,* one of the most expensive and extremely enjoyable wines, so easy to drink. Merlot is the basis for the *St-Emilion* and *Pomerol* wines of Bordeaux.

The Merlot grape has always been used to blend into Cabernet Sauvignon-based wines whether from France or California, and today it is blended with Italy's Sangiovese grape to make their Super Tuscans. The grape is a little darker than Cabernet Sauvignon, but has thinner skin and less acid, so it produces wines that can be drunk younger, are softer in your mouth, but still pair well with most foods calling for red wine.

The Merlot grape clusters are more prone to rot than Cabernet, and need more spraying. It buds earlier, does better in damp, clay soils and is harvested earlier than Cabernet Sauvignon so it avoids being diluted by early autumn rains.

Merlot is grown just about everywhere in the world, and is made as its own variety or blended with other grapes to enhance it. Washington State is making excellent Merlot wines at present, and because so many places produce this grape, prices remain stable. Because of its softer tannins, the wine is easy to drink and since the 1990's, it has become America's top choice as a red restaurant wine. Samples from every country that grow grapes can be found.

From Bulgaria to Australia, Merlot has become the "go to" wine for gift giving, and is stored by the case in every home that drinks wine with most of their meals.

The better Merlot examples almost always have some Cabernet Sauvignon and Cabernet Franc blended in to darken them and to increase the aroma. Remember, in most of America, you need only 75% of a grape used in a wine to call it by that name.

All smart wine drinkers know that Merlot will work with almost any dish from red meats, chicken, fatty fish and even pasta and cheese creations. It's just smart to seek out quality Merlot priced in the $12 to $20 price range. It is easy to taste a difference between a $5.99 sample and a $15 Merlot. It's much harder to tell the difference between a $19 bottle, and those costing between $30 and $40. Because of the new popularity of Malbec and Carmenère wines, Merlot pricing has remained stable. Carmenère was actually sold as Merlot for decades before the Chilean wine makers realized it was a different grape. They look so much alike, only DNA testing proved the difference. Malbec is bolder and is never as soft as Merlot when sipping it. Each wine has its own place as a partner with food, but gaining knowledge of Merlot is a good academic road to follow. Be smart.

You can sample a different Merlot every day of the year and still not try them all.

Pinot Noir has become so popular because it is so sexy. As far back as the 1300's, a vine with the name Pinot was noted in

Burgundy. The species has many variations with regards to its genetic makeup, and growers of Pinot Noir, now in every country of the world, use a number of different clones for different sections of their vineyards.

Of the 46 different clones of this grape, the best tasting wines come from those that love limestone, and produce the world's sexiest red wine. Pinot Noir, along with Chardonnay produce the world's best sparkling wines as proven in Champagne.

Oregon and New Zealand are making great New World Pinot Noirs. The French *Pommard* clone is used throughout most of the new world, and because every Pinot Noir is very soft on the palate, filled with cherry aromas, and ages gracefully, it is becoming the most sought after red food wine. Nothing can best it when paired with grilled salmon. Pinot Noir makes an excellent sipping wine and with dishes like duck breast, or fondue, it is a marriage made in heaven. It's called Pinot Nero in Italy and it produces Italy's finest sparkling wines.

The 2004 movie *Sideways* helped make Pinot Noir famous. Each character in the movie has the personality of a different grape. The star of the film has the sensitive, and subtle qualities of the thin skinned Pinot Noir, a grape that can easily fail while maturing to become an accomplished wine. When successful, however, it produces a heavenly nectar fit for only those who learn about and appreciate the winemaker's artistic creations.

Syrah makes some of the world's greatest wines, and every intelligent wine lover should collect and drink as many different styles as he or she can find. Legend has it that the Crusaders brought the grape back from the city of Shiraz in Persia. Sometimes labeled as Sirah, and in parts of South Africa and especially in Australia, it's called Shiraz.

Note: The wine from California called *Petite Sirah* is really the *Durif* grape. Like Syrah, it is a black grape, but with smaller berries producing a rich higher tannic wine with hints of black pepper and spice. It's easy to see why some thought it was the Syrah of France's Rhône Valley.

The Australians mass produced its Shiraz, and made it the most imported wine into North America from about 1990 through the early 2000's. This mass-produced jammy easy drinking red wine has since lost much of its appeal. Since that time, California's Lodi, and surrounding counties, are producing what they call the Rhone Ranger wines. They've tried to imitate the great northern Rhône wines of *Cote Rotie, Hermitage* and *Crozes-Hermitage*. Syrah is also used in southern sections of that French district where it's added to the Grenache-based wines of Châteauneuf-du-Pape and other village wines around Avignon.

Note: During the fourteenth century, the Popes were mostly French and they moved the papal seat from Rome to Avignon, France, hence the castle of the Pope, or in French, *Châteauneuf-du-Pape*.

The Cote du Rhone wines are made mostly with the Grenache grape, and lack the rich complex character of northern Rhone wines based on Syrah.

Syrah is the perfect match with game meats, and pairs well with hard cheeses. They age very well and should always be laid to rest for eight to fifteen years. Many will last decades. Start today on the road to learning more about and enjoying the plethora of Syrah wines.

Sangiovese is the soul of the best Tuscan wines. It's the most widely planted grape in Italy, and can now be found in the USA from New Jersey to California.

It is sometimes named with its different clones: Brunello, Morellino and Prugnolo Gentile are all the same grape called the "Sangiovese Grosso" clone. It is the majority of all Chianti blends. My favorite Sangiovese wine is *Vino Nobile di Montepulciano*, where, I believe, it shows its noble characteristics.

Note: If the name *Montepulciano* comes first on an Italian wine label, it refers to a grape name, most famously grown in the *Abruzzi* region, for example, *Montepulciano d'Abruzzi*. It has low tannin, and drinks easily while young. However, if the name *Montepulciano* is at the end of the wine's name, it is referring to a city in Tuscany where it is make into a fuller-bodied, cellar-worthy classic Italian red wine with centuries of history behind it. The wine, *Vino Nobile di Montepulciano* is made from the famous Sangiovese grape.

The name "Sangiovese" translates as "the blood of Jove" telling us that the grapes must go back as far as the Etruscan period long before the Roman Empire. The grape produces lots of sharp acid, so it is usually softened with the *Canaiolo* grape, especially when making Chianti.

Note: Chianti was first made in 1716. There are eight Chianti zones even though most Americans know best the zone between Florence and Sienna called Classico. The others are (2) Colli Florentini, (3) Rùfina, (4) Colli Aretini, (5) Colli Senesi, which includes the Brunello and Vino Nobile areas, (6) Colline Pisane, (7) Montespertoli, which was set up in 1996, and (8) Chianti Montalbano

The Sangiovese grapes blend well with Cabernet Sauvignon or Merlot, the concoction they call Super Tuscans. Wise wine drinkers stick to the historical forms of Chianti and the other Sangiovese-based wines because when the popular western grapes are added to it, the wine loses its Italian *terrior,* and becomes just a more expensive bottle of any modern-styled Californian red wine. However, Robert Pepi and the Atlas Peak winery in Napa are making fine food worthy examples of Sangiovese.

Zinfandel is the sixth and final red grape to know, taste, and understand if you want to belong to the top bracket of knowledgeable wine drinkers.

Native Hungarian, Agoston Haraszthy is said to have brought Zinfandel to California. This black grape produces high sugars, capable of making wines with high alcohol. It exhibits wine with black fruit aromas, spice, and pepper on the nose. Depending on the total number of days of full sunshine while growing, Zinfandel's pepper scents and its taste will reflect either black or white pepper.

Zinfandel is a red wine that can replace nearly every Italian wine served with any Italian dish. At worst, examples over 15.5% alcohol won't age to add complexities. At best, it is a great medium alcohol wine to consume rather young with meats, pastas, cheese dishes, and game, especially venison.

The grape seems to be similar to the Italian *Primitivo* and was thought to be the same, but in the late 1900's, DNA fingerprinting didn't prove it. Instead, the research traced Zinfandel back to the *Plavac Mali* grape of Croatia.

It was Napa Valley's Sutter Home Winery, who had the fermentation stall (as when yeast stop converting grape sugars into alcohol) so they pulled off the wine to see what they could do. It had plenty of residual sugar making it pleasantly sweet. It was very soft because it hadn't absorbed much tannin, and it was just pink, not red, because it hadn't had time to leech enough of the color pigmentation out of the black skins. They called it "White Zinfandel," bottled it, and sold millions of bottles over the next few years to younger new wine drinkers. It may not be a good food wine, but when chilled, it is fine for beach or pool parties. Most importantly, it stopped the removal of older Zinfandel vines that were being torn out and replaced with the more popular

Merlot and Cabernet Sauvignon grapes. It saved many "Old Vine" Zinfandel plants from being destroyed.

The trend of new popularity for the "real" red Zinfandel has continued, and many of the warmer places in California now specialize in producing Old Vine Zinfandel.

Knowing the facts presented in this chapter alone, easily puts you among the top 19% of the world's wine experts. Drink a glass of real Zinfandel, the red one, when you re-read this chapter.

10 LET'S TALK DIRTY
Terroir

If you plant Chardonnay in Chablis, and also plant the same clones of Chardonnay in the Burgundy village of Meursault, you will end up making two distinctly different white wines. The first will be crisper with a "tongue on stone" taste while the Meursault will be rounder, fuller, and creamier with a note of chalk in the aftertaste. Why? Well the first vineyard, the one in Chablis, will be planted on a mostly granite-based soil, while the second vineyard will be growing over an ancient seabed filled with limestone. Talking dirty with regards to wine means discussing the different soils where grapes are planted. I'm sure you've heard the quote, "You are what you eat." It's true, and it is also true for grapes because they eat from the soils in which they're planted. The same Chardonnay can stab at your tongue, or flow like perfect iambic pentameter across your palate. That's why Robert Louis Stevenson said, when writing about the wines of California, "that the wine is bottled poetry."

The vineyard site and the direction in which you plant the rows of vines will determine the final quality of the product. As with real estate, it's "Location. Location. Location."

For decades, I've hosted Corporate Seminars and the one I call; "Let's Talk Dirty" is always a big hit. Maybe the guests expect some funny crude jokes, but it's all about the dirt! I present the same grape grown in a number of different soils from different places around the world and in just a few minutes, the audience quickly understands that where a grape is grown can make a world of difference. Most times, even the newest novice will leave the seminar understanding enough to place themselves in the top half of America's wine drinkers with regards to vinous understanding.

The French coined the term, *terroir* (tehr-wahr) to indicate that every vine produces grapes indicative of the place, soil type, wind direction, amount of rainfall, and the total number of sunny days during the growing season, along with the altitude and slope of the vineyard. It's a hard word to translate. For example, Pinot Noir loves the soil, weather conditions, and locational longitude of Burgundy, but Cabernet and Merlot thrive better in Bordeaux's coastal soils of gravel and clay, its weather conditions, and the southern location.

Over the centuries, grape growers learned which grapes grew and ripened best in certain locations, and the wine made from those select spots produced the richest, most complex wines. For example, the Gamay grape was banned from northern parts of Burgundy, but permitted in its lower sections to make the basic Beaujolais; it just couldn't compete with Pinot Noir for making kingly Volnay, Chambertin or Pommard wines.

Wind

Strong winds can dry out and burn the life out of a grape vine. Over the centuries, local people have devised ways to protect their vines. Much of Greece and all its islands train vines on the stony ground in the shape of a bird's nest. Each plant resembles a doughnut or a bird's nest, and the grape clusters, trained in the *koulara* method, will survive against the strong winds by developing inside the protective ring. The *stefáni*, as each plant is called, that I saw on Santorini and Crete, will grow that way for up to twenty years.

On the Azores, they build four-meter by four-meter stonewalls and plant five or six vines inside each cubicle to protect them from the endless wind. As I walked around a half-acre vineyard doted with stone cubicles, I noticed that the leaves of vines that grew above the walls were burned brown from the stinging winds.

In north central Spain, they dig large circular holes across the open plain and plant, then bush-prune, a single vine in each hole. Their Tempranillo grapes need to be protected from the burning winds.

Even the French built *Clos*, walls to enclose their Burgundy vineyards, not just to mark off great locations, but also to protect the vines from hillside winds. The strength and frequency of wind is an important part of the *Terroir*.

Soil

The soil type in a vineyard is just part of what we call *terroir*. The large stony fields where grapes are planted in the Rhone area of France help reflect the sunlight back up onto the grapes. This rocky soil also forces the vines to grow deep and seek out water and nutrients that develop the wines from Syrah and Grenache grapes. That's why Chateauneuf-du-Pape, Cote Rôtie, and Hermitage wines from the Rhone are so special and unique. It's the *terroir.*

The gray-marl in Chablis is reflected in the wines' flintiness as is the chalk noted in Chardonnay grown in Meursault. The type of soil, as found out by trial and error over the centuries in Europe, proved to determine where certain grape species grew best. This in turn, permitted the best possible wine to be made from that area. There is no Pinot Noir growing in Southwestern France around Bordeaux. Cabernet Sauvignon and Merlot grow best there and can produce wines of the highest quality, while there is no Cabernet Sauvignon or Merlot in Burgundy where Chardonnay and Pinot Noir grow best.

When a particular grape and wine from that grape becomes popular, winemakers all over the world want to plant and make wine to sell from that currently popular grape. It's taken California decades to learn that Napa produces good Cabernet Sauvignon, but not so great Pinot Noir. The Eastern Coast of America can make high quality Cabernet Franc, and New Jersey, New York and

Virginia could produce great examples of that wine, but too few winemakers have yet to do it as their best-featured wine!

Malbec is a blending grape in France, but in Argentina, it has found a home and the soil, altitude, water, sunshine, well, the *terroir*, has permitted the grape to stand out on its own. It found a better home, as Carmenère has done in Chile.

Temperature

Zinfandel thrives in really hot areas and produces big juicy red wines with high alcohol, black pepper and spicy aromas, whereas Pinot Noir likes much cooler temperatures. Chardonnay can grow well in both types of areas, but it will produce distinctly different types of wines in both areas.

If the winemaker is set on producing a Sancerre-like Sauvignon Blanc, whether he or she is in South Africa, Australia, New Zealand, or North or South America, the location's temperature must fall within the same range as Sancerre, or they will end up with an entirely different smelling and tasting wine. Remember, to get natural higher acids, the average temperature must be cool.

Over the centuries grape growers have developed different rootstocks, and different clones best suited to each *terroir*. The most knowledgeable wine drinkers know that within single vineyards, the soil, slope and water content can greatly change, and different types of rootstocks and clones need to be planted to produce the best possible grapes if the goal is to make the best possible wine. Rootstocks and clones are a study unto themselves, and that research is more necessary to a wine grower than a wine drinker.

Just as the term *Climate* is complex, so too is *terroir*. It is the surface and sub-surface types of soil and stone beneath the surface; it's the number of days and the angle at which the sunshine hits the vine, the altitude, and the average rainfall. Even the angle of the slope of a hillside versus a flat plain helps make each location unique with regard to it special *terroir*. For any bright individual, that's enough said. The top 15% of wine lovers certainly know about and understand *terroir* and they also know how it makes every wine smell and taste differently. Imagine how boring life would be if every Syrah tasted the same. Intellectuals need variety, and they're happy to know that the wine journey is endless.

Note: *Clone* used as a noun means genetically identical. When *clone* is used as a verb, it means to propagate or make another that closely resembles the original. An example is, "Of the dozens of new plants, all similar, the best one was chosen." This is how *clone* is used when talking within the wine world.

11 SHARING YOUR WINE KNOWLEDGE

The Mahoney-Value-Ratio, Wine Lists,
Hosting Tastings and Wine Parties

If you skipped the first ten chapters and wanted to jump right into savoring some wine, because this chapter talks about tastings and wine parties, well that's quite all right. "Fools rush in where angels fear to tread."

Let's begin. Start by knowing that intelligent wine lovers understand what value is. You can impress a sommelier or wine waiter at a restaurant, or when buying wines at your local wine shop, by using the *MVR* or the *Mahoney-Value-Ratio.* The value of anything is always a ratio of the cost of something compared to its quality. We all do this analysis with automobiles and artwork, but with wine, we most often, just check its score or rating. To figure my *Mahoney-Value-Ratio*, simply **divide the cost by the rating** (the score it was given on the 100-point-scale that wine magazines so often use, by the price you are paying). I do this at retail wine outlets to draw a fair conclusion. Restaurant markups are so highly absurd that the *MVR* will never show anything worth buying. A ten dollar wine given 90 points produces a *MVR* of 0.1, which is an excellent *MVR*. Buy as many of these as you can get. A $150 bottle divided by its 94 score has a *MVR* of 1.6, seldom, if ever, worth it.

Lower is better. You'll quickly find a range that you prefer.

A point of interest: wine lists in restaurants have their highest markups at the lowest end. The lowest priced wine on a list usually has had the highest markup. The wines just above the middle of a list are your best buys, examples with much lower markups, unless you want the $750 or $2,500 bottle that have the least markup. Those wines are usually found at the bottom of a wine list in every over-priced restaurant.

A prefixed menu makes it easier to select a wine to enhance the meal. When you are dining with a partner or a few friends, it gets harder to select a wine to pair with two, or more different items. One solution is to order two different wines, say a Sancerre for those having fish or light meats, and another bottle like a Syrah for those ordering meat or pasta. If the group wants to keep it a lighter alcohol evening, then select one wine that will weigh in at the middle of the most extreme flavors. Lighter or fuller dishes can do well with Pinot Noir from France, or Oregon with a sensible level of alcohol ideally below 14 percent. Brut sparkling wines will also go with, and pair nicely to nearly everything, so I often have only sparkling wines with a larger group at multi-course dinners.

Wine by the glass is convenient, but the price of one glass is usually what the restaurant paid wholesale for the entire bottle. Now, let's return to and learn what the *MVR* is all about.

If a bottle of wine cost you $16, and you saw in a wine magazine or wine site that the wine you bought scored an 88; you divide the cost (16) by the score (rating) it received, and you get a decimal: 0.18 which is the *Mahoney-Value-Ratio*.

If a bottle cost $100 and it had a score of 95, you can just do the math: the price divided by the score, and you get 1.5 for a *MVR*. The higher the *MVR*, the lower the value of your purchase! The closer you get to zero, the better. Expensive, famous wines will score above one, but the *MVR* says they're not really worth it.

Note: Paying a lot of money to drink the summer sunshine turned into wine from the year you were born or married may be worth it if you're astute enough to know it's the history you're experiencing and not the value of the wine. Anytime you're paying double or triple the price of your entrée for something to drink, you have to question it.

Let's evaluate another one. I bought two bottles to share with friends. One cost $50 and I saw it was rated at 91 points. The second bottle cost $15, and it scored an 86. The first one is 50 divided by 91 giving a *MVR* of 0.55, while the second one is $15 divided by the score of 86 resulting in a *Mahoney-Value-Ratio* of 0.17. Remember the smaller the decimal, the bigger the value.

How about a bottle of Screaming Eagle costing $1,500 with an average score of 96 versus a $60 bottle from Enriquez Winery in Sonoma County, California? The $1500 divided by the 96 points it scored, is a woppingly high 15.63 while the second wine is $60 divided by its score of 90 points, giving it a 0.67 for the *MVR*. That means the $60 bottle has 23 times the quality-value of the absurdly expensive bottle. Wines with an MVR of 0.9 down to 0.3 are always excellent values.

I can usually tell the difference between a $45 bottle of Cabernet Sauvignon and a $15 bottle of Cabernet Sauvignon, but it's really hard to pick out major differences between a $50 bottle and one costing over $500, or even one costing just $100. Keep your own record of the *MVR*s on the wines you buy for even a short while, and you'll soon see that too many people are paying for the status of the label, and not for the wine inside the bottle.

The Spanish Rioja 2009 Reserva from Vina Eguia runs about $18 and scored an 89 giving it a MVR of 0.2 while a Vega Sicilia Ribera del Duero Valbuena 2009 cost as much as $850, and usually gets 94 to 96 scores. Do the MVR, the price divided by the rating and you get 8.94, or at least eight times higher than a good value drinking wine. Smart people have to make a decision based on something rational. The Vega Sicilia is a very nice drinking wine, loaded with high quality French oak. It's hard to tell it's even Spanish, but it's more rare than the charmingly smooth Vina Eguia, aged in less expensive American oak. It does, however, express its true *terrior.*

These is just some examples of a hundred thousand possibilities; each wine has its merits, but remember you drink what is inside a bottle, not the famous label, and as you refine your tasting abilities, you will be less impressed with excessively priced wines and see that the MVR really makes sense for wine lovers who enjoy it everyday. Now let's taste some wines.

We'll do white wines first, going from light and easy, to wines with fuller flavors that have more depth and body. Then, we'll do the same with red wines.

Believe it or not, you are now, most likely, among the world's top fifteen percent of knowledgeable wine drinkers. So few people have made your effort to learn more about wine. Yes, you're in the top 15%.

Now you understand wine, want to share your knowledge, and also share a few of your favorite wines with friends who are just starting to do the same things you are doing: drinking less but better, and seeking out good quality for reasonable prices. You also want to continue to learn more, and taste as often as possible.

There are a number of ways to do this and all are fun, easy to do, and not too expensive. You and a small group of wine-loving friends should set up home wine tastings. Try your best to have a separate glass for each wine. Then pour all the wines at once so you can compare them at the same time. Tasting them one at a time is still better than not tasting them at all. It's just harder to learn about the differences that way. At least two wine glasses per person is a necessity to be able to quickly notice differences in shades of color, aroma, and mouth feel, as well as the length of each wine's aftertaste.

Join a chapter of the American Wine Society and attend their regular tastings.

Form your own "Wine Friends Group" and have each member arrange a bi-monthly tasting. If you try for every month, you'll start to feel too much pressure and lose some of the anticipation and excitement.

Check out the Society of Wine Educators if you really want to study wine like you would a college course. They offer certifications too. However, titles don't always prove an intellectual understanding of wine.

Have a different wine with dinner as often as possible; save one glass from last night's bottle, and pour a new wine in the second glass. Comparing two different wines is the *only* way to really learn. This technique makes it easy to understand the different grapes, styles, and sources of the wines. You'll quickly notice that one of the wines nearly always matches better with the food because its body or weight is more similar to what you're eating.

Tastings

The ideal tasting has a number of wines, six to eight are perfect, but as many as a dozen can work if you're doing a vertical or horizontal tasting. Glasses should be pre-poured before guests sit. It's very hard to pour wine over someone's shoulder. The wines should be on a white placemat so colors can be discussed, saltless crackers, water and a very small food item can be also set out ahead of time. Never use anything hot or spicy at wine tastings.

When friends arrive, ideally, serve a glass of sparkling wine to cleanse their palates. Then sit, and taste through the wines going from the lightest to the most bold, youngest to oldest, or driest to sweetest. Only then, should you use a food item to teach how the food can change the taste of the wine. The spit cup is very important if you want to learn. After swallowing even a few ounces of wine, your sensual abilities begin to fade, and it may be a fun, relaxing time, but not worthy of a worthwhile learning experience. Suggest to your friends that they learn first, and then they can swallow at the end of all the discussions. This casual social period after the formal tasting will reinforce many of the topics discussed during the tasting seminar. Learning is fun, and it increases your ability to find greater pleasure in every future wine and food experience. There is no limit to learning about, understanding, and appreciating wine. It will become a life-long endeavor, especially for intellectually curious people. The top 15% of bright active wine drinkers should belong to some wine club or organization. Maybe some Mensa-like wine club, or at least try, if possible, to get involved with some Dionysian Society activity or an American Wine Society chapter near you.

Share your wine and your wine knowledge. Help all your friends to live better.

12 UNIQUE WINES

Little known grapes, Faulty wines

Pinot Noir, one of the six Red Grapes noted in Chapter Nine, is the red grape to start with if you're just changing from all white wines and trying to learn to enjoy some red wines.

Note: Red grapes provide seven times the health benefits of white grapes because of the compounds found in their skins. You'd have to drink seven glasses of white wine to equal the health benefits of one glass of red wine.

Pinot Noir makes wine that even your White Zinfandel-only drinking friends can easily start to enjoy. Since white wine drinkers are used to drinking chilled wines, they can easily drink Pinot Noir, and also red Beaujolais made from the Gamay grape, slightly chilled. Remember, lowering the temperature hides the aromas and flavors so don't over do it. Pinot Noir has obvious fruit aromas and soft tannins making it smooth and easy to drink. So, taste it as often as possible, and use the 5-S's to help absorb the qualities offered in the wine. Consider your tastings as the nicest homework that you've ever had. As Alexis Lichine said, "There is no substitute for pulling corks."

We learned in Chapter Eight that wine is food. You drink water to quench your thirst, and use wine to enhance flavors, cleanse your palate, and to complement or contrast the essence of the meal. There are more than a thousand other wine grapes besides the most famous and key ones we pointed out in Chapter Nine.

Red Grapes To Try

The Greek Agiorgitiko, also know as St. George, has a spicy plum taste. It's found in most Greek wines from Nemea. It will help any highly spiced meat dish.

Barbera, from the Piedmont region of Italy, is an all-purpose red that can age a few years, but also be drunk when quite young. It has a sour cherry aroma and pairs well with tomato based dishes.

Bobal is little known. From the southeast sections of Spain around Valencia, it makes a delightful Rosé and a red wine lighter than Rioja, but fuller than Beaujolais.

Cabernet Franc is a personal favorite. The best are from *Chinon* in the Loire Valley in France. It has more perfume, rose petal, and less tannin than Cabernet Sauvignon. Excellent examples come from Virginia and even New Jersey.

Dolcetto is another Italian grape with moderate tannin and pleasant acidity. Even though the name means *the sweet little one*, the wine is dry and refreshing. It's always better than Beaujolais with meals that have some weight.

Gamay is the grape of Beaujolais. Seek out one of the ten Grand Cru Beaujolais to see how nice this lightweight wine can be. It's the perfect party red.

Note: The 10 Grand Cru Beaujolais are St.-Amour, Juliénas, Chénas, Moulin-a-Vent, Fleurie, Chiroubles, Morgon, Régnié, Brouilly and Côte de Brouilly.

Grenache is added to many Spanish (called Garnacha) and French reds. It makes the most delightful Rosé. Drink it all summer with salads and fish.

Lagrein from Trentino-Alto Adige in northern Italy has bitter cherry and hints of chocolate. It goes with big game or roasted meats.

Malbec, usually added to Bordeaux, shows its best in Argentina. It's perfect with steak dinners. It's called Côt in Cahors and in the Loire Valley in France.

Monastrell, as it's know in Spain, is called Mourvèdre in France's Rhone Valley. From Spain, it can stand alone producing a dark blackberry nosed wine, and in France it adds backbone to many of the best Rhone reds. It goes with any cheese, meat or pasta dish.

Montepulciano is the grape when the word appears first on the label. It's light and fruity, and not meant to age. It's ideal with a ham sandwich. The best examples come from Abruzzi in Italy. Remember, as stated earlier, if the word is at the end of the name, it refers to a Tuscan village and not the grape; Vino Nobile di Montepulciano is an excellent red food wine made with Sangiovese grapes in the village of Montepulciano.

Morellino is a synonym for Sangiovese and this clone has softer tannins than most of the Chianti wines.

Nebbiolo grapes make Barolo in Italy's Piedmont. They say it's "the wine of kings and the king of wines." It ages for decades and highlights anything with truffle oil. The best have rose petal and hints of fresh road tar on the nose, which is considered very positive.

Négrette is grown near the city of Toulouse in southwest France. It makes a superb Rosé that has hints of watermelon. It's ideal with spicy cuisine, Asian food, salads, chicken and fish. It's a unique, rare wine.

Nero d'Avola, from Sicily, is the perfect pasta wine.

Periquita, from Portugal, is the name you'll see most often on labels, but it's really the Casteláo grape. The soft raspberry notes make it an enjoyable wine with grilled meats and even heavier weighted fish.

Petit Verdot is added to Bordeaux and Californians add it for color and body into their red blends. A few places, especially on the American East Coast, make it as a single variety wine.

Pinotage is a cross of the Pinot Noir and Cinsault grapes, and is the basic red from South Africa. It matches well with red meats.

Primitivo is similar to Zinfandel. It comes from Italy and is usually lighter with lower alcohol than the Californian examples. Pair it with pasta, turkey, or game.

Tannat, the core of most Basque wines, has a nutty taste and aroma, and it also does very well in Uruguay where the dessert style is filled with coffee and rich chocolate flavors.

Tempranillo is charming. It makes the greatest red Spanish wines, and it pairs with nearly everything.

Touriga Nacional is at the heart of the great Porto wines. It also is made into a dry red filled with violets and black cherry. Enjoy it with grilled dishes, both meat and vegetables.

White Grapes To Try

Albariño ranks among my favorite white wines. It has mineral and white peach aromas, great acidity, and is the perfect seafood wine. The best come from Spain's northwest Rias Baixas district.

Arneis is elegant. It comes from the Barolo area of Italy's Piedmont, and *Vietti* is one excellent producer to seek out and try with chicken, pork, or soups.

Chasselas, also known as Fendant, is a Swiss white that reflects its *terroir*. It's believed the grape came from Egypt through Byzantium. It's an easy drinking white and goes with light dishes.

Fiano is a southern Italian grape with hints of honey, flowers and spice. *Fiano di Avellino* is one of the best examples with its peach aroma: a really nice first course wine.

Gewürztraminer means "spicy traminer" and its herbal nose is easy to remember. It is perfect with all Asian food. The samples from Alsace, France are the best; Californian examples can be a bit too sweet. Dry and spicy is how to describe it.

Grillo from Sicily makes Marsala, but unfortified, it is finding a place as an American opening wine because of its lemony taste, so it's ideal for seafood.

Grüner Veltliner of Austria is best from the *Wachau* district. It has some white pepper and mango aromas. Filled with minerality, shellfish meals demand it.

Insolia is another charming white from Sicily. It has citrus notes, and when drunk fresh and young, it's delightful. It too was part of the Marsala blend, but now can easily be found on its own in a fresh light style.

Macabeo is called *Viura* in Rioja, and it's one of the key grapes in Spanish sparkling Cava along with the *Parellada* and *Xarello* grapes. It is just beginning to become know in North America. I use it as a reception wine for guests.

Marsanne, along with *Roussanne*, are two of the nine grapes that make great Rhone white wines. *Marsanne* does well in Virginia, Australia, and in California, but samples from the Rhone area are what you should seek out, if you want to try the highest quality.

Muscat, in all its variations, from Italy to Greece, makes soft, sweet dessert wines that pair well with sweet creams and pastries. It makes Italy's famous *Asti Spumante*.

Moschofilero is Greek and has a nose between *Muscat* and *Gewürztraminer*: floral and spicy. These pink grapes can also make a salmon-colored Rosé, and even produces a charming sparkling wine. It's balanced with refreshing acid that makes it easy for beginners to enjoy.

Pinot Blanc from Alsace in France is the milestone for this grape. Pear and wet stone are easily noticed on its nose. It's a very enjoyable food wine.

Pinot Grigio, called *Pinot Gris* in France, are the same grape. The *Gris* usually has a hint of wood on it, as do some Oregon styles. Today, the *Grigio* style is over-cropped and over-priced, so it has lost its quality. I drink very little of it, but you should know it if only for intellectual curiosity. The *Gris* style is better with food.

Rkatsiteli is mostly planted in Georgia (the country, not the state) and may be the most widely planted white grape anywhere, equal to or just behind, Spain's *Airén* grape. You'll seldom, if ever, see *Rkatsiteli*. Many times it's simply a basic white with little complexity or flavor. It's just something the top 15% of the world's wine drinkers know and talk about. Also, *Tomasello Winery* in Hammonton, New Jersey, makes a charming sparkling wine from this grape if you'd like to sample it.

Sémillon has a fig aroma and is blended with Sauvignon Blanc to make the best Sauternes. In the Hunter Valley of Australia, you'll find excellent examples of this grape.

Steen is what the South Africans called *Chenin Blanc*.

Silvaner or *Sylvaner* does well in both Germany and in Alsace, France. It makes most of the German Franken area whites. It's not as good as *Riesling*, but it has its place.

Torrontes came from Spain but does better on its own in Argentina. It has citrus aromas and good acidity as a seafood match. They seem to get better with each new vintage that South America puts out. Try one with crab cakes.

Vermentino is known to be the wine for fish. The better samples come from Italy's Liguria and mid-east coastal areas. Drink them young.

Vernaccia, another Italian, shows its best when from the *San Gimignano* village of Umbria. It's a nice, not great, everyday wine.

Viognier is planted nearly everywhere now. The best come form France's Rhone Valley around *Condrieu*. Yalumba of Australia produces an excellent example. Kunde and Alban Wineries from California also make excellent samples. Its pear and honeysuckle aromas make it a good choice for chicken, veal and fish selections. Bellview Winery of Landisville, New Jersey produces one of America's best, and is often compared to the *Viognier* of Virginia's Horton Winery, another top selection.

There are thousands of other grapes to experience and learn about but these examples and the selections noted in Chapter Four, are all you need to be an expert. Because wine is food, you always want to experience it with some type of meal or snack no matter how little. See how food changes the wine and remember, smell each wine for at least 30 to 45 seconds, before sipping it, to help your brain remember and record its aroma. There is no greater intellectual endeavor.

Major Faults

What is a faulty wine? Well, quite a few things can go wrong when making, bottling, shipping, and storing it. Remember, wine is a food item.

Let's assume the winemaker started with ripe, well developed grapes with high sugars and good natural acid, fermented the juice in a cool environment and kept oxygen off the fermenting must, then racked (moving the wine off the dead yeast lying at the bottom), fined (cleared the wine with egg whites or bentonite clay) and maybe even filtered it (with thick pads of cellulose, diatomaceous earth and sometimes perlite) to remove any other impurities. Many wines are then "cold stabilized" to have any excessive tartaric acid drop out. Finally, they're bottled and corked (or sealed with a number of different closures) to prevent oxygen from getting in and breaking down the wine.

Note: The darker the color of the glass wine bottle, the longer the wine is expected to age. Porto bottles are black and can age decades. Light green or brown glass is used for wines needing limited aging. Clear glass, as used to bottle many white and Rosé wines, is telling us to drink them very young, or soon after being purchased.

Every wine needs to be stored in a cool dark place. Direct sun and fluorescent light can alter the aromas of a fine wine. Heat is a killer of both aroma and flavor. If a bottle stands upright for too long and the cork dries out and shrinks, oxygen can get in and turn the wine to vinegar.

The following are some of the terms smart, knowledgeable wine drinkers will pick out when a wine has developed a problem:

A "Corked" wine smells like wet cardboard or old gym sneakers. It doesn't mean there are pieces of cork in it; it means the cork caused the problem. Some corks have TCA or *Trichloroanisole* in them. Just one part per billion, not million, can destroy a wine's aroma. Faulty corks were prolific during the 1990's, and into the very early 2000's. Now, those faulty corks have been greatly eliminated, and it happens way less often.

Fingernail polish on the nose is *Ethyl acetate,* and it is caused during the winemaking and bottling.

Vinegar is Acetic acid and the excessive volatile acidity has ruined the aroma and taste of the wine. Excessive oxygen, before or after bottling, has started to turn the wine to vinegar, which you'll pick up on the nose.

Maderized wine has been exposed to air and developed Sherry flavors; sometimes when a wine was stored in a hot kitchen, the "cooked" flavors will show maderization.

Sometimes you'll smell strong Geranium in the nose of a wine; it is *2,3ethoxy,3,4hexadiene* that developed as trouble when potassium sorbate was added during the malolactic fermentation.

A wool nose, hurting the fruit notes, is caused by UV light exposure.

Slight leather scents will develop in old Bordeaux and is a pleasant addition, but wet leather, Et*hyl-4-phenol,* is a fault.

Barrel funk stems from dirty wine barrels with evil bacteria living in them. The only solution here is to burn the old barrels. Brettanomyces, called Brett, adds a barnyard scent.

Sulphur is used to preserve the wine. White wines have much more sulphur than reds because the red wine's natural tannins will work as a preservative. If you smell a burnt match when first opening a bottle of a nice Italian white, just swirl it and the smell will blow off. If the wine is totally colorless, almost like water, you can be sure too much sulphur was added.

Excessive volatile acidity and corked wines will be the two most common faults you'll experience during your wine tasting journeys. Don't let them stop you from learning more. If in a restaurant you find that the wine is corked, the odds are a thousand to one that the next bottle from the same case will also be bad. Try another bottle of the same wine after explaining the problem to the waiter or wine steward. If the bottle is maderized, smells like finger nail polish or vinegar, ask for an entirely different wine because not only that bottle, but most likely, the entire lot is faulted.

I've used faulty wines as a great learning experience, and even hosted Faulty Wine Seminars to show exactly how these wines smell. Recall the old quote, "The nose knows." Is a study of chemistry really needed to enjoy wine? No, but knowing some of the chemistry noted in this chapter easily places you among the top 12% of the world's most knowledgeable wine lovers.

13 DESSERT WINES
The nectar of the Gods

Dessert wines are unique and very special! Many people will tell you they don't like sweet wines, but the odds are, they've never had any good ones. They're most likely thinking of the sugar-filled plunk they tried in high school or during college. Wine coolers are not dessert wines. We won't discuss any of the sweet Concord grape wines like Mogen David or Manischewitz, or Boone's Farm, Annie Green Springs or even Mateus, which was a step up at the time is was popular, or any other of the once youth-influenced popular wines. The world's best dessert wines derive their sweetness from the grape's natural sugars.

Research has shown that the older you get, the more you will appreciate sweeter wines. It may be reverting back to your early youth, but the nose knows and the tongue supports the concept. However, added sugar is used to hide faults, and if it's just used to disguise a faulty wine, as sometimes happens, you'll pay for it later that night and into the next morning.

Use this chapter as a homework assignment and taste your way through all of the noted wines during this wine study semester whether it's over just a few weeks or all year long. Experience some quality dessert wines.

Moscato d'Asti is a still wine – no bubbles, that is usually low in alcohol. Try it with any apricot or peach dessert you can devise. Its low alcohol and refreshing taste makes it a good wine to conclude an evening. A key point to remember is that American restaurants always quickly push after-dinner coffee as you order dessert. Coffee deadens your taste buds, makes you think your meal is over, and gets you out of the restaurant faster so they can reuse your table for a second seating. Have coffee or tea *after* dessert, *not with* it. If you sip coffee with your dessert wine, you'll force your culinary senses to compete with each other.

Riesling may be the most famous dessert wine. Riesling sold in blue colored bottles is usually the bulk-produced examples of the lowest quality; their cloying sweetness hides their limitations. Avoid blue bottled wines. As we've learned, added sugar is used to hide faults in lesser wines. Quality Riesling is a grape that matures best on rocky soil with slate. It does well in cooler areas like Germany, France's Alsace, Hungary and Austria, New York's Finger Lakes, the Niagara Peninsula into Canada, parts of Michigan and Washington State, as well as the cooler areas in Australia and South Africa.

To be a good dessert wine, fruit aromas should excite the nose and the sweetness will excite the front tip of the tongue. The most important factor is that the wines have enough natural acid to cleanse the sugars away so the finish leads into a far less sweet aftertaste, and has a refreshing conclusion that gets the mouth ready for the next spoon or forkful of dessert. Riesling has both sweetness, at many different levels, and great refreshing and concluding acids.

German examples tell you the ripeness levels on their labels, and help you decide on just how sweet you'd want it. If it says **Halbtrocken**, meaning "half-dry", or **Trocken**, which means, "dry", then these Rieslings are best served with fish or other lighter dishes instead of using them as a dessert wine.

When it says **Kabinett**, shown clearly on the label, the wine has a lighter body and noticeable acids with low levels of sweetness. Use this category as a reception wine or with desserts that are not very sweet like nut cakes.

Spätlese Rieslings are not too sweet, but noticeably not dry. They have more body (re-read Chapter Eight about a wine's Body) and higher sugars. Fruit cocktails with some tartness work with this level of Riesling.

Auslese levels are riper, rounder and can work with so many desserts that it's best to keep one in your refrigerator all the time. All of these Rieslings usually have alcohols under 11.5%, and are easy to drink. At this level, it can pair with fruits, cakes and pies that are not soaked with sugary creams. It is also a lovely sipping wine all by itself.

Beerenauslese referred to as BA's, exhibit a charming sweetness, all from natural sugars, that is luscious when sipped. It is a dessert in itself, or can pair with rich custards and creams. German words get longer by adding separate parts together. The rule here is that the longer the word noting the ripeness or sweetness level, the sweeter the wine will be. The name means "shriveled clusters of grapes that were picked during a selected late-harvest."

Trockenbeerenauslese, simply called TBA's, are the late-harvested, raisin-like shriveled *individual* grapes picked by hand. They are the sweetest of the series and pair with rich cream desserts. However, they are best savored by themselves *as* dessert, not *with* dessert! They will also age very well, and decades after harvest they become deep golden in color, and will have very complex bouquets.

Canada, as well as New York's Finger Lakes, is cold enough to imitate the German **Ice Wine.** The Riesling grape and some white hybrids, grown in colder parts of North America, are left hanging on their vines until they freeze. Then, they are handpicked and the pulp and sugars are separated from the frozen water. This remaining juice is then fermented into an ultra sweet wine with a full body and an aftertaste that lasts forever. These final three categories of Riesling dessert wines all have enough natural acids so that the wines do not become cloying in your mouth, or deaden your ability to continue tasting. They are truly nectar for the Gods.

Sauternes, some *Madeira* and *Tokaji*, and Vintage *Porto* can be blatantly sweet, but are heavenly when paired correctly.

Well-aged **Sauternes**, served with crème brulée, is a dessert fit for a deity. Few, if any wine and food pairing, can match this combination. All educated wine lovers cellar some Sauternes to be able to serve and enjoy this godly dessert union. Sauternes is luscious. *Sémillon* and *Sauvignon Blanc,* are the grapes used to make this dessert wine.

Some producers also include portions of *Muscadelle.* The region of Sauternes is about 25 miles (40.2 kilometers) below Bordeaux in the southern part of the Graves District. The **Barsac** district is next-door, and it makes similar but less costly dessert wines and therefore Barsac is a good buy in this category. Morning fogs along the Ciron River running through the district help promote a mold they call the *noble rot.* It is *Botrytis cinerea* and it reduces the amount of water in each grape, but it leaves all the sugar. The vineyards are handpicked a number of times to gather just the shriveled grapes, which is labor intensive and costly. The resulting wines are higher in alcohol than the German examples, but are golden and sweet with very long aftertaste that conclude with a dry mouth-refreshing acid. Sauternes can age for decades and are ideal wines to cellar from birth years so your children can enjoy them when they turn 21 or even older. They are ideal to toast with at your daughter's wedding.

In 1855, Chateau d'Yquem was listed alone as the Grand Premier Cru. Eleven others were noted as First Growths, like Chateaus Suduiraut, Coutet, Climens, Guiraud and La Tour-Blanche. Thirteen Chateaus were listed as Second Growths. They're just as good, I think, but cost less. Chateaus Doisy-Daëne, D'Arche, Nairac, de Malle, and Romer are all smart wines to try and cellar. A non-listed House, Chateau Raymond-Lafon, is a favorite of many of my very knowledgeable wine friends

A special treat is to serve any well-chilled Sauternes with *Foie gras* as an *Amuse Bouché* or an "entertainment for the mouth" as a teaser before, or as, an opening course at dinner. Of course, Sauternes is the perfect dessert wine with egg custards and creams. There is no greater match than older Sauternes married to a well-made crème brulée.

Note: Late-harvest **Banyuls** from France, and Italy's **Vin Santo** can be enjoyed just prior to and sometimes even with a concluding coffee breaking the rule I stated earlier about enjoying dessert wine *before* a concluding coffee.

Banyuls is a fortified French dessert wine from France's Mediterranean town of Banyuls-Sur-Mer in the Languedoc region. It's been made since the 13th century when they learned to add brandy to heighten the alcohol, and kill the yeast before they consumed all the sugar. It's made mostly from the Grenache grape but can have Macabeu, Tourbat or Muscat blended in and also 15% can be Carignan, Cinsault, or Syrah.

The best **Vin Santo** comes form Italy's Tuscany region. It's not the same as the Greek *Vinsanto*. It's an ideal after-dinner wine with notes of hazelnut, honey, and apricot and it's usually served before coffee with biscotti. The name means "Holy Wine" and it's made from dried grapes laid out on mats from harvest until early spring. These raisins are pressed into wine with around 19% alcohol, and can have as much as 225 grams of residual sugar per liter. The best are made from Sangiovese and Malvasia Nera grapes.

Uruguay makes a late harvest dessert style wine from the **Tannat** grape. It is reddish brown, full-bodied, has thick slow-moving legs and pairs with any chocolate dessert. Its aroma is a flood of mocha and dark chocolate. It's easily a dessert by itself.

Port-style wines are made nearly everywhere, but real traditional ports are labeled as **Oporto,** the Portuguese city where they're made. Well, they are really made across the Douro River in *Vila Nova de Gaia,* but are shipped from Oporto to the rest of the world. Port also pairs with dark chocolate, blue cheese and walnuts. Few drinks are as enjoyable after dinner, in front of a fireplace on a cold winter's night. The wine is fortified by pouring distilled brandy into the fermentation vats. This kills the yeast and leaves loads of natural residual sugar. It also raises the percentage of alcohol to 19 or 20 percent by volume.

New world port style wines are often made from Zinfandel, Shiraz, and even Merlot or Pinot Noir; none of these succeed as well as the classic Portuguese varieties: *Tourgia Nacional* (the best), *Tinta Barroca, Tinta Roriz* (which is the same as the Tempranillo of Spain), *Tourgia Francesa* and *Tinto Cão.* Three other grapes, *Sousão, Mourisco* and *Tinta Amarela* are permitted but not always used.

Few people know about or even enjoy white Porto, which is made from *Malvasia, Verdelho* (which they call *Gouveio*) and *Viosinho* grapes. White Porto, served chilled with salted almonds, also makes an excellent aperitif.

Intellectual drinkers should also know that 10, 20, 30 or 40 year-old Tawnies are a blend of younger and older wines averaging the years named on the bottles. I serve friends the 20-year-old Tawny because it is the Best Buy of the four. The 40-year-old samples have, many times, too much of a Sherry nose, and I'd buy old Cream Sherry if I want that flavor. Tawny wines are left in barrels much longer, turning slightly brownish, thus the name, and are mostly sediment free because the tannins had time to fall out of the wine before bottling.

Porto labeled *Colheita* is from a single year. The word means, "harvest." They're aged in wood at least seven years making them tawny in color and free of most of the sediment.

LBV stands for "Late Bottled Vintage." They're Port wines that came from a single year, and not a blend of vintages, as the simple Ruby Ports are. They also have less sediment than vintage Porto does because of the aging prior to release. Ruby Ports are introductory everyday examples of Porto.

Vintage Porto, the king of all Porto, is all from a *declared vintage*, meaning it was thought to come from a harvest with perfect growing conditions. They are bottled quite young and will always have to be decanted because all the sediment will fall to the side of the bottle. They are wines for special occasions, like birthdays and anniversaries because they shouldn't be drunk for at least ten to twenty years and the greatest vintages like 1977, 1994 and 2011 will last past 50 years. Be sure to get a few and put them on their sides in a dark cold place to sleep for decades. You'll never be happier about anything else than cellaring Vintage Porto for your old age!

Tokaji is the Hungarian dessert wine, and its *Eszencia* style was once served to dying Popes, who many times recovered for a while. In America, it is called Tokay. It's made mostly with the *Furmint* grape, but *Hárslevelü* and *Muscat* are grown and also used in Tokaji.

The labels of this golden sweet nectar will note how many wicker baskets, or *Puttonyos* were added near the conclusion of the fermenting must to increase residual sugars. Three *Puttonyos* will have up to 9% residual sugar. The 4, 5 and the 6 *Puttonyos* have up to 18% residual sugar in the wine. They also make an *Aszu Eszencia* style, when the same *Botrytis* mold that helps make Sauternes, infects the Hungarian vineyards. Lastly, the Tokay that comes from raisin-like shriveled grapes, where only tiny drops of almost pure sugar drips out, is call *Tokay Eszencia*. It can have up to 70 percent residual sugar. These wines are desserts unto themselves, and no other food need be paired with them at the conclusion of a meal.

Cream Sherry is not as popular as it used to be, but wise wine lovers should know that Sherry is made mostly with the *Palomino* grape. The sweetest examples, called Cream Sherries, have the *Pedro Ximénez* grape in them. You can also get a dessert Sherry made with all *Pedro Ximénez* grapes that has a raisin and prune aroma. Sherry is bottled from a *Solera* series of wine barrels where it's drawn off the oldest barrel on the floor to be bottled, and that barrel is refilled from the ones stacked above it. *Soleras* can be stacked three, four and even five barrels high.

The newly bottled wine will always have small amounts of very old wine in it along with medium aged and even some newer wine. This system helps maintain a similarity from year to year.

Dry Fino Sherries are called: *Fino, Manzanilla, Amontillado* and *Palo Cortado* and the sweeter Sherries are all of the Oloroso Class: *Oloroso, Cream* and *Pedro Ximénez*.

Madeira comes from the Portuguese island of Madeira in the Atlantic off Africa. *Sercial* is quite dry and nice with shellfish. *Verdelho* is semi-dry, and both styles come from grapes of the same name. It's not until you taste Madeira made from the *Bual* and *Malmsey* grapes that you experience the richest, sweetest dessert types that can age for one or even two centuries.

There are Five-year, Ten-year, and Fifteen-year-old Madeiras available, but the greatest is the classic Vintage Madeira that Ben Franklin and Thomas Jefferson loved. It's said that without Madeira, we wouldn't have had a Declaration of Independence because those two patriots drank it every night while writing.

Old Madeira pairs well with caramel and toffee laced desserts. When you savor old Vintage Madeira, the summer sunshine that helped grow the grapes lingers in each glass. Enjoy dessert wines and know that nearly every country on earth makes their own style or imitations of these famous examples. Seek them all out during your academic journey through the world of wine like the other top 10% of wine lovers do. You've truly become a wine intellectual. Congratulations!

14 QUOTES, NOTES AND GENERAL REFERENCES

Items for an Intellectual's Wine Conversations

Now that you understand what wine is, how it's made, and why there are so many differences, you'll find yourself explaining a lot of your newfound knowledge to your family, and wine-drinking friends. Well, just your friends because your family seldomly wants to hear about anything you want to share. In any case, you'll want to quote some wine references to support your intellectual opinion that wine is a symbol of true civilization, and it has been noted in art, literature, and music throughout the ages.

As you scan through Chapter Fourteen, I'd suggest you use a yellow, or any favorite color, highlighter to mark quotes you really like or find interesting, and might be able to use when next talking about wine at a favorite restaurant with friends, at a formal wine tasting, even a casual wine party, or dinner at home. It makes it so much easier to remember the quotes you want to use while sharing your wines, and your wine knowledge, once you've highlighted them.

Great Wine Quotes

Ernest Dowson, the 19th Century author wrote, "They are not long, the days of wine and roses." Do you have to know that's where the movie title came from? No, but if it slips into a wine dinner conversation, you'll show that a knowledge of wine is more than simply drinking it, and your fellow intellectual friends will love it.

"A flask of wine, a book of verse and thou," is from Omar Khayyam's *Rubaiyat*. C_2H_6O is the alcohol found in every wine. Before Robert Mondavi built his eponymous winery, he was a partner at Charles Krug Winery with his brother Peter. The red grape Portuguiser comes from Germany.

Wine is referred to 155 times in the *Old Testament*. Cadillac is not just an automobile; it's a wine-growing village across the river from Sauternes. The *Quran* says that, "There's a devil in every berry of the grape." In the 1600's, Champagne produced mostly red wines. You don't need this data to enjoy wines, but it's just fun to know some of it.

A Methuselah holds eight bottles of Champagne, as you've learned in this text, and the name comes from the long-lived Biblical figure. He lived 969 years and died seven days before the Great Flood. Pablo Picasso designed the 1973 label of Chateau Mouton-Rothschild and never picked up his liquid commission for doing it. Charles Dickens called Champagne, "one of the elegant extras of life." In the Bordeaux region of France, only Sauternes is served with Roquefort cheese. And, it's nice to know that Leonardo DaVinci lived out his final years in the French wine region of the Loire.

A *wine thief* is a tool, not a person, that's used to take a small sample from a wine cask. *Puttonyos* are the Hungarian baskets of very ripe unfermented grapes added to Hungarian Tokay near the end of the fermentation process to sweeten the wine. The number of baskets used is usually printed on their wine labels. The Roman poet Ausonius started Chateau Ausone in Saint-Emilion, more than 2000 years ago. In Alsace, a "gourmet" refers to a wine broker. *Blanc de Blanc* is white wine produced from white grapes, *Blanc de Noir* is white wine produced from red or black grapes.

Vitus, from Latin, is a grape's scientific *genus* name. It was Ernest Hemingway who said, "A person with increasing knowledge and sensory education may derive infinite enjoyment from wine." Quote that one when friends ask why you spend so much time talking about and drinking wine.

Cocteau, Laurencin, Miro, Chagall, Picasso and even Warhol have all done wine labels for Chateau Mouton-Rothschild. The Cyclops was pacified by wine in Homer's *The Odyssey*. Appellation means the name of the region where the wine was grown. A "Kir Royale" is a shot of Crème de Cassis topped off with Champagne served in a flute.

The name of a fine white wine vineyard in Burgundy's Cote de Beaune is *Pucelles* and it means "Virgins." In *Silverado Squatters*, Robert Louis Stevenson talks about his visit to the Napa Valley in California. In "On Her Majesty's Secret Service," the James Bond movie, Telly Savalas poured Dom Pérignon Champagne for Diana Rigg. The only Grand Cru Bordeaux to be elevated from Second Growth to First Growth was Chateau Mouton-Rothschild in

1973, so the 1974 vintage was the first Mouton with that top classification. There's simply no limit to the topics of interest for wine-lovers.

Jesus was offered some spoiled wine while suspended on the cross. Barsac is the largest commune in the Sauternes region. The English Romantic poet Lord Byron said, "Let us have wine and women, mirth and laughter, sermons and soda-water the day after." For wine lovers, the year 1919 is known as the "Great Curse" because Prohibition stopped "most" of the wine production in the United States. Bordeaux bottles have square shoulders while Burgundy bottles have sloping shoulders.

Charlemagne owned quite a few vineyards in Burgundy. Cultivar is the South African term for grape variety. The Shiraz grape takes its name from an ancient village in Persia (Iran). The Petite Sirah grape is actually the Durif grape from France's Rhone Valley. In 1475 in Venice, the first dated cook book suggested eggs poached in wine. In Kenya, hippos, giraffes and termites are the three major vineyard pests. That's important because who knows when you'll do a wine tour in Africa?

If you didn't know about carefully handling Port and decanting it through cheesecloth to remove the sediments, you'd never understand why Lord Wimsey, in Dorothy Sayers's novel, goes crazy when his maid shakes his bottle of Port before opening it. Sayers's book is *Busman's Honeymoon*. A wine scientist is called an Oenologist. Crémant means the wine is less sparkling but more creamy. Don't confuse it with *Cramant*, which is a tiny village in the Côte des Blancs within the Champagne region where only Chardonnay is grown. Because King Henry II married French Eleanor of Aquitaine, the British became aware of Bordeaux wines. Henry was Richard the Lion-Hearted's father. Both drank a lot of wine.

The famous playwright and ambassador to Italy, Clare Booth Luce, stated her favorite wines were Chateau Haut-Brion and Chateau Pape-Clement, both French Bordeaux. Cava is the Spanish term used to indicate a wine made in the classic Champagne method. The German wine term *weingut* means wine estate. Sherry wines were first developed during Shakespeare's lifetime. The Romans are most responsible for spreading viticulture throughout Europe. The aristocratic character played by Louis Jourdan in the movie, *Three Coins in a Fountain*, drank only his favorite Italian wine called, Lacrima Christi, which means the "tears of Christ." It's a charming food wine and I too really like it with Italian dishes. Sebastiani Winery, in Sonoma, has America's largest collection of hand-carved wine casks. *Disgorging* is the name of the process for removing the sediment from a sparkling wine just before the bottle is corked and caged.

Wine matures more slowly in larger bottles. That's important to know if you want to age wines for your children. *Porto* is the same as *Vinho do Porto*, and either is required on a label coming into the US. It's pretty certain that a red wine was served at the Last Supper. Any Champagne marked "Naturel" is drier than one marked "Brut," as you've learned in Chapter Seven. Every continent on Earth except Antarctica produces wine. The "Legend of Jamshyd" tells us that the Persians first discovered wine, but more modern research says it may have started in Soviet Georgia. I'm just happy someone did it.

Yul Brynner always kept bottles of Chateau Gruaud-Larose with him on tour. It's one of the best Bordeaux from St. Julien. Champagne was poured in every nightclub scene at Rick's Café in the movie *Casablanca*. Stag's Leap Wine Cellars outscored all the top Bordeaux in the famous 1976 Paris Blind Tasting. Madeira is only made on the Portuguese Island of Madeira in the Atlantic Ocean off North Africa. The small metal cup worn on a chain and used to taste wine is called *Tastevin*.

The first miracle that Jesus performed was at the Wedding Feast of Canaan where He turned water into wine. I think about this one every time I see it raining in a vineyard where the grapes soak up the water and swell with their natural sugars before being crushed and fermented into wine. The miracle continues.

Lucille Ball (I Love Lucy) is said to have loved her Pouilly-Fuissé. Joan of Arc always downed a glass of local wine before leading her army into battle. After Champagne is disgorged, the *Dosage* or *Liqueur d'Expedition* is added before corking to give it the desired level of sweetness.

The Persian poet Omar Khayyam wrote, "Wine is also a beauty spot on the cheek of intelligence." Now that demands some thinking. Chasselas is the grape used to make the French Loire Valley Pouilly-sur-Loire. The Solera system is a blending of new and mature wines in making sherry. It was Alexander Pope who said, "Wine awakens and refreshes the lurking passions of the mind." That's why you spit at large tastings and drink moderately at meals.

Sack is what Shakespeare called Madeira and Sherry.

A French *barrique*, or wine barrel, holds 24 cases of wine. *Appellation Contrôlée* is a term on a French label that tells us the wine was made under French vineyard controlled rules of law. Another name for the Ugni Blanc grape, as used in Cognac, is Trebbiano. In *Sparkling Cyanide*, Agatha Christie has the murder perpetrated by using poisoned Champagne. The letters "RD" printed on a Champagne label means that the wine was "Recently Disgorged." This is used when they want the Champagne to lie on the dead yeast cells a long time to pick up a creamier flavor. I love them even though I can seldomly afford them.

Tartrates will settle in a wine bottle or stick to the cork when a wine has not been cold stabilized enough. They are tartaric acid crystals and cannot hurt you. The most expensive Burgundy comes from Romanée-Conti, a four and a half acre vineyard in the village of Vosne. The oldest operating winery in the USA is Brotherhood Winery. It's found along the Hudson River in New York.

Fumé Blanc is made from the Sauvignon Blanc grape. White is the recommended color for tablecloths at wine tastings and for dinner. Jerez in Southern Spain is the birthplace of Sherry. Native US grapes called *Vitis Labrusca* grow wild along the East Coast and always produce a Concord-like foxy aroma. It's not a species to be used in quality winemaking. It makes a good jam to put on peanut butter.

Sonoma County's Korbel sparkling wine was poured at the eight exclusive Inaugural Balls for President Reagan in 1984. Sercial is the driest Madeira. It goes well with soups and opening fish courses. The Roman king Coriolanus in Shakespeare's play says, "I am known to be the one that loves a cup of hot wine with not a drop of allaying Tiber in't." This meant he did not dilute his wine with any water, which was the custom at the time. It's unbelievable how many people have made references to wine. I'm certain by now that you can tell the study of wine is not for dullards. Truly interesting people study the pleasures of wine, and the most interesting people seek out the most interesting and unique wines.

"Wine maketh glad the heart of man," comes from Psalms 104:15. George Gordon, Lord Byron, wrote, "Few things surpass old wine." Having gotten used to old mature wines, I fully agree. I was lucky to have cellared some in my youth and had the patience to let them sleep for a few decades.

"I sell well it is necessarie, where that we go, good wyn with us carie," was written by Geoffrey Chaucer in Middle English as part of his *Canterbury Tales*. John Keats' statement, "Give me books,

French wine and fine weather, and a little music out of doors," is good advice for enjoying life to its fullest!

Cervantes wrote, "I drink when I have occasion and sometimes when I have no occasion," while Johann Strauss said, "A waltz and a glass of wine can invite an encore." Of course he meant more of both, the music and the wine.

Some wines can heighten emotions: "This wine is too good for toasting, my dear. You don't want to mix emotions up with a wine like that. You lose the taste," wrote Ernest Hemingway, but King Edward VII said, "One not only drinks wine, one smells it, observes it, tastes it, sips it, and one talks about it." In Ecclesiastes 10:19 we find it written that, "A feast is made for laughter and wine maketh merry."

"Wine is one of the most civilized things in the world and one of the natural things of the world that has been brought to the greatest perfection, and it offers a greater range of enjoyment and appreciation than, possibly, any other purely sensory thing which may be purchased," wrote Ernest Hemingway, and very little can be said after that.

In Bizet's *Carmen,* the Gypsy lures Don Jose by promising him Manzanilla, one of the driest types of Sherry. Impress your Opera friends with that one. A *Petillant* wine is one that is just slightly sparkling. When President Nixon opened the doors to China, they took along cases of California's Schramsberg sparkling wine to serve to China's leaders. It seems to have worked.

Lord Peter Wimsey proved his identity by correctly identifying six different wines in one of Dorothy Sayers's whimsical mysteries. The tulip, flute and the coupe, which went of out style at the end of the 20th Century, are the only three types of glasses from which you should drink any sparkling wine. The coupe, said to be designed from a casting of Marie Antoinette's breast, is too shallow for wine with bubbles, and lets the wine go flat too quickly. No pun intended. Champagne is the northernmost wine region in France. Don Pérignon was a Benedictine monk.

This next one is really obscure and I cannot prove it, but I learned that the wine Cleopatra served to Caesar was *Mareotic* wine. It's also said that Cleopatra bathed in wine, which gave her smooth beautiful skin. I wouldn't waste that much wine. However, you should do whatever you feel like doing. Salvador Dali wrote an entire book in honor of his wife: *The Wines of Gala,* which was her name. President Nixon's favorite wine was Chateau Margaux, and it was also Hemingway's favorite Bordeaux. I too, used to love it, when I could afford it.

Giovanni Boccaccio, in his *Decameron,* talks of the mountain Bengodi, where streams flow with red wine. Julia Child always said that only young Beaujolais goes with Bouillabaisse. The Hunter Valley is the Napa Valley of Australia. The bulk process of making sparkling wine is the *Charmat* process named after Eugene Charmat. Here's a wine pun for you: if you ever entertain a Blue Nun at home with dinner, the only wine you should serve is

Liebfraumilch. This one is hard to understand if you're under forty, but it's easily researchable. Remember, this book is for intellectual people, not nincompoops.

German wines bottled in green glass are traditionally from the Mosel areas while wines in brown glass come from the Rhine areas. Willie Nelson recorded the country and western song, "Yesterday's Wine." If you're the host or person who ordered the wine bottle, the waiter will fill your glass with a sip to test it, and after you approve it, he'll finish pouring your glass last. The Egyptians attributed wine to Osiris, as a gift to mankind. The Greeks got it from Dionysus.

Côte is the French word for slope. It was Lord Byron who said that love is to marriage as wine is to vinegar. That's one to meditate upon. It was the New Christy Minstrels that recorded the hit song called, "Bottle of Wine." The most costly wine from Spain is Vega Sicilia, and it's never released until ten years have past since its harvest. White Chateauneuf-du-Pape should always be sold in a Burgundy-shaped bottle. Shakespeare's famous drinking character, Sir John Falstaff, always referred to Sherry as "sack." *Palomino* is the grape used to make most of the Spanish Sherries. The Lur-Saluces family has owned the most famous Sauternes house, Chateau d'Yquem, since 1785. That's a lot of generations to continue working one enterprise.

People who like wine usually also like literature and should know that Ralph Waldo Emerson wrote, "Give me wine to wash me clean of the weather-stains of cares." The French word *Clos* means a "walled-in vineyard" and goes back to the monastical Middle Ages. Epernay and Reims are the two key cities in the heart of the Champagne district. The richest, sweetest Madeira comes from the Malmsey grape.

"It wasn't the wine, it was the salmon," said Mr. Snodgrass in Charles Dickens' novel, *The Pickwick Papers*. In Edgar Allan Poe's, "The Cask of Amontillado," the Sherry lover gets buried alive in a wine cellar. The wine style "vermouth" comes from the German word, *wermut* meaning Wormwood. Vermouth is spiced wine. It was Madame Veuve Clicquot who invented "riddling," also called, *remuage,* to help clear Champagne. *Veuve* means, "widow."

Note: If you find yourself marking too many lines with your yellow highlighter, I'd suggest you use two different colors with yellow meaning "ones I'll definitely use" and green for "ones I might use."

Pindar wrote, "…even the wealthy find their hearts expanding when they are smitten by the arrows of the vine."

Le Montrachet is the greatest French white Burgundy, and according to Alexander Dumas, "should be drunk on your knees with your head bared." During the few times I've gotten to taste it, I have to agree, even though I sat while enjoying it.

Shakespeare's *Two Gentlemen of Verona*, would have drunk Bardolino, Valpolicella or Soave. Armagnac was the home of d'Artagnan, one of the Musketeers. "Chateau-bottled" is a Bordeaux term while "Estate-bottled" is used in Burgundy. The German term, *Qualitatswein* means "quality wine." Ronald Reagan used Dom Pérignon to toast, "one for the gipper." When Champagne is *Sur Pointe,* it means it is upside down and ready for *disgorging.*

The 12th Century Gothic wine presses inspired the printing press. Printing shared ideas and freed our minds; where would be without words or wine?

It was St. Peter, the first Pope, who said, "Drink no longer water, but use a little wine for the stomach's sake." Still good advice. The term, *ullage,* is the space between the wine and the bottom of the cork in a full bottle of wine. One of Plato's greatest quotes was, "No thing more excellent nor more valuable than wine was ever granted mankind by God."

"Stewball was a race horse and I wish he were mine. He never drank water; he always drank wine," sang Peter, Paul & Mary. *Plonk* is the English slang term for cheap, low-quality wine. The Spanish word, *Tinto,* refers to red wine. Wine ages more slowly in larger bottles; age 750ml bottles for yourself and Magnums (1.5L) for your children.

"After wyn, on Venus I thinke," wrote Geoffrey Chaucer. Notice, he put wine (*wyn*) ahead of love (*Venus*) even though they're closely tied together. Prohibition was the result of the 18th Constitutional Amendment. The 17th Century poet and playwright John Gay's very first poem was entitled, "Wine." Cabernet Franc is the most common name in the world for Pomerol's grape variety called Bouchet.

The Franciscans are responsible for starting grape-growing and wine production in California. The Californian jug wine called "Chablis" is made from Thompson Seedless and French Colombard, not Chardonnay like the real Chablis. The Greek playwright Euripides wrote, "Where there is no wine, love perishes and everything else that is pleasant to man," whereas the Quran calls wine an abomination. You decide.

Ninety percent of all the wine made in the world is expected to be consumed within one or two years. The Romantic poet Henry Wadsworth Longfellow wrote "Catawba Wine." The oldest existing literature referring to wine was written on stone. *Copita*, the tasting glass for Sherry, in Spanish means, "little cup."

Always hold a wine glass by its stem. Stemless wineglasses are better used for votive candles. There are 31 Grand Cru Burgundies. It's said that Noah drank wine everyday and lived to be 950 years old. Remember, the Vikings first called America, Vineland. The place was loaded with wild vines growing everywhere.

"Will you be sending me a Valentine – Birthday greetings bottle of wine," sang the Beatles. Odysseus used Maronean wine to drug Polyphemus. The German *Eitelsbacher Karthauserhofberger* is the longest name of any wine. Wine bottles should be recorked every 25 to 30 years. Wine is mentioned ten times in the *New Testament*. The Crusaders liked a Yugoslavian wine so much, they named a local vineyard, "Jerusalem" upon return from the Holy Land.

The Greek word, *Symposium*, means, "drinking together." The German grape *Spatburgunder* is really Pinot Noir. The Portuguese wine term *Vinha*, means "vineyard." Charles Krug Winery was the first winery established in Napa Valley, and they're better than ever.

The first person to talk about wine in the *New Testament* was Jesus. The French word, *Sommelier*, means "Wine Waiter." Oenology is the science of wine. In Hemingway's, *The Sun Also Rises*, the Count says, "All I want out of wine is to enjoy them." The Native American grape variety, *vitis labrusca* was commonly called the Fox Grape. The two-pronged cork puller is called an "Ah-So."

Dionysus granted King Midas his wish to turn everything into gold; sadly even his food and wine were turned into gold. The Hungarian red wine called *Egri Bikaver* translates to mean, "Bull's Blood of Egri." It takes two fermentations to make Champagne. The Cistercian monks created modern Burgundy during the Middle Ages. "VSOP" on a Cognac label means "Very Special Old Pale." Wines are stored on their sides to keep their corks wet and swollen tight. Winston Churchill's favorite Champagne was Pol Roger. Apollo and Zeus drank "Mead," the wine made from honey. Provence is famous for its Rosé wines. *Schloss*, in German, is the equivalent of "Chateau" in French.

Henry Wadsworth Longfellow made more than 300 references to wine in his works. England's, "Wine and Spirits Education Trust Limited," confers the Master of Wine certificate. The "Society of Wine Educators" confers the CWE or Certified Wine Educator certificate. Europe uses the term, "Hectare" instead of acres to measure their landside; a hectare is 2.47 acres. French Vermouth is made from Grenache, Clairette and Picpoul grapes. They are three of the 13 grape varieties permitted to make Chateauneuf-du-Pape.

"The Wasp" is the name of Picasso's well-known etching of a grape vine. "Kosher" is the name of wine supervised and made under rabbinical rules. The French, *sec* and the Italian *secco* both mean, "Dry." It was Yugoslavia, and not any place in India, that made a wine called "Tiger Milk." A "refractometer" measures the sugar content of grapes. *Frizzante* means semi-sparkling wine. Most wine grape varieties contain two seeds. All of Champagne was nearly destroyed during the Battle of the Marne in WW I.

Ancient Romans stored their wines in a smoke house to improve their flavor. Iago exclaims in Shakespeare's *Othello*, "that wine is a good creature, if it be used well." Wine was used as currency during the Middle Ages. *Stravecchio* in Italian means "Very Old." "Wine is good for women," say the *Chevaliers du Tastevin* of France, "when men drink it." You might have to think about this one a bit.

It's the skins of grapes that produce the color of a wine; the juice of white, pink and red grapes is clear. St. Vincent is the Patron Saint of Wine Growers and Wine Cellars. Mark Twain said, "Too much of anything is bad, but too much Champagne is just right."

Thomas Jefferson said, "No nation is drunken where wine is cheap." Caviar and Champagne are the *classic* wine pairing. The French, *chai*, or Spanish *bodega* and Portuguese *adega* all mean "wine cellar." Lastly, the Latin phrase, *in vino veritas,* means, "In wine, there is truth."

This concluding chapter, filled with run-on thoughts about wine, are the references that intelligent wine-lovers can incorporate into their discussions during meals with wine, answering questions about wine, or simply points to make when you have to defend your wine collecting hobby, which you'll do for decades. Wine drinkers exhibit the lowest rate of dementia. Taste as many wines as possible. Enjoy wine, and never stop learning. Share what you've learned with others. It will reinforce your wine memory. I toast to you, because you should consider yourself among the world's top 10% of intelligent wine drinkers. *In vino veritas.*

RECOMMEND READINGS

Adams. Leon D., *The Wines of America, (3rd Ed)* McGraw-Hill, New York, 1985.

Anderson, Burton, *Italian Wines*, Simon and Schuster, New York, 1982.

------ *Wines of Italy, An Adventure in Taste*, Italian Trade Commission, New York, 1986.

Asher, Gerald, *Gerald Asher on Wine*, Random House, New York, 1972.

Baldy, Marian W., *The University Wine Course*, The Wine Appreciation Guild, San Francisco, 1993.

Baxevanis, John J., *The Wines of Bordeaux and Western France*, Rowman & Littlefield, Totowas, NJ, 1987.

Bespaloff, Alexia, *Complete Guide to Wine*, A Signet Book, New York, 1994.

------*Wine A Complete Introduction*, A Signet Book, New York, 1971.

Blumber, Robert S., Hurst Hannum, *The Fine Wines of California,* Doubleday & Company, Inc., 1971.

Broadbent, Michael, *Michael Broadbent's Pocket Guide to Wine Tasting*, Simon and Schuster, New York, 1968.

------ *The New Great Vintage Wine Book*, Alfred A. Knopf, New York, 1991.

------ *Wine Tasting*, Christie's Wine Publications, Thanet Press, Margate, Kent, England, 1979.

Cass, Bruce, Ed., Jancis Robinson, *The Oxford Companion to the Wines of North America,* Oxford University Press, 2000.

Chemlminski, Rudolph, *I'll Drink To That: Beaujolais And The French*

Peasant Who Made It The World's Most Popular Wine, Penguin, New York, 2007.

Chroman, Nathan, *The Treasury of American Wines,* Rutledge-Crown, New York, 1976.

Clarke, Oz, *Oz Clarke's Encyclopedia of Grapes,* Harcourt, Inc., New York2001.

Collier, Carole, *505 Wine Questions,* Walker and Company, New York, 1983.

Conaway, James, *Napa,* Houghton Mifflin Company, Boston, 1990.

Dallas, Philip, *The Great Wines of Italy,* Doubleday & Company, Inc., 1974.

Darlington, David, *Angels' Visits,* An Inquiry into the Mystery of Zinfandel, Henry Holt and Company, New York, 1991.

De Groot, Roy Andries, *The Wines of California, The Pacific Northwest and New York,* Summit Books, New York, 1982.

Dorozynski, Alexander – Bibiane Bell, *The Wine Book.* Golden Press, New York, 1969.

Govaz, Michel, *Encyclopedia of the Great Wines of Bordeaux,* Julliard, Bernard Neyrolles, Paris, 1981.

Elkjer, Thom, *Adventures in Wine,* Travelers' Tales, San Francisco, 2002.

Fonseca, A. Moreira da, A. Galhano, E. Serpa Pimentel, J.R.P. Rosas, *Port Wine,* Instituto do Vinho do Porto, Porto, Portugal, 1982.

Gaiter, Dorothy J., John Brecher, *The Wall Street Journal Guide to Wine,* Broadway Books, New York, 1999.

Gluckstern, Willie, *The Wine Avenger,* A Fireside Book, Simon & Schuster, New York, 1998.

Hanson, Anthony, *Burgundy,* Faber and Faber, London, 1982.

Hazan, Victor, *Italian Wine*, Alfred A. Knope, New York 1982.

Henriques, Frank E., *The Signet Encyclopedia of Wine,* The New American Library, Inc., 1975.

Immer, Andrea, *Great Wine Made Simple*, Broadway Books, New York, 2000.

Jamieson (Ed), *The Concise Atlas of German Wines*, Mitchell Beazley Publishers, 1986.

Jefford, Andrew, *Port An Essential Guide to the Classic Drink*, Exeter Books, New York, 1988.

Johnson, Hugh, *Vintage: The Story of Wine*, Simon and Schuster, 1989.

------ *Hugh Johnson's Pocket & Encyclopedia of Wine,* Simon & Schuster, New York, 1977.

------ *The World Atlas of Wine*, Simon and Schuster, New York, 1971.

Kladstrup, Don & Petie, *Wine & War,* Broadway Books, New York, 2001.

Kramer, Matt, *Making Sense of Wine,* William Morrow, New York, 1989.

Lausanne, Edita, The *Great Book of Wine,* Galahad Books, New York, 1969.

Lee, Susan, *Inexpensive Wine*, A Signet Book, New York, 1974.

Lichine, Alexis, *Alexis Lichine's New Encyclopedia of Wines & Spirits,* Alfred A. Knopf, 1977.

Lord, Tony, *The New Wines of Spain,* The Wine Appreciation Guild, San Francisco, 1988.

MacNeil, Karen, *The Wine Bible,* Workman Publishing, New York, 2001.

Manessis, Nico, The *Illustrated Greek Wine Book,* Olive Press Publications, Corfu, 2000.

Massee, William E., *McCall's Guide to Wines of America,* McCall Publishing Company, New York, 1970.

------ *The Red, White & Rosé* of Wines, Dell, 1972.

Mayson, Richard, *Portugal's Wines & Wine Makers,* The Wine Appreciation Guild, San Francisco, 1992.

Morrell, John, *An International Guide to Wines of the World,* John Bartholomew and Son Ltd, Edinburgh, 1974.

Muir, Augustus (Ed), *How to Choose and Enjoy Wine,* Bonanza Books, New York1972.

Muscatine, Doris (Ed), Maynard A. Amerine (Ed), Bob Thompson (Ed) *The University of California Sotheby Book of California Wine,* University of California Press, Berkeley, 1984.

Olken, Charles, Earl Singer, Norman Roby, *The Connoisseurs' Handbook of California Wines,* Alfred A. Knopf, New York, 1980.

Perdue, Lewis, *The French Paradox and Beyond,* Renaissance Publishing, Sonoma, CA, 1992.

Peynaud, Emile, *The Taste of Wine,* The Wine Appreciation Guild, San Francisco, 1983.

Pinney, Thomas (Ed) *The Brady Book,* Nomis Press, Santa Rosa, CA, 2003.

Prial, Frank (Ed), Rosemary George, Michael Edwards, *The Companion to Wine,* Prentice Hall, New York, 1992.

Price, Pamela Vandyke, *Guide to the Wines of Bordeaux,* Monarch, 1978.

Quillen, Jacqueline L., George H. Boynton Sr., *The Magic of Wine,* Taylor Publishing Company, Dallas, 2000.

Ratti, Renato, *Asti,* A.G.V. Group Mondadori, Vicenza, Italy, 1985.

Ray Cyril, *Bollinger, Tradition of a Champagne Family,* William Heinemann Ltd., 1994.

Robards, Terry, *The New York Times Wine Book,* Avon Books, New York, 1976

Robinson, Jancis, *The Oxford Companion to Wine*, Oxford University Press, Oxford- New York, 1999.

------ *Concise Wine Companion*, Oxford University Press, Oxford, 2001.

Roby, Norman, Charles Olken, Earl Singer, *The New Connoisseurs' Handbook of California Wines*, Alfred A. Knopf, New York, 1991.

Roncarati, Bruno, *Viva Vino 200+*, Wine and Spirits Publications, London, 1986.

Sarles, John D., *ABC's of Italian Wines*, Wine Books, San Marcos, CA., 1979.

Seldon, Philip, (Ed), The *Great Wine Chateau of Bordeaux*, Vintage Magazine Press, Hastings House Publishers, New York, 1975.

Seward, Desmond, *Monks and Wines*, Crown Publishers, Inc., New York, 1979.

Silverman, Harold I., (Ed) *Pride of the Wineries*, California Living Books, San Francisco, 1980.

Schoomaker, Frank, – Julius Wile, *Frank Schoonmaker's Encyclopedia of Wine*, Hastings House, 1978.

Sherbert, Felicia M., *The Unofficial Guide to Selecting Wine*, IDG Books Worldwide, Inc., 2000.

Sokolin, William, *Liquid Assets*, MacMillan Publishing Company, New York, 1987.

Stevenson, Tom, *The Millennium Champagne & Sparkling Wine Guide*, DK Publishing, Inc., London, 1998.

------ *Sotheby's World Wine Encyclopedia*, Little, Brown and Company, Boston, 1988.

Suckling, James, Vin*tage Port*, Wine Spectator Press, New York, 1990.

Taber, George M., *A Toast to Bargain Wines*, Scribner, New York, 2011.

------ *Judgment of Paris*, Simon & Schuster, Inc., New York, 2005.

------ *To Cork Or Not To Cork*, Scribner, New York, 2007.

Thompson, Bob, *California, Oregon and Washington, The Complete Touring Guide*, Simon & Schuster, Ltd., London, 1987.

Voss, Roger, T*he Wines of the Loire,* Faber and Faber, London, 1995.

Wiegand, Ronn R., *Wines and Your Restaurant,* German Wine Information Bureau, New York-Mainz, 1985.

Zraly, Kevin, Windo*ws on the World Complete Wine Course*, Dell Publishing, Inc., New York, 2014.

66066113R00111

Made in the USA
Charleston, SC
14 January 2017

SEEING
THE
SUPERNATURAL

SEEING

—— THE ——

SUPERNATURAL

How to Sense, Discern and Battle
in the Spiritual Realm

JENNIFER EIVAZ

Chosen

a division of Baker Publishing Group
Minneapolis, Minnesota

© 2017 by Jennifer Eivaz

Published by Chosen Books
11400 Hampshire Avenue South
Bloomington, Minnesota 55438
www.chosenbooks.com

Chosen Books is a division of
Baker Publishing Group, Grand Rapids, Michigan

Printed in the United States of America

Library of Congress Control Number: 2017941812

ISBN 978-0-8007-9854-3

Unless otherwise indicated, Scripture quotations are from the Holy Bible, New International Version®. NIV®. Copyright © 1973, 1978, 1984, 2011 by Biblica, Inc.™ Used by permission of Zondervan. All rights reserved worldwide. www.zondervan.com

Scripture quotations identified AMP are from the Amplified® Bible, copyright © 2015 by The Lockman Foundation. Used by permission. (www.Lockman.org)

Scripture quotations identified ESV are from The Holy Bible, English Standard Version® (ESV®), copyright © 2001 by Crossway, a publishing ministry of Good News Publishers. Used by permission. All rights reserved. ESV Text Edition: 2011

Scripture quotations identified MOUNCE are from THE MOUNCE REVERSE-INTERLINEAR NEW TESTAMENT Copyright © 2011 by Robert H Mounce and William D Mounce. Used by permission. All rights reserved worldwide.

Scripture quotations identified NASB are from the New American Standard Bible®, copyright © 1960, 1962, 1963, 1968, 1971, 1972, 1973, 1975, 1977, 1995 by The Lockman Foundation. Used by permission. (www.Lockman.org)

Scripture quotations identified NIRV are from the Holy Bible, New International Reader's Version®. NIrV®. Copyright © 1995, 1996, 1998 by Biblica, Inc.™ Used by permission of Zondervan. All rights reserved worldwide. www.zondervan.com

Scripture quotations identified NKJV are from the New King James Version®. Copyright © 1982 by Thomas Nelson, Inc. Used by permission. All rights reserved.

Scripture quotations identified NLT are from the *Holy Bible*, New Living Translation, copyright © 1996, 2004, 2015 by Tyndale House Foundation. Used by permission of Tyndale House Publishers, Inc., Carol Stream, Illinois 60188. All rights reserved.

Scripture quotations identified KJV are from the King James Version of the Bible.

Cover design by Dan Pitts

20 21 22 23   7 6 5

green press
INITIATIVE

I dedicate this book to Jesus Christ,
who is forever faithful
to complete His work in me.

Contents

Foreword

Many books have been written on the gifts of the Holy Spirit that have helped the Church understand the functions and importance of these spiritual manifestations. Certain gifts have been emphasized more than others, and our understanding of certain gifts is greater than others. This is especially true of discerning spirits.

I have heard teaching on the discerning of spirits that has simplified it to the realm of discerning angels, demons or human spirits. Many people teaching on this subject have not gone beyond this level of understanding. The teaching in this book will expand your understanding of this subject as the author takes you deeper into the spiritual realm.

Jennifer Eivaz teaches from personal experience on the importance of the discerning of spirits, and her firsthand experience is invaluable. She has a unique approach to this subject that I have never read or heard before.

She emphasizes the importance of training your senses to discern between good and evil. This training is a process and requires spiritual maturity and growth.

11

Whether you are beginning the process, in the intermediate stages or have come to a level of maturity, this book will benefit you greatly.

John Eckhardt, overseer, Crusaders Church Chicago;
founder and presiding apostle, IMPACT Network

Acknowledgments

I first want to thank my wonderful husband, Ron, for his endless support after my many hours away writing this book. Thank you for believing in me and encouraging me to keep going and not quit.

I also want to thank my church family, again for their perfect support, prayers and encouragement while I wrote not only my story, but also many of theirs in this book.

Thank you, Steve Shultz from the Elijah List, for being a divine appointment and catalyst for God's plan in my life as a writer.

Thank you, Virginia and Justin Meyer, for allowing me to use your spare home to write when I just needed to get away so I could think clearly and write without distractions.

Thank you, Tom Hammond, for giving me a word of encouragement at just the right time, when I was fighting the hardest to accomplish this book.

Thank you to the many people who prayed and fasted for me, especially Andrea, Catherine, Charlene, Elaina, Emmanuel, Mary, Michelle, Nathan and Joe.

Introduction

A Gift with a Purpose

It was my first attempt ever to teach on the gift of discerning of spirits. I remember it being a Sunday night service at my home church, Harvest Christian Center, in Turlock, California. My husband and I had been ministering there for approximately five years, and we were teaching our church about the gifts of the Holy Spirit, which included the gift of discerning of spirits (see 1 Corinthians 12:7–11).

My teaching about this gift was quite simplistic. I gave a standard definition of the gift—that it is a supernatural ability from the Holy Spirit to see and distinguish between spirits: the Spirit of God, the spirit of man and the spirit of devils. I then gave several biblical examples of the discerning of spirits, as well as some testimonies. I felt deep down that my teaching was somewhat lopsided and shallow. I just could not yet explain in plain language how I discerned what I discerned. There were so many variables and so many strange feelings and physical sensations involved. Trying to package that in an understandable way seemed almost impossible. At the same time, I felt I could only effectively present how to discern the demonic realm because I had only enough clear language to explain that side of this gift. Since then, I have gained the experience and found the language to explain both sides of the gift, the discerning of both the positive and the negative, as you will see when you read on. But even back then, my teaching was still well-received, and it opened the eyes of our congregants more than they had been before.

The night after I spoke, I had a disturbing dream. In the dream, a strong angel named Jeff was escorting me. Jeff means "the peace of God." This angel was muscular, but the size and appearance of a man. He wore regular clothing, but his clothes were white, and so was everything else about him. He escorted me through the air to a large city. I did not know the name of the city or have any idea where I was. He then escorted me into a high-rise building located in the center of the city. We went up the elevator to the very top floor and then stepped out of the elevator, right into a penthouse office suite. There we met a physically short man wearing business attire. When he saw us, he stood up firmly from behind his desk and walked briskly around it, coming right in front of me to look me square in the eyes. He had the meanest countenance I have ever seen. The fierce hostility radiated off him.

"Why are you teaching this?" the man demanded nastily and with force. "Don't you ever teach this again!"

Here the dream ended, and I woke up realizing that I just may have encountered Satan himself in a dream. Why was the gift of discerning of spirits such a threat to him?

As time progressed, I began to realize the price tag for those who operate in this gift. Most everyone loves you when you spiritually discern their more positive attributes, or the presence of the Lord or the angels. When you have the ability to discern the hidden things, however, it can bring a very real level of persecution by those who do not want you to see the things that you see. In addition, that vile deceiver, Satan, will do anything he can to stop you from blowing his cover. Still, it is immensely worth it to be in the know spiritually.

The dream also showed me that Satan still occupies very high places in the earth. He was in the tallest building, at the very top floor! Whoever occupies the high places overshadows the people with his presence—in this case, Satan's wickedly deceptive presence. For this reason, the gift of discerning of spirits will be challenged from the high places—that is, until we, Christ's Church, rise up and occupy them. This is what this gift is all about. You see and discern so you can respond. You see and discern so you can battle. It is a gift with a purpose: to advance Christ's Kingdom in the earth.

1

Seeing Both Sides
of the Supernatural

My daughter and I were having a serious discussion about Santa Claus. We were approaching Christmas Eve, and she had asked to leave Santa a glass of milk and some baked cookies. Like many young kids, she expected Santa to visit our home in the middle of the night to leave her a surprise gift. Now, my husband and I do not have a problem with those who bring Santa into their Christmas family fun. It just was not something that we made a big fuss about in our home. Still, my daughter had become a wholehearted believer in Santa Claus, having been educated by her preschool teacher and classmates. They told her about the large white-haired man from the North Pole who flew around the world on a magic sleigh with reindeer. They let her know that Santa would leave every child a gift, including her, as long as she was not on the naughty list. She was sure that she was not on the naughty list.

And so I explained about Santa more accurately, which led to further discussion not only about Jesus, but also about the tooth fairy, the Easter bunny, angels, witches and ghosts. It turned out that my daughter was a true believer in all things mystical and supernatural in an age-appropriate way. I had already begun restricting her cartoon watching, having firmly said, "No witches, wizards or ghosts!" The children's shows seemed to carry an abundance of such themes. I clarified that although some of these things (not all) can be real, they are evil. I then pointed out how Santa and the Easter Bunny are fun, but not factual, and then I joked, "I'm the tooth fairy and will gladly hide money under your pillow for each tooth!" Finally, I reemphasized the reality of Jesus, the Holy Spirit and the angels. I was grateful to be experiencing a genuine miracle with angels in that season. We had seen bursts of small white feathers appearing several times in midair during our worship services, prayer services and even at home. We understood this phenomenon to be a visible manifestation of angels in our midst. This was positive reinforcement with our daughter, who enjoyed collecting these feathers to show her friends at school. It also kept alive our firm belief in the supernatural.

Keep in mind that I have experienced the supernatural my entire life. My experiences clearly changed in scope after I became a Christian during my freshman year of college, but nevertheless, I have always had them. And perhaps you have, too. The Bible, which is our guide, shows us how normal it is to have supernatural encounters of a wide variety. It even helps us know what experiences to accept and what to reject, and why. The Bible shows us that it is normal to see and experience both angels and demons, it is normal to have visions and dreams from God, and it is normal to encounter a wide variety of miracles. Understand that the supernatural is not a limited, one-time experience for us as Christians, because our God is supernatural and He has no limits. At the same time, many unbelievers also experience the supernatural, but in a much different context.

When non-Christians experience the supernatural, it creates a hunger in them to know more. Only they do not know how to discern or sort through it. If their home becomes haunted, for example, they do not know how to cast the spirit out. They often do not know they need to cast the spirit out! Or if they start exhibiting psychic or telepathic abilities, they do not know how to classify what is happening, and they often reach out to occult and New Age sources for answers. People desperately needing physical healing or personal deliverance from spirits might go to brujas, shamans, exorcists and the like to try to get relief, instead of going to Jesus and His Church. Countless television shows, books, radio programs, blogs and more attempt to provide spiritual counsel for such issues. Only they do not lead you to Jesus, so they ultimately harm you much more than they help you. And many people, including me, have found themselves wandering down wrong paths, looking for answers and still not finding any.

My first spiritual experience took place when I was only three years old. I lived with just my mother, as my biological father had gone absent. I do remember being a happy and energetic toddler during the day, but I was troubled at night. The reason is, I could always see *her*, and I am not referring to my mother. There was another woman in my bedroom who appeared to be sleeping on the floor of my closet. And then sometimes she would float off the floor. I could not see her until it was dark and the lights were off, but she was always there. She never made a sound or moved around. I remember that she had pale skin and long dark hair, and she appeared to be nude.

Once I shouted out something like, "Mom! There's a woman in my closet!"

My mother investigated and then replied, "Just shut the closet door!" And that was the end of the conversation.

The following year, my mother moved us from Nevada to her home state of California. The good news is that the woman in the closet did not come with us. I never saw that apparition again. Mother also remarried a man who was an active member of the Latter-day Saints Church (LDS), also known as the Mormon church, and naturally we became an LDS family. Once my mother remarried, life seemed pretty normal for her, my new stepfather and me. I was still highly energetic, now a five-year-old, and I did not think much about it when the following happened.

One day I was playing and doing what normal five-year-olds do, when I heard two men talking somewhere in my house. They were having a full-on conversation with each other, and I went to investigate out of curiosity. I looked all over, but I could not find them. I could still hear the conversation quite clearly, however. No worries; I just went back to my playtime. I never heard these two men converse again, but off and on I would hear voices in or around the house, or feel as though I were being pulled into conversation with someone whom I could not physically see. This would take over my reality from time to time, so much so that my mother ended up taking me to the doctor to have my hearing tested. I had become habitually unresponsive to her when she would try to talk to me or get my attention. She thought I had a hearing problem, but the doctor said I was fine. Some of this was probably my not listening to her. But the other side of it—and it was something I could not explain at that age—involved my strong connection to the spirit world, which did absorb my attention.

At age seven, I was playing with some neighborhood friends in my bedroom. We all attended the LDS church together. I have no idea what prompted me to do this, but I told my friends something like, "Do you want to see me call a ghost into the room?" We all just laughed and squealed, as little girls do. No one said no, so I just called it in. "Come here, ghost! Come here, ghost!"

We all watched as my school papers tacked up on my bedroom wall began to flutter up and down as what seemed like a wind entered the room. Surprisingly, none of us were scared when this happened. The papers stopped fluttering within just a few seconds, and we returned to our playtime as if it were nothing. Only it was not just nothing. I was not playfully inviting Casper the Friendly Ghost to come over for a visit. I was inviting demons into my life in sheer ignorance.

As time progressed, heading into my teen years I was dabbling more intentionally in some occult activities. For example, I had tried to use a Ouija board to obtain information about the future. A Ouija board is typically used in séances and involves a board printed with letters, numbers and other signs, to which a movable planchette points in response to your questions. My use of the Ouija board did turn into a séance when a spirit named itself through the board, pretending to be a long-dead relative of mine. This really was not a long-dead relative, but a familiar spirit, which the Bible describes as a demon (see Leviticus 19:31; 20:6). It was also the last time I did any conjuring through this method, as it had a dark presence attached to it.

On other occasions, my friends and I would attempt various incantations to conjure specific spirits, levitate and induce trances. These incantations were spells many teenagers do as a form of entertainment, such as the traditional "Bloody Mary" spell or the recently popularized "Charlie Charlie" spell. These incantations did work on occasion, which meant we were successfully conjuring spirits to perform magic. In addition, I was venturing out on my own into astrology, ESP, the paranormal and psychic powers. I never considered these activities wrong, because I did not do these things to try to harm anyone.

The heavier stuff came in when I began participating in rituals for the dead at the LDS temple on a regular basis. These rituals are not perverse or scary, but are believed to secure eternal benefits for the deceased as you stand in proxy for specific persons and perform the various rites. These rituals typically invoke the spirits of ten to twenty deceased persons at each temple visit and require that you be baptized in water for each one. Some participants would say they could see the spirits of the dead in the temple facilities, but I never saw such apparitions. The ritual is then complete once the LDS elders lay their hands on you to impart their version of the Holy Spirit upon you. These rituals did carry and release a spiritual presence upon me, but now, on this side of the cross, I can certainly distinguish that it was a false presence.

By the time I turned sixteen I was rebelling at home in re-action to family issues, and I became conscious of a tangible darkness around me. What I mean by this is that I was aware of a canopy or cloud of darkness around my person, and I could not see or feel any hope for my future. For example, I was in honors classes but no longer cared about excelling. I chose un-stable friends over stable ones. I also put myself in dangerous situations several times because, at the time, I felt no personal worth. I was also experiencing an increase in dark spiritual encounters, usually at night. I would hear eerie voices outside my bedroom window—the kinds of voices that left an instabil-ity in your mind once you heard them. And then my bed would sometimes shake on its own while I slept. This was absolutely terrifying and would jolt me out of sleep. I could also sense the coming and going of dark spirits, and I was bottoming out emotionally. Jesus gave warning not to let darkness overtake us, because those in darkness cannot see where they are going (see John 12:35). He then said, "I have come as a light into the world, that whoever believes in Me should not abide in dark-ness" (John 12:46 NKJV). The word *abide* in this passage means to live and dwell in darkness. Darkness, then, is a place and a state of being, not just a metaphor. And darkness, in my situ-ation, had become a perceptible presence.

Through the fervent prayers of relatives, neighbors and some high-school acquaintances, not only did I survive this period of my life, but I was also introduced to Jesus Christ. I gladly surrendered my life to Jesus as a freshman in college, and the Light of the world truly began to destroy the darkness in my world. The stronghold of Mormonism came off me instantly, I did away with all occult practices, and I learned how to let go of wrong friendships. I was also baptized in the Holy Spirit, which is an infilling of God's power (see Acts 1:8). I could genuinely feel God's light working inside me instead of that foul darkness. I had godly hope and could see with clarity for the first time.

As a new Christian, I did undergo a very serious deliverance from spiritual bondage in direct connection to my occult past. It happened innocently enough during a weekly house prayer meeting, after one woman in attendance expressed that she saw a spirit of sorcery standing over me. When she said that, something picked me up and threw me against the wall. Next, I went into a grand mal demonic manifestation, mine being one of the worst in comparison to those I have personally witnessed in all my days of ministry. I wrote about this incident in more detail in my book *The Intercessors Handbook* (Chosen, 2016).

What happened to me at this prayer meeting was challenging to my pastor and to others in my church. They believed that Christians could not manifest demonically if they truly had the Holy Spirit. (I discuss this very issue in more detail in the appendix that I have included at the end, "Can a Christian Be Demon Possessed?") I did have the Holy Spirit, but I still manifested demonically since those areas of occultism had to be firmly addressed and dealt with. The good news is, I found my spiritual authority in Christ during that season and learned to walk out my freedom.

After my deliverance, the Holy Spirit gave me a very powerful gift. It is called the gift of discerning of spirits, and you can see it listed with other supernatural gifts in 1 Corinthians 12:8–10. This is a gift that allows you to see and sense the truth about the spiritual realm. It reveals to you what spirit, whether good or evil, is motivating people, opportunities, conflicts, supernatural experiences and a whole lot more. It is a gift that came to me without a set of instructions, but with a clear invitation to listen to the Teacher, the Holy Spirit, day by day and moment by moment in order to experience this gift's truths and benefits. And it is this gift that I want to introduce to you throughout this book in ways you may have never considered before.

Understand that this gift from the Holy Spirit is intended for "the good of all" (1 Corinthians 12:7 MOUNCE). The word *good* in this verse is the Greek word *symphero*, which means to bring together (as in a symphony) and to be profitable, beneficial and advantageous.[1] And it is true. This gift gives you a tremendous advantage as a believer in Christ. It allows you to see what is in the dark so you will not stay in the dark. It supernaturally puts you in the know and gives you the upper hand in difficult circumstances. It gives you the right information so you know how to pray, prophesy and battle intelligently.

Unfortunately, this gift has been highly misunderstood in its operation. Those who have it often do not know they have it, and they have mislabeled themselves as crazy. Others have misused this gift and gone on to harm people instead of building them up. The Holy Spirit wants to open our eyes and shift our understanding. He wants to activate this gift powerfully, but properly, in the Body of Christ. I have written this book to help you understand and operate in this gift. By the time you are finished reading it, you will become aware of and equipped for seeing the supernatural, so that you can effectively sense, discern and battle in the spiritual realm.

2

The Gift of Discerning of Spirits

Midway through my second year of college, I was invited to serve on a campus ministry leadership team. I was thrilled to be asked and immediately said yes. A few months had flown by when the campus ministry director called an emergency leadership team meeting at his home to discuss a difficult matter. He said, "We have to pray for Easton (not his real name), and we have to pray now!" He explained that Easton was being tormented by a demon almost every night.

Easton, a leader just like me, went on to describe the hair-raising details of each incident. Incidentally, Easton attended a local congregation and had plans to attend seminary at a popular Christian university. While renting a room at the campus ministry director's home, he found himself being spiritually attacked in the night. What added to his dilemma was that Easton came from a theological paradigm in which people did not believe in the supernatural, or at least did not experience it personally. Being forced to set his paradigms aside, he was now in a genuine spiritual battle of eerie proportions. In short, he described a giant black snake that would wake him up in the middle of the night and threaten his life over and over.

As Easton shared his story, I began feeling as though I were being pulled to the back of the house. I recognize now that the One pulling me was the Holy Spirit, but back then I only knew it was an unusually strong feeling. I interrupted Easton and asked if I could go look in his room. He agreed, but the campus ministry director wanted to test me in what I was sensing. He said with enthusiasm, "Sure! Go ahead! But I'm not telling you which room is his."

Without mistake, I walked straight into Easton's room and then into his closet. I normally would not go into someone's closet without permission, but in this situation it seemed appropriate, and the outcome proved it was true. As I reached toward the back of his closet, I discovered his personal collection of heavy metal band LPs tucked neatly away under some clothing. I handed the LPs to Easton and said, "I think I found the source of your problem!"

Easton responded by breaking each record into pieces, realizing that he had cohabitated with compromising music that clearly hosted both sexual and occult themes. He repented of his sin, and that spirit never came back.

What took place in Easton's life that day all began with the gift of discerning of spirits being in operation. Because of this, he was freed from a tormenting demon. I still did not know yet that this gift existed. I did know enough, however, to follow the leading of the Holy Spirit and do what Jesus did: "Jesus went around doing good. He healed all who were under the devil's power" (Acts 10:38 NIRV).

This story also presents us with several questions, namely, "How could secular LPs sitting in a closet be the cause of a demonic attack?" And, "Is this something that could happen to me?" This is where we need to expand our paradigms to *include* and not *exclude* the spiritual. We do not live in just a natural realm; we also live in and are affected by the spiritual realm. Spiritual laws that the Bible defines for us govern both realms. Honoring God's Word creates conditions in which we experience natural and spiritual blessings. On the other hand, violating God's Word nullifies His promises to us, including His promise to protect us from harm and torment (see Deuteronomy 28; Romans 2:6–8).

Easton had violated God's clear word about sexual impurity and false religion through his choices in music. The apostle Paul commands us, "But among you there must not be even a hint of sexual immorality," and he tells us to "flee from idolatry" (Ephesians 5:3; 1 Corinthians 10:14). Ignorance or dismissiveness about the spiritual does not absolve us of consequences, either. When we violate God's holiness, it is like leaving the front door to your house unlocked. A thief might not discover it immediately, but eventually the thief comes to your neighborhood, looking for opportunity. And when he finds an unlocked door, he will enter in and try to steal, kill or destroy (see John 10:10). Fortunately for Easton, his situation was short-lived because the gift of discerning of spirits was in operation.

The Gift Explained

A common description for the gift of discerning of spirits is that it is a supernatural ability from the Holy Spirit to distinguish between spirits—divine, demonic and human. It also enables us to discern the hidden motives of the heart. Since this gift embraces the "hard to explain" and the "intangibles" of the spiritual realm, it has historically been difficult to teach since we have lacked adequate language to explain it properly.

The apostle Paul shared a similar struggle in discussing visions from the Lord, specifically visions of the third heaven and paradise. He referred to both places as "inexpressible" (see 2 Corinthians 12:1–4). I believe this was the apostle John's challenge, too, as he attempted to detail the visions and revelation of the end times in the book of Revelation. If John had been able to use clearer terms with which to express the ideas, we probably would understand this book more fully, rather than having continual arguments over what in heaven and on earth he was pointing to. This is the same challenge we face in describing the workings of the gift of discerning of spirits. We are still engineering vocabulary to explain the formerly "inexpressible" aspects of the spiritual realm. I humbly pray and believe that this book will be a forerunner in this regard by giving words to your experiences, thus enabling you to walk out the fullness of this gift.

There are numerous examples of the gift of discerning of spirits in both the Old and New Testaments. Remember, this gift sees past the natural realm to reveal the spiritual realm, causing us to know what is really behind our circumstances and how to respond. For example, the prophet Elisha prayed an unusual prayer for his servant during a time of battle: "O LORD, please open his eyes that he may see" (2 Kings 6:17 ESV). Elisha was not referring to his servant's physical eyes, but actually to his spiritual ones. Elisha and his servant had been targeted for certain death by an enemy army. The servant had become terrified with that strangling fear that manifests when you know the worst is about to happen. Elisha could see into the spiritual realm, which is the gift of discerning of spirits in operation, and he saw the true spiritual conditions of the matter. The truth was that a fierce army of warlike angels had jam-packed the spiritual horizons, ready to fight on their behalf. Their physical enemies were completely outnumbered, which dispelled all thoughts of death and execution. This is what Elisha wanted his servant to see, and God answered the prophet's prayer.

We also see how this gift operated in other lives in the Old Testament. We see it in the life of Lot, when he encountered the two angels God sent to rescue him. We see it in the life of Samuel, when he heard the audible voice of God—something that was rare in those days. It operated in the lives of Saul's attendants, who saw the evil spirit that was tormenting him (see Genesis 19; 1 Samuel 3:1, 4; 16:15).

In the New Testament, Jesus not only cast demon spirits out of their helpless victims; He also could identify them by their kind—unclean spirits, spirits of infirmity, deaf and mute spirits, etc. This, too, was the gift of discerning of spirits in operation. You cannot identify a spirit unless the Holy Spirit reveals it to you. Later, the apostle Paul did the same thing by identifying a spirit of divination that had possessed a young female fortune-teller in Ephesus, more specifically a python spirit.[1] He cast the spirit out of her, which caused the entire city to go into an uproar (see Acts 16:16–22). Finally, the apostle Peter knew by the gift of discerning of spirits that a husband and wife by the names of Ananias and Sapphira had brought him a deceptive offering. They had pretended to sell their land at a certain price, but had secretly held back a portion of the proceeds for themselves. He addressed their sin openly, but unfortunately, their actions brought the judgment of the Lord upon their lives and they both died for it (see Acts 5:1–10).

These examples exhibit the gift of discerning of spirits in operation, but they don't explain how this gift operates or how to distinguish one spirit from another. We see the end point, but not the process. And it is the process of discerning that is often misunderstood, ignored or rejected. The reason is that this gift is a sensory process before it is an intellectual one. And in our Greek-thinking culture that elevates logic and reason above emotions and the spiritual, we have inadvertently shut down the internal mechanism by which this gift flows.

Training Your Senses

The writer of Hebrews provides us with some insight about how the gift of discerning of spirits works, which is primarily through your senses: "But solid food is for the mature, who because of practice have their senses trained to discern good and evil" (Hebrews 5:14 NASB). In other words, this gift from the Holy Spirit causes us to discern good and evil through our physical senses. That would be through our eyes, ears, smell, taste and touch, as well as through our emotions. And then the mature have learned through practice how to accurately sort out what they are sensing, so they can respond to the information appropriately. This implies that the gift of discerning of spirits has a learning curve to it and requires community and accountability in order for a person gifted in it to grow in accuracy.

Around the same time as the incident with Easton, my neighbor, Patricia, invited me over to her home. Now deceased, she had prayed for the salvation of my family for years. She had felt the assignment of the Lord to pray faithfully for us and was now enjoying the fruit of her prayers. She also was an avid garage sale shopper and had decorated her home with several objects she had purchased over the years. Patricia began to recognize that I might be walking in the gift of discerning of spirits and decided to put it to the test. She asked me, "Are any of these objects in my home spiritually unclean for any reason?"

I looked around her kitchen and her living room and picked out only four or five objects that irritated my spirit, even though I had no reason for it. When I identified them for her, Patricia said, "Hmm . . . all those objects were purchased from the same home."

Neither of us knew exactly why I felt that irritation, but it prompted Patricia to pray. She prayed that anything unholy or demonic still lingering on those household objects would be removed, and then she asked God to bless them instead. To her, that seemed like the right way to handle it.

I also had a friend who suffered with diabetes around this same time frame. Once when I sat near her, I suddenly had a strange physical sensation. I became uncomfortably warm and began to feel unwell all over. When I voiced my physical feelings, she explained that she often felt the same way when her blood sugar was doing the wrong thing. I put it together, although at a much later date, that what I was experiencing was the gift of discerning of spirits in operation. I was sensing the presence of a spirit—specifically, a spirit of infirmity—but I detected it by feeling it in my own body as if it were my own.

Jesus once described a woman as having this same kind of spirit of infirmity, which was the reason she was bent over and could not stand up straight. A spirit of infirmity does not cause just one kind of physical illness; it stands behind many physical ailments. Jesus then cast the spirit out of the woman, and she stood up straight again (see Luke 13:10–13). What we don't know is how Jesus knew this information and how He distinguished that it was a spirit instead of a physical condition that would have needed the Holy Spirit's gift of healing instead. Having had that experience with my diabetic friend and others, I believe that Jesus, too, may have felt the woman's problem within Himself. He thus could accurately diagnose its source, because He is "touched with the feeling of our infirmities" (Hebrews 4:15 KJV).

It is important to point out that the gift of discerning of spirits is not just the discerning of evil. It is a supernatural ability to discern both good and evil. The evil and the demonic just seem to stand out more once you have tasted of heavenly things and finally know the difference. Steve Shultz, founder of the Elijah List, shared with me that while reading something on his computer, he suddenly experienced a fragrant scent all around him. He thought it might be soap on his hands, but he checked it out and realized his hands did not smell like anything at all. He knew through his sense of smell that he was experiencing the presence of the Lord.

I also have smelled the fragrance of Christ in worship and have even tasted a sweetness in my mouth, knowing that I was sensing the Lord's presence by "taste." These simple but profound experiences bring the Scriptures to life. We can experience the "aroma" of Christ (2 Corinthians 2:14), and we can "taste and see that the LORD is good" (Psalm 34:8 NKJV). Many people have cited that they felt goose bumps or electricity on their skin and recognized these feelings as pointing to the presence of the Lord. Others have heard the voices of angels singing in heavenly chorus, or they have felt the wind of the Holy Spirit upon their person. The gift of discerning of spirits is very multifaceted in its expression, but it works powerfully through our senses to reveal the spiritual realm.

Keep in mind that the gift of discerning of spirits is listed alongside other power gifts such as the gifts of healings, the gift of faith, and the working of miracles (see 1 Corinthians 12:8–10). We all know of persons who have moved in these powerful gifts in profound ways. With that said, what would happen if someone received the gift of discerning of spirits in the same strength of anointing as the anointing we have seen on some people for healing or miracles, such as Maria Woodworth-Etter, Smith Wigglesworth or Jack Coe? I believe we are seeing something like this just beginning to emerge in the Body of Christ, only we have not yet fully grasped it.

Also, if this gift is something that flows mostly through your senses, could it be possible to become anointed but not recognize it at first? The answer to that is yes! It happened to me. The Holy Spirit anointed me with this gift well before I ever knew it. And because it works through your senses, your senses begin to react and resonate to the "spirit" of your surroundings—whether good or bad—before your mind can even explain what you are reacting to. This can be quite disturbing, until you know what is happening to you and why.

You're Not Crazy; You're Gifted

After my deliverance, I went into a kind of spiritual and sensory overload that is somewhat hard to describe. Hearing voices was not abnormal for me, but it escalated into unmanageable proportions. I would hear voices in the air, in my mind, on objects and more. My emotions would also shift erratically from one moment to the next. Crowds, shopping malls and classrooms, for example, often became a sensory avalanche crashing against my mind and senses. For those reasons, I began to crave being alone and finding silent places. I honestly thought this was temporary and reasoned how this must only happen to those who have just gone through a demonic deliverance. Only it did not go away, and things never did quiet down. My best efforts to cope with it were now turning into desperation as I seriously wondered if I were losing my mind. On top of it, my symptoms mimicked those of medical schizophrenia and bipolar disorder, both in my family history.

There just happened to be an emphasis in the Body of Christ on "spiritual warfare" during that time period. There were fresh waves of teaching about how to pray and combat the devil, what to do if you were under demonic attack, and how to deliver people from demonic spirits. Because of this emphasis, and through some basic teachings on spiritual discernment, I grew to accept the idea that I might not be crazy; I might have a gift from the Holy Spirit since I did see and sense demons. I will also add that spiritual discernment back then was mostly about discerning the demonic and not much else.

But what about the rest of it? Erratic mood shifts, hearing voices, seeing strange sights and feeling unexplained physical

35

sensations. Literally no one was talking about this side of the gift of discerning of spirits. For years this became my secret strange world, by which I knew spiritual and hidden information but could not explain how I knew it. It is only in the last few years that I have been able to find words to teach, activate and give identity to those who are given this gift in the strength and manner that I have received it.

Melissa Villegas attends Harvest Christian Center in Turlock, California, and also has the gift of discerning of spirits. She describes this gift as overbearing at times because it involves all her physical and emotional senses. Melissa will feel, literally, what another person feels. For example, if she were to read a news article about someone who attempted suicide, she would find herself agonizing in the deep anguish of pain that the person could not see past. This intensity of feeling, of course, pushes her into places of deep intercession.

"This gift is not a 'feel great' gift, but a gift that goes deep," Melissa said. "That's where our heavenly Father is. He's in our deep places, the places that need His cleansing."

My friend Sid Widmer, a business owner, describes himself as always having an awareness about people and a sensitivity to the spirit realm. In his twenties he could often be found in his pastor's office, "emotional and stormy," describing various burdens he felt for the church and the people in it—burdens about situations he had no prior knowledge about. He finally realized in his thirties that he discerned a lot through his emotions, picking up things that were going on in the spiritual environment and processing them through his feelings.

"I used to think I was becoming unstable or bipolar," Sid said. "My moods would shift so fast and disproportionally to the situation I was in."

Sid began to make mental notes about his mood shifts, noticing repeated patterns and realizing that his mood would shift in reaction to certain spirits in the vicinity. He is still learning about this gift and how to remain anchored to the Holy Spirit when these things take place, something most will say is easier said than done.

I take great joy in helping people such as Melissa and Sid dispel the lies that something is wrong with them and that they are crazy. They are not crazy, but are powerfully anointed with the gift of discerning of spirits. They are chief agents in setting the captives free and healing the land. As most of those gifted with it have discovered, however, this gift is something that requires time and diligence on the part of those who are gifted, so that they develop the emotional stamina and accuracy they need for operating in the gift effectively.

Wrong Discernment

The fruit of this gift is just as important as learning how the gift processes. Are people being set free? Is the Kingdom of God being established in greater measures? Too often, this gift has been credited for shaming and blaming people and/or falsely accusing them. Because the gift of discerning of spirits works primarily through the senses, it requires practice and maturity to know what you are sensing and why. It also needs a redemptive application. Unfortunately, wrong discernment happens. Let's look at some of the reasons why.

1. Having a loveless heart

As I looked to the Holy Spirit on how to be effective in walking this gift out, He first pointed to my heart and instructed me "not to judge." Be aware that not judging something is not the same as ignoring it. A proper response, however, requires a right heart condition in order to be effectual. He was directing my heart toward love and redemption, especially when I encountered negative spiritual information about people or circumstances. I think Francis Frangipane says it best in his book *Discerning of Spirits*:

> There is a false discernment that is based on mistrust, suspicion, and fear. You can recognize false discernment by the coldness around it. False discernment may be packaged in a type of love, but it does not originate in love; it comes out of criticism. True discernment is rooted deeply in love.[2]

Let's say, for example, that I am discerning a disloyal and greedy heart with an acquaintance or a business peer. I don't have any evidence yet for what I discern, but it truly feels like a point of discernment from the Spirit of God. Regardless, I first need to discern my own heart to determine if I am functioning out of mistrust, an unhealed past experience or a competitive attitude. If not, then I need to ask the Holy Spirit, *What does love look like in this situation?* And the answer will depend on context. There is no one-size-fits-all solution, except to be led by the Holy Spirit and wisdom.

I will say that when you discern by the Holy Spirit something negative about another person, remember that God has just told you a secret. Secrets remain in the secret place, unless God gives you permission otherwise. Remember that God loves that person even if he or she is demonized, struggling or wicked. There will be times you are called on to deal with the situation more openly, but prayer is usually all that is required of you.

2. Looking on outward appearances

One of the key mistakes associated with the gift of discerning of spirits is looking at someone's outward presentation and presuming a spiritual condition, either good or bad. It is true that you can make some general assumptions by observing how people carry themselves over time, how they habitually dress and act, and how they communicate. This is not spiritual discernment, however, but natural perception. It can provide helpful information, but it is not the gift of discerning of spirits.

Jesus said, "Look beneath the surface so you can judge correctly" (John 7:24 NLT). The gift of discerning of spirits therefore goes deeper than outward appearances. It bypasses our intellect and logic to reveal what is imperceptible to the natural eye. It discloses the spirit of the matter and the real motives of the human heart.

When Mary of Bethany anointed Jesus' feet with fragrant spikenard oil and wiped His feet with her hair, the disciple Judas raised a terse complaint. He said, "Why wasn't this perfume sold and the money given to the poor? It was worth a year's wages" (John 12:5). But Jesus knew the truth behind both Mary's and Judas's actions. Mary was not being wasteful at all. She had been moved upon by the Holy Spirit to anoint Jesus prophetically for burial. Judas, on the other hand, was a thief and would often steal from the offering. That was the real reason he complained (see John 12:6–7). The gift of discerning of spirits revealed the truth behind their actions, and Jesus responded by defending Mary's honor.

3. Being inexperienced with the spiritual

Just before Jesus went to the cross, He spoke to those around Him about His impending death. He was troubled and vexed, but had determined within Himself not to ask our heavenly Father to spare Him the cross, but rather be glorified in it. When He shared that out loud, our Father in heaven responded audibly, saying, "I have glorified it, and will glorify it again" (John 12:29). Amazingly, the crowd heard the audible sound of the Father's voice! Only they had trouble distinguishing it. Some heard it as thunder, while others thought it was an angel speaking (see verse 29). Jesus was experienced in our Father's voice and therefore discerned it more easily than the crowd did.

Recognize that there is a continuous learning curve when it comes to the gift of discerning of spirits. Walking out this gift is like learning a new language; only it is a spiritual language that requires time, practice and commitment for us to become fluent in it. Discerning the spiritual realm and doing it well is the mark of the mature believer (see Hebrews 5:14). Compare this thought to the attitude of committed musicians who practice their gift and train their ears to distinguish the notes correctly. We, too, need to do the same with this gift.

We will wrongly discern, or not discern at all, until we have first developed a grid for what is spiritually possible through the study of the Bible. For example, we read how God was in the fire of a bush, in the wind, in the earthquake and in the still, small voice (see Exodus 3:2; 1 Kings 19:11–12). We also read how Satan killed Job's family with a whirlwind, tempted Jesus in the wilderness, and possessed Judas to betray and murder our Lord (see Job 1:19; Luke 4:1–13; 22:3). We further read about angel armies, about the Holy Spirit falling like a dove on Jesus and then like fire on the disciples, and a whole lot more (see 2 Kings 6:17; Luke 3:22; Acts 2:3–4). Armed with biblical knowledge, we then need to pay attention to what is happening in our senses and emotions.

You will come to discover that things like numb hands, strange fragrances, certain headaches, unusual sights and sounds, or feelings of sudden joy or unusual heaviness may or may not have a spiritual parallel behind them. This is intended to draw you into dialogue with the Teacher, the Holy Spirit, who will gladly lead you into all truth and assist you in managing your spiritual sensitivity.

Kingdom Principles

1. The gift of discerning of spirits comes from the Holy Spirit and enables us to distinguish between spirits—divine, demonic and human. It is also a supernatural ability to discern the hidden motives of the heart.

2. This gift works primarily through our physical senses (see Hebrews 5:14). That would be through our eyes, ears, smell, taste and touch, as well as through our emotions.

3. You can become anointed with this gift just as strongly as those famously anointed with the gifts of healings or working of miracles. Only you might not know it at first because of the way it manifests.

4. Walking out this gift is like learning a new language; only it is a spiritual language that requires time, practice and commitment for us to become fluent in it. Discerning the spiritual realm and doing it well is the mark of the mature believer.

5. Because the gift of discerning of spirits works primarily through the senses, we can wrongly discern the spirit motivating people and circumstances if we have a loveless heart, are looking on only outward appearances, or are inexperienced with the supernatural.

Thoughts for Reflection

1. Do you have the Holy Spirit's gift of discerning of spirits? If so, how do you know?

2. How have you discerned good or evil through your senses and/or through your emotions?

3. Has this gift ever left you wondering if you were going crazy? How has this teaching helped you settle that issue?

4. Have you ever wrongly discerned something, thinking it was the Holy Spirit? What did you learn from that situation?

5. Do you struggle not to condemn people when you discern something that is negative? If so, how can you cultivate a redemptive heart toward them?

3

The Fundamentals of Distinguishing between Spirits

During my stint as a leader with a college campus ministry, I developed a strong friendship with another leader on the team by the name of Ron Eivaz. We had first met at an on-campus worship service, services that we both attended regularly prior to our leadership roles. Ron claims that during one of these worship services, I turned to him and gave him a too-friendly hug. It is something I cannot remember taking place, but it is a fact that he shares freely with almost everyone. He humorously claims that this is how I made the first move.

Ron and I were both invited to teach Bible studies on the college campus as part of our leadership responsibilities. We both agreed, but as a new Christian I obviously did not know very much about the Bible. And it was evident that Ron knew the Bible backward and forward. I would attend his weekly group and take copious notes before teaching his notes to my own Bible study. Ron often taught using material from well-known teachers such as Kenneth Hagin, Kenneth Copeland and Jerry Savelle. These men were referred to as "Word of Faith" teachers and were controversial at the time. This caused a mild degree of tension for our campus ministry director, but Ron was allowed to continue teaching from these sources. These well-known teachers laid a strong foundation in our hearts "to have faith in God and not to doubt"—a truth that grounded us through every obstacle we were going to face in the future.

The Holy Spirit then spoke to Ron's heart and said, *You are going to marry Jennifer.* Ron was not too sure about me as far as marriage was concerned, and he also questioned if he had heard correctly.

I, too, heard the Holy Spirit, but He had a different message for me. I approached Ron and said, "The Holy Spirit told me to tell you that He really did show you who your wife is going to be." I did not know the message referred to me, but God has a terrific sense of humor. Long story short, we fell in love and began to plan the rest of our lives together.

Ron and I both loved the move of the Holy Spirit, but this was something we rarely experienced in our home church, let alone anywhere else in our city. For that reason, we decided to leave Turlock, California, for good and go where we knew the Holy Spirit was moving. With much zeal and excitement we relocated to Tulsa, Oklahoma, so we could finish our education at Oral Roberts University (ORU). We also believed God would respond to our zeal with a well-suited, dynamic ministry position for us upon graduation.

While we were still attending ORU, the Holy Spirit spoke to us both. He said that we would return to our home base in Turlock, California, and eventually pastor the church that we had both attended. Actually, Ron did not hear a voice. But during his morning prayer time, he had a vision of himself preaching on our church platform. When that happened, he reacted in shock by jumping backward and shouting, "No!"

For me it was a strong internal knowing, and like Ron, I was very apprehensive. Ron and I knew this church well, and we knew it would not be an easy assignment. In reality, it was an impossible assignment! The church had become spiritually sick with legalism, sin and strife and was very close to dying. Upon our graduation, however, it was the only door of ministry that opened to us, as if God was making His point. My soon-to-be husband accepted the senior pastor's offer to become an associate minister alongside him, and we were married soon after.

What began to unfold through many trials, tests and decisions was a deeper understanding of the spiritual realm in connection to purpose. The gift of discerning of spirits flows the strongest and with the most impact when it is attached to purpose; only it is hard to discern what you don't yet understand. With that said, as a means of increasing our understanding, let's dive more into the fundamentals or the "hows" of distinguishing between spirits.

Recognition through Perception

Just to review, the gift of discerning of spirits is a supernatural ability from the Holy Spirit to distinguish spirits—meaning to differentiate, tell apart or discriminate between them, whether a spirit is divine, demonic or human. This gift is necessary to determine spiritual origins, which in turn will determine outcomes. When we fail in our recognition, we miss out on what God is doing, or we allow demonic harassment to continue out of ignorance.

James and Michal Ann Goll wrote this in their book *Angelic Encounters*:

In general, discernment always involves the evaluation of some kind of evidence. We can only accomplish this by using our five bodily senses: sight, hearing, smell, taste, or touch. We notice something; then we start sifting quickly through the incoming data. We discriminate between the pieces of evidence and we detect patterns. Then we decide what to do, based in large part on what our discernment tells us.[1]

Our first encounters with the Holy Spirit are often in the form of "goose bumps," a feeling of electricity or perhaps a prickly feeling on our skin. Two of my neighbors were saved around the same time, and both would proclaim with excitement how they felt goose bumps during church services. It was exciting to them because they knew they were sensing the presence of God. They could distinguish their connection with Him through goose bumps and other sensations on their skin.

Conversely, our encounters with demonic spirits are not so pleasant. Sometimes we can sense them through a bad taste in our mouths, or we feel an unpleasant coldness in a certain location, or we might experience a nauseous feeling whenever we come around a certain person or group of people. While ministering at a conference in Latvia, for example, I began to experience a certain feeling around one of the attendees. I would compare the feeling to a rubber band being stretched around my forehead and temples. I also remembered this particular feeling, through past experiences, as being connected with occultism. At the end of the service, I went to this person and began to pray with her. I also asked her some pointed questions to determine her involvement, or not, in magic or sorcery. It turns out this person was practicing forms of witchcraft. After our discussion she left the service with a friend, to whom she confessed, and then she surrendered her life to Jesus.

We also will discern the attitudes and struggles of people, good or bad, which can be a directive for prayer or an opportunity for ministry. While I was traveling with a ministry partner to a conference, she predicted that we would encounter a homosexual woman in need of ministry while there. I asked her how she knew that. She replied, "Well, I can tell by where my thoughts are going."

This can be tricky, because such thoughts are often mistaken as your own thoughts unless you know yourself really well. But in this case, my ministry partner was discerning very accurately. Right before the conference session, I felt drawn by the Holy Spirit to a particular woman in the room. I walked up to her and began prophetically to call out her gifts and talents. I then revealed God's heart for her and His plans for her future. Tears began flowing down her face, and she gave her life to Jesus. Later we found out that she was the woman my ministry partner was discerning before we ever even got there.

Once you realize how much spiritual information you perceive through your senses, you begin to pay attention. Gut feelings and hunches that were once ignored are now examined for their meaning. We sift more carefully through our random thoughts and feelings, asking questions like, *Why am I thinking that? Where did that come from?* We also begin to notice coincidences and patterns involving our senses, now investigating them for spiritual possibilities.

Examine Your Senses

With the Bible as our foundation, let's begin to pair up biblical precedent with our modern-day experiences, to better identify how the gift of discerning of spirits flows through our senses (sight, hearing, taste, smell and feeling). What follows is only a snapshot of illustrations, but it provides a framework to help you begin recognizing when this gift is operating in your individual world.

What do you see?

Discerning through sight involves our inner eyes, also known as the eyes of our heart, as well as our two physical eyes. The apostle Paul prayed for the Ephesians, that their spiritual eyes would be opened by the Holy Spirit, resulting in knowledge and understanding: "And [I pray] that the eyes of your heart [the very center and core of your being] may be enlightened [flooded with light by the Holy Spirit], so that you will know . . ." (Ephesians 1:18 AMP). This is a prayer we can also pray for ourselves—that our eyes would be opened, and that we, too, would know what is happening in the spiritual realm and would respond accordingly.

Afraid of the Israelites, Balak, a Moabite king, hired Balaam to curse them. Balaam waited on God for permission to curse them, but God instead said that He had blessed them. King Balak was persistent, however, and summoned Balaam to a meeting to try to change his mind. As Balaam traveled on his donkey to meet with the king, the angel of the Lord stood in his way to oppose him. Balaam's donkey saw the angel, but he did not. The donkey then stopped cooperating with Balaam, and Balaam punished his donkey severely enough that the angel intervened. The Lord caused the donkey to speak like a human and to argue his case with his master, and He also finally opened Balaam's physical eyes to see the angel as well. This sight is what led to Balaam's repentance (although short-lived), and he did not proceed in cursing the Israelites. Once Balaam saw the spiritual realm, he could see things properly. What he saw changed his direction (see Numbers 22).

Have you ever had your eyes opened to the spiritual realm in a way that radically changed you? There was a young hippie by the name of Lonnie Frisbee who was on one of many LSD acid trips, this time in the Tahquitz Canyon in Southern California. While high on LSD, he had a life-changing vision where he saw himself evangelizing a sea of people who were crying out to the Lord for salvation. Much like the apostle Paul's Damascus Road experience and subsequent conversion, what Lonnie Frisbee saw in the spiritual realm—namely a vision of himself as Jesus intended him to be—changed the course of his life. He converted to Christianity and became an unusual evangelist who helped birth two major Christian movements, the Jesus Movement and the Vineyard Movement. (You can watch his full story in the movie *Frisbee: Life and Death of a Hippie Preacher*.[2])

Through the gift of discerning of spirits we will see angels, visions of Jesus and even the Lord through signs in nature. When Jesus was born, for example, a new star rose high in the sky. Three kings from the East, astrologers according to tradition, saw the new star and came to Jerusalem in search of Him. They asked King Herod, "Where is the one who has been born king of the Jews? We saw his star when it rose and have come to worship him" (Matthew 2:2). They discerned a sign in nature and through it found their King and worshiped Him, offering gifts of gold, frankincense and myrrh.

Have you ever noticed something in nature and wondered if God was trying to show you Himself? I have experienced this over and over, from rainbows to cloud shapes to insects, birds and more. He opens our eyes to distinguish the spiritual realm, both good and bad, by causing us to see it in nature. The summer before the 2016 election, for example, I distinguished such a thing. It was just after 3 a.m., and I was walking up to my front porch, having just completed a night-watch prayer shift at our church. The Lord had been speaking to my heart all week about "change," only I did not know what He was referring to. As I headed toward my porch, my eyes gazed down to the ground and to a dragonfly lying on the pavement. I thought it might be dead and gave it a little nudge with my foot. Apparently, it was only napping, and it gave me a loud, angry buzz in response. Strangely, I felt the anointing of God in that moment.

I rushed inside my home and googled the symbolic meaning for *dragonfly*. I was pleasantly surprised to discover that this beautiful insect was often a sign for "change." I distinguished God's heart through interaction with His creation. He was saying that we needed to prepare for significant change. Looking back, I believe He was pointing to the 2016 election.

We also will distinguish demonic spirits through sight, often as shadowy shapes, dark mists or actual demons. When this happens, don't be afraid or overwhelmed, and always remember your spiritual authority. As a new Christian, I would see demons in and around my church almost every Sunday. When I say that I could see demons, what I mean is that I could see our natural surroundings, but also our spiritual surroundings at the same time. These spirits were typically about two feet tall, hideously ugly and obnoxious in countenance, and they would hide behind stairwells, inside closets and underneath furniture. I tried to warn our pastor about this, but it only irritated him. At the time, his reaction was hurtful to me, but now I understand why he reacted that way. He did not need me to tell him there were demons in and around the church all the time. For most leaders, hearing that is distracting and very discouraging. He needed me to pray discreetly and use my God-given authority to command these spirits to leave the premises—something we all have the authority to do as believers in Jesus Christ (see Mark 16:17).

When we surrender our inner eyes and physical eyes to the Holy Spirit, He will flood them with light and we will see beyond, into what is imperceptible to the natural eye. Sometimes we will see something in our mind's eye that is crystal clear and applicable to the situation. Other times, we will just see a glimpse of something in our imagination and almost miss it. These sightings should always draw you into dialogue with the Holy Spirit, who will joyfully teach you how to respond.

What do you hear?

Just like our eyes, we also will discern the spiritual realm with our inner and outer ears. What I mean by this is that sometimes you will hear the spiritual realm as a sound or a voice, perhaps, but you may hear it internally or you may hear it audibly, outside yourself.

The young Samuel was sleeping in the house of the Lord, where the Ark of God was. Three times he heard a voice call his name in the night. Each time, he woke up, found the priest Eli and asked him, "Did you call me?"

Eli had not called the boy but realized what was happening, so he told Samuel, "Go and lie down, and if he calls you, say, 'Speak, LORD, for your servant is listening'" (1 Samuel 3:9). The Lord called out to Samuel again, and Samuel, now able to distinguish His voice, responded as he had been instructed. God spoke to Samuel even further, telling him the things to come in regard to both Eli and Israel.

Many people have experienced what Samuel experienced. They have heard the invisible, and they have even heard someone call their name. Or they have heard other things such as doorbells, a telephone ringing or bells sounding, only to be unable to find the source of the sound upon investigation. These sounds are typically a call to you from heaven to listen further. The Holy Spirit has something more to say to those of us who have the spiritual ears to hear (see Revelation 2:7, 11).

Other biblical examples of hearing God's voice include Moses, who heard God speak to him from the burning bush (see Exodus 3). This is another example of discerning the supernatural in nature. We then read about Ezekiel, who heard the mighty sound of angel wings, and Elisha, who supernaturally heard the secret plots of an enemy king against the nation of Israel (see Ezekiel 10:5; 2 Kings 6). Mary, the mother of Jesus, saw an angel and heard the angel's voice (see Luke 1:26–38).

The disciples heard the sound of a mighty rushing wind in the Upper Room in Jerusalem (see Acts 2:2).

One woman in our church learned to discern the spiritual realm by what was actually happening to her ears. When her ears would ring in a certain way, it meant there was the presence of an evil spirit. This kind of thing was something she originally mistook for tinnitus, the medical condition of hearing ringing in the ears, before she received clarity from the Holy Spirit. On the other hand, when her ears had the sensation of popping open, she discerned this to mean there was the presence of an angel.

What do you taste?

Discerning spiritual realities through our sense of taste, although biblical, is probably a new concept for many and one in need of more exploration. King David exhorted us to "taste and see that the LORD is good" (Psalm 34:8 NKJV). We can readily accept "seeing" His goodness, but "tasting" His goodness? How does that work?

Whenever we discern something good or bad by the Holy Spirit, even if we have discerned it through taste, we have received knowledge from His treasury of wisdom. That is always His goodness being revealed to us. I have heard some people, myself included, describe how they have identified the presence of the Lord through a sweet taste in their mouth. This experience has biblical precedent. The Lord instructed the prophet Ezekiel to eat a scroll with prophetic writing on it. Ezekiel described the scroll as tasting sweet, like honey (see Ezekiel 3:1–3). The apostle John experienced something similar. An angel gave him, too, a scroll to eat. John said, "It tasted as sweet as honey in my mouth, but when I had eaten it, my stomach turned sour" (Revelation 10:10). I don't know of anyone whose stomach turned sour after tasting the sweetness of God, but it is something to note.

On the negative side, perhaps you have experienced an un-settling situation that "left a bad taste in your mouth." That, too, is a point of discernment, even if it seems obvious. Others have discerned heart issues in people through a bitter taste. For myself, I have identified the spirit of violence in people and in certain cities through a metallic, gunpowder-like taste in my mouth.

As an activation exercise, I once asked a group of people to partner with another person in the group and discern through their sense of taste something about their partner. One woman shared how she distinctly tasted wood oil in her mouth. She discovered how accurate that was once her partner revealed that he was a wood sculptor.

What do you smell?

Have you ever been in worship before the Lord, only to be overcome by the distinguishable scent of His fragrance? This experience is a common one for discerners and is a tangible expression of this gift.

Cari Perazzo, for example, who attends our church, had a powerful experience during a prayer service with our ministry leaders. "As we prayed together in the Spirit, all of a sudden this heavy scent fell down," she said. "It was musky, like a frankincense and myrrh blend, and it lingered in the air."

Others have discerned the Lord's presence as the scent of roses (i.e., the rose of Sharon in Song of Solomon 2:1). Still others discern His presence as a sweet fragrance, like the smell of fresh-baked cookies (see 2 Corinthians 2:14–15).

The demonic realm has often been distinguished supernaturally through the smell of death, sulfur, rotten eggs, rotting garbage and dirty laundry, just to name a few. These odors are clues to help us identify what spirit we are dealing with, so we can respond in prayer and bring deliverance to those being affected. Maria Carlson from Ohio, who formerly interned at our church, had such an experience. She and her family encountered an obnoxious smell in their home, and it seemed to jump from one family member to another. They believed it was physiological and genetic. Maria described the smell as "extreme halitosis mixed with bad body odor and burning plastic." She added that it was an odor that filled the house even with the windows open. Finally, Maria discerned that this was not a bodily malfunction, but a demonic spirit. After a lifetime of harassment, Maria and her family commanded the spirit to leave their home "in Jesus' name," and the smell left.

Other points of discernment that help identify how to minister to someone could be the smell of something familiar to you, such as your grandmother's perfume. Is there something you recall that was notable about your grandmother? Or was there something she specifically struggled with? If you are with someone and this happens to you, ask the person a few questions and you will most likely discover why you smelled that scent. In this case, you are discerning a heart issue that the Holy Spirit wants to highlight or heal in that person through an odor already familiar to you.

What do you feel?

This area of the gift of discerning of spirits is actually twofold in its function. You can discern the spirit of something through physical touch and external sensations, or you can discern spiritual information through your emotions.

There was a new family attending our church, and the father came forward for prayer and ministry. I greeted him by first shaking his hand before asking him what he needed prayer for. When my hand made contact with his, I discerned something that I have never discerned before or since. I distinctly felt the presence of money in his hand, except there was not any. To test my experience, I took my hand away and then grabbed his hand once more. There it was again! Here I blurted out, "Ooh! I can feel money in your hand!"

Thankfully, this man was a strong intercessor and fluent enough in the gifts of the Spirit to receive my random behavior. He was also a businessman. The following week he had a business deal go through, something he had been waiting on for months. Only what took place for him in the natural realm had already taken place in the spiritual realm. That is how I could discern the presence of money in his hand before he physically had it.

Pasqual Urrabazo, a pastor at the International Church of Las Vegas, described an encounter he had while ministering at a conference in Texas. He grabbed hands with a man in order to pray for him, and when he did, they both discerned something powerful from the Holy Spirit. The man being ministered to made this comment to Pasqual: "You see with your hands, don't you?"

Pasqual replied, "You do, too! I can feel it!"

Both this man and Pasqual had the same ability to discern by what they felt in their hands. Pasqual often discerns physical and emotional pain just by laying his hands on someone. He can also feel through his hands if there is the presence of demonic spirits or not, and he has delivered many people from demons as a result.

Scripture shows that both good and evil can be discerned by touch. Peter saw, heard and felt the presence of an angel. An angel appeared in his prison cell, striking him on the side to wake him and saying, "Quick, get up!" (Acts 12:7). Eliphaz the Temanite encountered a spirit that made the hair on his body stand up (see Job 4:15). A young boy possessed with a deaf and mute spirit manifested physically at the sight of Jesus (see Mark 9:19–26).

Shaking, tingling, heat, cold, pressure and the like could all be connected to something spiritual. I have felt the playful poking of angels before, and I have felt the brush of their wings. I have also felt the headache and nausea that come when someone is operating in a spirit of religion or has a hidden vice. You can discern spiritually through touch and physical sensation. Pay attention to what you feel, take note of patterns, and ask the Holy Spirit for clarity.

You can also discern the spiritual realm through your emotions. Jesus was touched with our infirmities, and we, too, will be touched with what others are feeling as an extension of His ministry on the earth (see Hebrews 4:15). This method of discernment requires patience, emotional stamina and some getting used to, because it is not the "feel good" part of the gift. It also requires much practice to sort out which emotion is yours and which is someone else's.

Elaina Ayala, my personal assistant and also one of our campus pastors, learned she had the gift of discerning spirits when she began to struggle on her ministry outings. She was a new Christian and was part of an internship program. On ministry days, the team would begin with powerful worship and testimonies in one city to prepare themselves. As they traveled to their target city, however, Elaina would shut down with anxiety, nervousness and foreboding thoughts. Her pastor began to notice her repeated pattern, since she only did this when they ministered in one particular city. He clarified to her that she was reacting to the spiritual atmosphere of the city inside her own emotions. He then taught her to stand in her identity in Christ, and to pray, minister and prophesy in the opposite direction of what she was discerning.

Do your emotions and thoughts seesaw depending on where you travel and what crowd you associate with? Pay attention to your emotions, thoughts and the short movies that play inside your imagination. You might be discerning much more than you think.

Anointed to Discern

What God appoints you to do, He will also anoint you to do. To be anointed means to be given supernatural ability from the Holy Spirit. This is what happened to Jesus when the Holy Spirit fell upon Him like a dove after John the Baptist baptized Him in water. Here, Jesus was anointed for ministry. "God anointed Jesus of Nazareth with the Holy Spirit and with power, who went about doing good and healing all who were oppressed by the devil" (Acts 10:38). This same anointing is available to you. Jesus said we would do greater works than even He did, and that we, too, would be given power by the Holy Spirit to do just that (see John 14:12; Luke 24:49). God will anoint you to establish His Kingdom in the places where you have influence and to heal those who are demonically oppressed. He will anoint you with the gift of discerning of spirits so you can see and discern spiritual conditions in order to be more effective.

Mavis, a Christian and former emergency room nurse, noticed a pattern in our city in regard to patients coming in for emergency care. She noticed that on any given day, there would be one highlighted kind of injury or emergency. For example, there would be a run on head injuries one day and then a run on broken fingers the next. She discerned this as being the "demonic assignment of the day" and would take this to prayer the moment she identified it. Her prayers targeted the unseen demonic powers trying to steal, kill or destroy the city residents. Recognizing her powerful assignment, she also took much opportunity to share her faith in the emergency room, even calling in reinforcements at times from our church to help her minister to certain patients and their families.

My friend Edwin Smith shared with me how he had experienced a flood of overwhelming concern for a young woman in the youth group of his church. "I discerned the spirit of suicide," he told me, "even feeling her anguish and that it was something planned out."

Edwin went to the youth pastor, pleading and crying for him to contact this young woman. Thankfully, the youth pastor acted on Edwin's discernment. He met with her and her mother, with the young woman tearfully admitting her plan to kill herself—a plan that was intercepted. The gift of discerning of spirits saved her life.

At my last secular job before being hired at my church, the gift of discerning of spirits operated many times to bring divine intervention to problems in my workplace. Once, I was in my personal prayer time at home when I felt a distinct jab in my right eye. It was an unusually sharp and painful jab, and through this I knew I was discerning something spiritual. I asked the Holy Spirit for clarity, and that night I had a dream. The dream showed me two people at my job who were planning to stir up trouble and involve me in it somehow. I also saw in the dream that their plans would just blow over and that there was nothing to worry about.

That week, my direct supervisor became very agitated and was communicating excessive rules to the staff about things that you would say and implement to protect yourself from false allegations. When I saw this happening, I explained to him that I had already discerned the matter, prayed about it and then had a dream. I even told him who was behind the false allegations, which confirmed for him that I really did hear from God. (My boss was already aware of the people involved, of course, but he could not identify them to us. What I revealed was just confirmation of my discernment.) I then assured him that it would all blow over. Later, I had the privilege of leading one of those persons to Christ.

Receiving the Gift

Is your heart being stirred for this gift? Do you want to become anointed with the gift of discerning of spirits? Or if you already have this gift, do you want it to grow stronger in your life? Here are a few things to help:

1. Desire the gift

God partners with our desires. If you are one who desires the gift of discerning of spirits or a stronger form of it, the Holy Spirit is eager to anoint you with it. If, perhaps, you are concerned that you are being prideful or grandiose in desiring this gift, you are not. We are strongly encouraged to desire spiritual gifts, and God promises to give us the desires of our heart (see Psalm 37:4; 1 Corinthians 14:1).

2. Ask for the gift

James teaches us that we don't have something because we have not yet asked God for it (see James 4:2). Ask God to anoint you with the gift of discerning of spirits. Ask for more of it! That is a prayer He most definitely will answer, because "I will do whatever you ask in my name, so that the Father may be glorified in the Son" (John 14:13).

3. Have someone with the gift lay hands on you to receive it

This is often called the prayer of "impartation" and implies the divine ability of someone to give, share or bestow what he or she has to another person, typically through the laying on of hands. For example, I could "impart" this gift to you by placing my hands on you and praying for you to receive the gift, and then by faith you would receive it for the first time (or receive even more of it). Through the laying on of hands, Joshua received an anointing from Moses, and the believers received the Holy Spirit through the apostles (see Numbers 27:18–23; Acts 8:18). The apostle Paul imparted spiritual gifts to Timothy in the same way and told him, "For this reason I remind you to fan into flame the gift of God, which is in you through the laying on of my hands" (2 Timothy 1:6).

4. Steward the gift

Stewardship involves studying the gift, using and practicing the gift, and being accountable for the things we discern. Reading this book, for example, is a form of stewardship, and you will see this gift activate and expand as a result. It is one thing to ask for the gift and receive it through the laying on of hands. It is an entirely different thing to apply it and develop in it. Peter teaches us to "use whatever gift you have received to serve others, as faithful stewards of God's grace in its various forms" (1 Peter 4:10). Through stewardship, we fan this gift into flame and become powerful servants to others.

The gift of discerning of spirits is amazingly multifaceted in its expression and function. We miss points of discernment most often because we don't recognize that we are discerning anything. We think it is just us, or we dismiss spiritual information because it does not make any sense. Once we connect the dots about how this gift can operate, however, we will find new opportunities for ministry. We also will discern spiritual atmospheres, both good and bad, which is the subject of the next chapter. Discerners act as watchmen and gatekeepers to such things, opening the spiritual gates to the right things and shutting them to the wrong things.

Kingdom Principles

1. Once you realize how much spiritual information you perceive through your senses (sight, hearing, smell, taste or

feeling), you begin to examine your senses more carefully for spiritual possibilities.

2. Discerning through sight involves our inner eyes, also known as the eyes of our heart, as well as our two physical eyes. We might see angels, visions of Jesus or signs in nature. We might distinguish the demonic as shadowy shapes, dark mists or actual demons.

3. When you discern the supernatural through hearing, you will hear either internally or outside yourself. Some hear the voice of the Lord or an angel; others hear the voice or thoughts of an enemy. Still others hear common sounds such as bells, doorbells, door knocks, etc., but the sounds are actually spiritual sounds and not natural ones.

4. You can discern good or bad through your sense of taste or sense of smell. The presence of the Lord is commonly discerned as a sweet fragrance or taste. The demonic might be discerned as the smell of death or something dirty, or it leaves a bad taste in your mouth.

5. Many discern the presence of the Lord through sensations on their skin or within their emotions. They feel goose bumps, electricity or overwhelming joy or peace. Others discern the demonic or a negative situation through a gut feeling, foreboding thoughts or through identifiable physical discomfort.

Thoughts for Reflection

1. Have you knowingly discerned the presence of the Lord before? How did you know it was the Lord?

2. Could your random thought patterns, thoughts that come into your mind seemingly from nowhere, be a point of

discernment? How would you know, then, what thoughts are yours and what thoughts are not?

3. When you discern the demonic realm, does it leave you fearful or with a sense of defeat? What is the Holy Spirit saying about that situation, and how, then, should you pray?

4. Through which one of your senses (sight, hearing, smell, taste or feeling) do you sense the supernatural the most and with the most accuracy?

5. How has the gift of discerning of spirits released ministry through you? Were you able to help someone else because of what you discerned?

4

Discerning Spiritual Atmospheres

It was payday, and I rushed to the bank during my work break to deposit my check. I did not tell anyone where I was going, knowing my personal errand would only take ten to fifteen minutes. Once inside the bank, I found myself nervously looking around the interior. I thought to myself, *I hope the bank doesn't get robbed while I'm here. I would be late getting back to the office!* That was a strange, irrational thought that came out of nowhere, and I dismissed it as soon as I had it. Over the next month or so, I went to the bank three more times. Each time, I had the same bizarre thought that I needed to get out of the bank as soon as possible in case it got robbed. I still did not catch on that I was discerning something in the bank's atmosphere, until I read about it in the newspaper. The bank actually was robbed! I was still learning, through this experience and many others, that when you discern something through your emotions, you can miss what you discern because it seems as though it is your feelings and is not rational enough for you to validate.

My friend Mary had a similar experience, but with a better outcome. One day she noticed what she described as an "odd, unsettled feeling" descending on her like a dark cloud. She knew by the Holy Spirit that she was discerning something in the atmosphere of her neighbor's home, but she could not put her finger on it. As the day wore on, Mary became more and more preoccupied with her neighbor's house, getting up several times to look at it through her window.

"I had no idea what I was watching for," Mary explained. "I began to intercede for my neighbors, while still looking through my window to try to identify what was bothering me."

Finally, Mary saw with her physical eyes what her spiritual eyes were discerning. That evening, she saw a man walking along the street. He made a sudden turn into her neighbor's yard and onto their porch. Within seconds a light went on in their living room, then in a bedroom, and then in the back room of the house. Mary's husband called 9-1-1, and the man was arrested for breaking and entering as he walked out the front door of the house. It turned out this was the same man who had robbed Mary's home a month prior.

Have you ever noticed an intrusive feeling or thought such as what Mary and I experienced? Did you doubt it was real, or did you dismiss it as being too irrational? When you operate in the gift of discerning of spirits, you will discern spiritual atmospheres through your senses, often through the vehicle of your thoughts and emotions. It is something you have to catch on to, because it is not logical or rational at all. These thoughts and feelings just show up, rather disconnected and unattached to any reality. Once you catch on to it, however, you can ask the Holy Spirit for more clarity.

An atmosphere can be defined as "a surrounding or pervading mood, environment, or influence."[1] A spiritual atmosphere is created by the outflow of the human spirit(s) and by the presence of spiritual beings, whether divine or demonic. Atmospheres have distinct and identifiable feelings attached to them. Those can be feelings like joy, generosity, hospitality and worship, or they can be depression, anger, greed and fear. You can sense and discern the atmospheres of homes, churches and cities, for example, and much more. Spiritual atmospheres affect your thoughts, feelings and actions, and negative atmospheres are something you have to guard yourself from yielding to.

Whenever I travel to minister, I distinctly discern each city's spiritual atmosphere in my thoughts and emotions, and even in my dreams. In one city I might discern an atmosphere of witchcraft, but then discern violence and murder in another. In still another city it will be homosexuality, and in another it will be a spirit of unbelief in God. In one city in particular, I discerned its spiritual diseases in a dream as if they were my own—gambling, pornography and addiction—and I woke up grateful it was just a dream and not really part of me! That can be unnerving if you don't understand why you would have a dream quite like that.

Overseas travel often involves a much stronger sensory experience for someone with discernment. In China, for example, I will encounter unusually perverse thoughts, but then in Central Asia I will discern deep anger and rage. Those who travel with me have similar experiences because we are discerning the same atmospheres. We have also encountered places that host the glory of God and His angels, and such atmospheres are always refreshing!

Discerning different atmospheres happens in different ways and varies from person to person. For myself, I often discern the spiritual atmosphere of a city by what I spiritually see and feel on the land. Where there is a strong local church, cities will host the peace of Jesus in such a way that you can feel it coming off the ground and in the air. I have even sensed that same feeling of peace while driving through certain cities, which tells me even before I have any tangible evidence for it that the Church of that city is strong. I have also heard testimonies from incoming travelers to my city, Turlock, who say they feel the tangible presence of God when they enter the city borders.

Cities that lack a strong local church will come under the influence of a demonic atmosphere, and this will show up in the personality of the city. This is why some cities become labeled with derogatory nicknames such as "sin city," "drug capital of the West," "religious city" or "party town." These labels are actually the personality of the demonic spirit ruling the atmosphere, "the prince of the power of the air, the spirit who now works in the sons of disobedience" (Ephesians 2:2 NKJV).

I once ministered in a city that was so bound to witchcraft that I could see with my spiritual eyes endless numbers of snakes coming out of holes in the ground. I spoke at a conference there, but I struggled emotionally and mentally throughout because of this issue. I know how to overturn that kind of spiritual problem in prayer and through other biblical methods, but this was such that it would require going back to that city several times to uproot it successfully. Likewise, I was ministering in a small city in the Midwest and noticed how many of the church people's children were in bondage to or were in jail for drugs, alcohol-related crimes, theft, etc. It is not normal for so many "church" children to be in jail, be unsaved and be in that much trouble. The Bible promises us a much better outcome (see Psalm 115:14; Acts 16:31). Yet this was their normal because this was the spiritual atmosphere of the city, and the Church there had not yet defeated it.

Spiritual atmospheres are real, and we discern through our senses what God and His forces are doing, as well as what Satan and his forces are doing. This is always a call to prayer. In her book *Unlocking the Gift of Discernment*, Australia's Helen Calder, founder of Enliven Ministries, put it this way:

> If we stayed in a place in Asia where strange spirits were wor-shipped, I encountered them in my dreams. If we ministered

in a region or church where spiritual warfare was occurring, I felt the battle acutely.

We were often led to wage spiritual warfare or intercede through my sensitivity to the spiritual realm.[2]

The Role of Discerners

Discerners are spiritual watchmen and gatekeepers. The Bible talks about the role of watchmen and gatekeepers in a very practical sense. In ancient times, watchmen were guards who would watch from high towers and walls over their grain fields and cities. One of the Hebrew words used for watchmen is the word *shamar*, which means to watch, protect, keep and guard.[3] Watchmen would watch for any sign of danger from potential trespassers or enemy armies who would want to invade, rob, spoil and destroy the fields or the city. Gatekeepers were attendants at the city gates or other designated gates who would control access to the city and other important places. Watchmen, then, would work with the gatekeepers to keep the gates shut and guarded at any sign of danger.

Those with the gift of discerning of spirits are both spiritual watchmen and gatekeepers for their church and city and beyond, as the Lord directs. They *"shamar"* the land and genuinely discern spiritual enemies, what they are presently doing or what they are about to do. Several years ago, our head usher had become agitated at a male visitor who had dropped off a young boy at our children's service. He began questioning the visitor and asking him the nature of his relationship with the young boy. Everything seemed to check out, but our usher could not get over it. He became so agitated that he asked the man to leave the church campus, which is something we never do without a tangible reason. I was really taken back by our usher's behavior and debated this within myself. Not long afterward, however, Megan's Law was passed, allowing the public to look up sex offenders by city on the Internet. Would you believe that the man who brought the boy was on the list? Now I understood the "*shamar*" reaction that our usher had, although it did not make sense at the time.

Several years after this incident, I had a dream of a very good-looking man asking me—more like begging me—for permission to come through my city. Remember that the gift of discerning of spirits also works inside our dreams. Through this gift, I knew that this charming, good-looking man was actually some kind of serial killer. He kept asking me for access through the city, and I kept saying no. He finally gave up asking, and the dream ended. A few days later, I read in our local newspaper that members of a terrorist sleeper cell had been caught and arrested in a nearby city. I also had the distinct impression that, by the grace of God, my dream and what happened with this terrorist cell may have been connected. In the dream, I refused to open the spiritual gates of our city to a serial killer looking for access. What was handled in the spiritual realm was immediately revealed in the natural realm. Through my gatekeeping and likely the similar efforts of some other such gatekeepers throughout the city, a religious enemy, an actual "serial killer," was not only locked out, but was also shut down.

Not only do discerners shut the spiritual gates to the wrong things; they also open the gates to the right things. Cindy Jacobs, founder of Generals International, and her companions were attempting to pass out Russian tracts in Moscow's Red Square. "To my amazement no one would take them," she wrote in her book *Possessing the Gates of the Enemy*. "In fact, they ignored me, staring straight ahead as though they had not heard or seen me." [4]

Cindy discerned that they had entered the territory of a spirit controlling Red Square, and that it was blinding the eyes of people to the Gospel (see 2 Corinthians 4:3–4). Cindy and her team used their spiritual authority to bind Satan in the name of Jesus and command spiritual blindness to fall off the people in Red Square. Then they prayed for God to open a door for them to share the Gospel. They saw results immediately! People readily received their tracts, even asking for more.

As spiritual watchmen and gatekeepers, discerners often become great intercessors. An intercessor is one who advocates in favor for another, and discerners passionately advocate for people and for their cities in prayer. What drives them so fervently into prayer is often the pain and discomfort they experience as they discern the spiritual realm through their senses.

Henry (not his real name) was working in an assisted living facility that had a separate locked unit for patients with Alzheimer's and dementia. Every time he worked that floor, he experienced tormenting fear in the atmosphere and was petrified even to be there. He also noticed a distinct change in a certain patient who had been transferred to that unit. The patient became deliriously afraid and tormented, and then quickly died. Then another patient kept saying over and over, "There's a spook in here!"

Henry finally clued in that he was discerning a spirit of fear in the Alzheimer's/dementia unit (see 2 Timothy 1:7 NKJV). He began to pray and command the spirit to leave. Thankfully, there was a quick turnaround. That oppressive fear no longer afflicted him as he worked the floor, and the patient who saw the spook, which was probably a demon, stopped seeing it. Again, this is the "not so great" aspect of this gift, but those who discern in this manner will pray diligently to get relief both for themselves and others.

Managing Overwhelming Discernment

It is one thing to be sensitive to spiritual atmospheres and quite another thing to be overwhelmed by what you discern. What I mean by that is that some people have been anointed so strongly with this gift that what they discern can become too painful to carry or too overwhelming to allow them to function. And when they don't know they have this gift, all too often they end up on medication and in psychiatric facilities, falsely believing they are going crazy. I have recovered many such persons to their place in the Body of Christ, helping them learn how to manage their discernment. They are shocked when they discover how strongly they are gifted, soon realizing that they pay a higher price for what they have been privileged to discern about the spiritual realm.

There was a widely spread news report about a South African sign language interpreter who was assigned to former President Barack Obama at South African President Nelson Mandela's memorial. As he signed Obama's speech, Thamsanqa Jantjie, 34, claims that he "lost concentration, and started hearing voices and hallucinating," according to Johannesburg's *The Star*.[5] Upon investigation, it was discovered that Thamsanqa reportedly suffered from schizophrenia and would see visions of angels. He also had some history of turning violent.[6]

Thamsanqa became widely criticized in the media, being labeled as a "fake" interpreter. I cannot argue for or against this man's credentials, as I have no knowledge of the situation beyond the media reports. I did watch his videos, however, both on and off stage. Since I have walked this kind of thing out personally and with others and I know what it looks like, I would like to suggest an alternative. Is it conceivable that Thamsanqa was not crazy, but had a gift from God? Could he possibly have had the gift of discerning of spirits instead?

People like Thamsanqa are often connected to the spiritual realm, but they don't know why. This is intended to be a blessing from God, but it becomes a point of defeat until you learn how to control it. Instead of discerning through your senses, it feels more as if you are being ransacked in your senses. You see apparitions, you hear voices, and it is overwhelming on your emotions. Nothing is yet filtered through the Scriptures, and you are therefore not exercising wisdom and self-control about it. This unfortunately brings disruption to your world, until you know what you have is a gift and you learn what to do with it. To make matters worse, the way this gift often manifests can be mistaken for symptoms of schizophrenia and bipolar disorders.

Jami Redman from Bozeman, Montana, believes she has had the gift of discerning of spirits her entire life, but did not know it or understand it. She said that when she gave her life to Jesus, her sensitivity to the spiritual realm then escalated beyond what was manageable. She thought she was cursed, crazy and schizophrenic. She was volatile with explosive rage because of the "voices." Totally desperate, Jami attended a conference where I was teaching about this gift. Hope filled her world again as she realized she was not crazy, but needed to learn how to manage and control her strong discernment in the context of a healthy church community. Jami still sees and senses things very strongly, but steadies herself through promises in the written Word and in prayer. She has also learned to look for ministry opportunity when she has had a rough day filled with overwhelming discernment. She knows that someone nearby is suffering with what she just walked through, or that she has experienced an atmosphere that needs her prayerful intervention.

Like Jami, Michael (not his real name) could see and sense the spiritual realm for as long as he could remember. His traditional parents, however, believed that what was happening to him was demonic and did their best to shut it down. Left without help, Michael was unable to process all the spiritual information he was absorbing. This left him severely depressed and overwhelmed as a teenager and young adult.

"I turned to psychiatric medication and alcohol to try to get relief, but couldn't get a grip on myself most days," he explained.

Michael climbed out of his severe depression when he broke rank to attend a charismatic church that believed in all of the gifts of the Spirit. Finally, he found acceptance for his unusual spiritual package and a healthy place to process the myriad of things he was discerning. Michael often discerns what is going on with people without having been told, and then he ministers healing and deliverance out of that supernatural knowledge. He also discerns spiritual atmospheres in his church, his city and his travels.

"It's still overwhelming, but now I have context," he shared. "I can usually pray through it and get to the other side, or I can get help when I need it."

I shared with you in the first chapter about how I have had supernatural experiences my entire life. These experiences would have been misdiagnosed as a mental disorder if I had ever talked about them. And the symptoms only escalated after my deliverance from demonic oppression, instead of diminishing. Having an extensive family history of schizophrenia, I naturally wondered if I were losing my mind. My late great-aunt, for example, spent the last years of her life in a mental institution with this diagnosis. Her religious denomination had made no room for the supernatural. If her schizophrenia was truly a medical condition, her church was not looking for supernatural healing for her (see Mark 16:17–18). If it was a misdiagnosed gift from God, her church could not redirect her. She was imprisoned for the rest of her life because she had been denied the freedom in her church to learn about the Holy Spirit and operate freely in His gifts. How sad and how true for so many people.

The Holy Spirit graciously taught me through the Scriptures and through His voice that I was not crazy, but had a gift from Him. He then began to teach me how to walk out this powerful gift in a way that was a blessing to me and to others. It has been a long road of discovery, with plenty of mistakes and victories along the way. I also learned that the things we discern are not the end of the story. We discern so we can respond. When we discern the presence of the Lord, we can worship. When we discern a demonic atmosphere, we can change it. We are supposed to change it.

Changing Spiritual Atmospheres

Jesus stood in a boat off the shore of Galilee and taught the multitudes until evening. He then told His disciples, "Let us cross over to the other side," and they got in their boat and left (Mark 4:35 NKJV). You probably know the story, but a terrific storm emerged along the way, making it appear as if the boat would capsize. The disciples panicked, while Jesus slept peacefully in the boat's stern. When they finally woke Him up, Jesus "rebuked the wind, and said to the sea, 'Peace, be still!' And the wind ceased and there was a great calm" (verse 39 NKJV).

Here we see the disciples becoming overwhelmed by an atmosphere. This atmosphere was a storm, but it was not just any storm. When Jesus told them, "Let us cross over to the other side," it was because they were on divine assignment. On the other side of the sea was a man possessed with a legion (thousands) of demons, a man Jesus would fully deliver. I believe these spirits sensed Jesus coming toward them and sent a killer storm to try to stop His arrival. Jesus shifted the atmosphere, however, by speaking to it. His disciples were in chaos, but He declared His peace to the storm. We can do the same.

When you encounter a demonic atmosphere, you, too, need to speak to it. You speak to the atmosphere out loud and with authority, going in the opposite spirit of what you have discerned. We read in Scripture, "Death and life are in the power of the tongue" (Proverbs 18:21 NKJV). We are also exhorted that if something is standing in our way, we can speak to it and it has to move (see Mark 11:23). God uses His words to give life to the dead and call things into being that are not (see Romans 4:17). Being created in His image, you and I will also use our words to change what needs to be changed.

David Jenkins, from Texas, served as an on-site intercessor at a men's retreat in Colorado. His job was to pray over the facilities prior to the arrival of the retreat guests, since many groups had used the location for different purposes. As he entered the various buildings and rooms, he would typically experience a wave of feelings, usually negative.

"It was fairly simple to remedy once I discerned it," David said. When he discerned hopelessness by feeling it within himself, for example, he spoke to hopelessness out loud. "Hopelessness, go away!" he commanded. "I release hope and faith instead."

He did this with many more issues as he discerned them. David was amazed at how his thoughts and feelings instantly changed from room to room, corner to corner, and even bed to bed. As he spoke to these issues, he could feel darkness shifting and being replaced by light.

Another way to purge an atmosphere is through praise and worship. Bible teacher and evangelist Perry Stone shared about the spiritual struggles he experienced while traveling around the country in his early days of ministry. He wrote in an article for *Charisma* magazine that he and his wife would have bizarre and disturbing experiences in hotel rooms, accompanied by strange and demonic dreams. He learned, however, that he could change the atmosphere of his hotel room if he would play praise and worship music in the room continuously.

"In Scripture, David's music brought refreshing and peace to a tormented king (1 Samuel 16:23)," Perry wrote. "If music had this effect in David's life and ministry, why would it not have the same effect today?"[7]

It sure did! This changed the atmosphere of his hotel room every time and made his stay much more peaceful.

Dr. Violet Kiteley, the late pastor of Shiloh Christian Fellowship in Oakland, California, discovered the impact of praise and worship on her troubled city when the police called on her, as well as on her church, to "do something" about Pleitner Avenue. At the time, Pleitner Avenue was notorious for gangs, drugs and prostitution; it was one of the most dangerous areas of the city. Dr. Kiteley and her congregation understood that this was first a spiritual problem and needed a spiritual solution. In Psalm 149, we read that the high praises of God work to bind kings and enemies. With that in mind, Shiloh Church held a block party on Pleitner Avenue for three weeks in a row. This block party included a barbecue and giveaways, praise and worship according to Psalm 149, and an evangelistic message. The results were so incredible that the police notified the media of the good news—70 percent of the drug pushers moved out of Pleitner following Shiloh's praise party that shifted the atmosphere.[8]

Spiritual atmospheres can and do shift instantly, such as in the case of David at the retreat site. Or a shift can occur in a matter of weeks, such as in the case of Dr. Kiteley. And then some shifts require much more. God called Ron and me to repurpose a difficult church environment in a historically "religious" city. Not only were we battling a demonic spiritual atmosphere; we were also dealing with strongholds of thinking and an inflexible culture. As a strong discerner, I suffered week after week in the atmosphere of my church. It was a cold, strife-filled atmosphere with a heavy, oppressive feeling. If you were to look at the congregants on Sunday, they, too, looked sad, bored or angry underneath their plastic smiles. Prayer continued to be my lifeline, because in prayer I could breathe in the heavenly atmosphere, which is peace, joy, love, etc., and in prayer I could get my feelings straightened out. That is, until the next church service, where the battle inside would start all over again. Shifting this atmosphere would need much more than a few one-time commands or a few weeks of praise and worship. We were engaging in a top-to-bottom spiritual overhaul, which largely began with discerning who was for us and who was against us. That will be our topic in the next chapter.

Kingdom Principles

1. When you operate in the gift of discerning of spirits, you will discern spiritual atmospheres through your senses, often through the vehicle of your thoughts and emotions. We often dismiss what we discern, though, because it is not rational enough.

2. Spiritual atmospheres are real, and we discern through our senses what God and His forces are doing, as well as what Satan and his forces are doing. It is always a call to prayer.

3. Discerners are spiritual watchmen and gatekeepers who shut the spiritual gates to the wrong things and open them to the right things.

4. The things we discern are not the end of the story. We discern so we can respond.

5. We can change most spiritual atmospheres through our words and with praise and worship.

Thoughts for Reflection

1. Have you ever noticed an intrusive feeling or thought that seemed out of place, only to discover you were discerning something real in the atmosphere?

2. Do you experience distinct shifts in your thoughts, emotions and dreams, depending on your location?

3. How have you acted as a spiritual watchman, opening or closing spiritual gates, depending on what you were discerning in the atmosphere?

4. Have you ever struggled with overwhelming discernment? If so, how are you learning to manage that?

5. Are you noticeably aware of how your words and your praise and worship change atmospheres?

5

Discerning Who Is for You and Who Is against You

I knew it would happen eventually, but we had been together only a few years when our pastor flew the coop.

"I've had enough!" he said. "I'm going to minister at another, much healthier church."

And that is exactly what happened. He returned to the church he had planted in another city, but this time as an associate minister. His sudden departure left Ron and me with that weird "dangling" feeling and the insecurity of not knowing what to expect next.

To my shock, the church board quickly turned to my young husband, asking him to become the interim senior pastor. It did not take long, however, for the board to fall into disunity over my husband's future with this church. As arguments began to stir, my husband sensed the tangible presence of the Lord enter those tense meetings. Again, this is the gift of discerning of spirits in operation. Ron described how the "felt peace" of God filled the room more than once, and those at odds with each other then would supernaturally come into agreement. The plan was for Ron to serve as interim pastor for a year, but within a few months the board invited him to take a more permanent role. Ron, at age 27, became the youngest senior pastor in the church's 80-year history.

God's word to us about leading this church had finally come to pass, but now we had a new word: "For a great and effective door has opened to me, and there are many adversaries" (1 Corinthians 16:9 NKJV). It would be years before we understood how this little church in a small town could ever become a great and effective door of ministry. It did not take long, however, to realize that our adversaries were many and they often came in disguise. What I mean is, our adversaries did not look like adversaries. They looked like ordinary people who could quote the Bible, pray and worship in church on Sundays. If we were going to thrive in this assignment, then, we had to see behind the masks. We had to know who was for us and who was against us.

The gift of discerning of spirits will reveal people's heart motives, whether they are sincere and genuine or evil and deceitful. To be honest, I have found that most people are somewhere in the middle. They are not all sincere, but neither are they all deceitful, and we can still have a relationship with them and they with us, knowing that we all are a work in progress. At the same time, there are those who are really, really deceitful and have evil agendas. They don't want you to succeed, or they want to take something from you. Some even want to destroy you. The gift of discerning of spirits is God's security system to let you know who is really who.

At first, this gift worked to reveal and expose malicious gossip that was rampant inside our leadership and fellowship. Some of that, of course, was exposed naturally as people came forward about it. Other times, Ron would rub his head as if he were feeling a headache and say by the Spirit of the Lord, "Mr. and Mrs. So-and-So are stirring people up over the change we made last week. I can feel it right here!"

Ron would discern rebellion and manipulative speech through a particular feeling of pressure against his mind. He even knew in his spirit who was involved and what it was about. This was his alert from the Holy Spirit to pray for the rebellious gossip to surface so he could confront it.

"I was confronting men and women who were two and three times my age on the sin of gossiping," Ron said of that time. "I had to call some of them into my office almost weekly until they stopped or left the church."

Backbiting is what had fueled devastating strife in the past, and it was strife that was being uprooted from the church in this season. The gift of discerning of spirits revealed it so we could deal with it. More than once, the gift of discerning of spirits revealed men and women sent on demonic assignment to harm my husband or me.

I need to point out here that there is a difference between a person sent against you by Satan and a person who is very broken and acts out of his or her brokenness. It can look the same on the surface, but the gift of discerning of spirits will reveal the truth. Discerning an actual demonic assignment against you can be alarming within your emotions, and you need wisdom and patience, not reactiveness, to handle it properly.

There was a middle-aged woman who began attending the church soon after my husband became senior pastor. She was eager, energetic, and had expressed her desire to be more involved in the ministry. I did notice some strange behavior on her part, however. She appeared to create situations on purpose that would set people up to be disappointed with me. She struck me as possibly having a divisive spirit, but then, like an alarm going off, I discerned her real motive. I said to Ron, "She's here on demonic assignment to destroy me! Please do something—anything!"

It sounded crazy, but I wanted her out of the church right then and there, and I did not care how that happened. You see, when you discern something that sinister, it causes panic and an inappropriate reaction inside you, until you become more experienced. If you are not careful, you might initiate a strong defensive action against someone without any tangible evidence for doing so. That is almost always the wrong thing to do. My husband, being the voice of reason, convinced me just to stay calm and wait it out. Not too long afterward, she popped up on a leadership team in one of the church's long-standing ministries. This ministry had neglected to check in with Ron or me before they appointed her, and it turned into their big mess. I also knew by the Holy Spirit that she wanted to lead this particular ministry so she could gain more power through that position. She became so bitterly divisive within that team that she was invited to leave the church.

The gift of discerning of spirits also sifts out the highly deceptive who see the church as a means for personal gain. A board member and his wife introduced one family to us who began attending our church. They acted very charismatic and quite "churchy." I never felt quite right about the guy, and one day in the hallway I just asked him flat out, "How do you make your money?"

I asked him that because I noticed his peculiar behavior when we received offerings during the church services. He would flamboyantly pull out of his jacket a large, folded stack of cash and then drop several large bills in the offering bucket in an almost choreographed fashion. When he shared with me how he earned his income, it sounded like garble and nonsense words. He did not make any sense! I knew I was discerning a lying spirit with a wicked financial motive. Soon enough, he began his "presentations" to others and to me about a hot investment, an investment that, thankfully, no one gave him money for.

I felt as if we were in a living Whac-A-Mole game. This is a game in which plastic moles mechanically pop up through a game board, and then you hit the moles down with a hammer.

The game itself is pretty satisfying because you can usually hit down all the moles. In the church, however, we would take care of one spiritually motivated problem, only to have two more pop up. That is because we really were not fighting with flesh and blood, as the apostle Paul described the battle, but "against the rulers, against the authorities, against the powers of this dark world and against the spiritual forces of evil in the heavenly realms" (Ephesians 6:12). At the same time, we faced unusual spiritual warfare, the kind you would hear about in foreign countries but not expect in your own conservative city. In response, we became very diligent and militant in prayer, and God answered us again and again.

The Tension of Two Extremes

During a conference in another town, I requested a private meeting with one of the speakers. The speaker was connected to a strong and impactful movement, so I trusted this person's perspective more than my own. I simply wanted counsel on how best to handle the high level of spiritual warfare we were dealing with in our church and city.

The counsel I received was that people such as those in my church and me, people who "see too many demons," are most likely out of balance. I was told that if we wanted to be spiritually effective, then we needed to look for God—Him only—and not be looking for demons. That thinking also needed to carry over into how we saw and ministered to people. We needed to "look for the good or positive" in people and not fixate on the negative.

I interpreted this counsel to mean that we should not actively look for demons in people. This sounded like solid advice and struck me as a much better option than what we were presently doing. It is true that we had become pretty negative and did see a lot of demons both spiritually and in people, and I was desperate to find a more comfortable balance.

The speaker also introduced a new model of prayer at the conference and called it "soaking prayer," which is quite different from intercessory prayer. Soaking prayer is an act of entering into the presence of God solely to experience His love and His voice. Intercessory prayer, on the other hand, is passionately advocating, keeping watch and enforcing God's promises on behalf of another. I noticed that many people around the conference room engaged in soaking prayer by casually lying down on the chairs or on the floor, as if asleep. It looked like a very peaceful experience.

I reasoned, then, that these concepts were exactly what we needed and began to teach them to my church and to our intercessors. I communicated how I felt that we had become spiritually out of balance and needed to look for what God was doing instead of what demons were doing, both in prayer and when we ministered to people. I then reconstructed our prayer services to look more like soaking prayer instead of intercessory prayer—again, just trying to balance everything out.

Seeing Only What We Wanted to See

It did not take long to realize what a mistake I had made. In trying to look for what God was doing, and Him only, we stopped discerning the hearts of people and the very real plans of the enemy. Rather than flowing in the gift of discerning of spirits, we began controlling the gift to see only what we wanted to see, instead of what we needed to see. And because we were mostly "soaking" in prayer instead of interceding in prayer, our spiritual hedges went down. A hedge is defined as something that provides a defense or protection. Job had such a spiritual hedge, lost it and then got it back (see Job 1:10). When he had this hedge, Satan could not touch him. When he lost the hedge,

Satan did all but kill him. We had lost our hedge because we were no longer seeing and interceding. I saw more evil come into our church during this time frame, in the form of people and spiritual attacks, than in any other time frame. It was a hard but valuable lesson.

Through this I learned that the truth is often found in the tension of two extremes. What is right for one church is not always right for our church. Remember, the apostle John in the book of Revelation gave seven different sets of instruction to the seven different churches. If these churches did not receive the same instructions, neither will we.

I am not saying that "soaking prayer" is a wrong kind of prayer or that we should stop seeing the positive in people. I am saying that our church was in a unique spiritual battle and needed the right strategy for what we were dealing with. We had stopped discerning our enemy, thinking this other strategy was the right thing to do. In so doing, we inadvertently had laid down our swords.

With that said, we reopened our eyes and hearts to see what the Holy Spirit wanted us to see, without filtering anything out. We had been trying to set the balance for our church, when God is the One who sets the balance. With swords back in hand, we were mindful again to keep watch over the gates by discerning who was for us and who was against us.

Discerning the Motives of the Heart

If you are new to the gift of discerning of spirits, here are some points to help you begin to identify who is for you and who is against you. Remember, this is a supernatural ability that goes beyond natural perception. You are not just reading people or their behavior. You are discerning by the Holy Spirit what the natural eye cannot see.

85

1. Pay attention to your "knower"

"I just know that I know," said Charlene, my external ministry administrator from Ceres, California. "It's never been that hard for me to know someone's intentions."

That is because Charlene has learned to pay attention to her "knower," that internal barometer that tells her whom she can trust and whom she should avoid. Some people call this intuition, a gut feeling or instinct. It is really the Holy Spirit's gift of discerning of spirits. Char once had a "knowing" about an event she planned to send her teenage daughter to. At the last minute, she decided to keep her daughter home because she knew in her knower that something about the event was deceptive. She found out a few days later that the event was closed prematurely due to the inappropriate behavior of an adult chaperone, which led to his arrest.

Nathan, a program specialist for an adult day program, also pays strong attention to his knower. "It can be difficult at times to explain how I discern if someone is for me or against me," he said. "I just know inside. My spirit is either drawn to them or repelled by them."

Still, Nathan tests his feelings with physical observations and observes a person over time to substantiate his initial reactions. Once, he even identified a witch masquerading as a Christian in his church fellowship. He identified her as such in his knower, but waited for evidence before he said anything. The evidence came soon enough, and she was revealed as a notorious witch, one who habitually infiltrated churches to stir up trouble.

Jennie, a parishioner also from Ceres, California, shared about the first time she met her best friend. "I had never felt such a sweet and gentle spirit before," Jennie explained. "I thought how strange it was to feel this good about someone whom I had just met."

This was significant for Jennie, because she does not trust people that easily. She knew in her knower, however, that she had met a real friend, and they have had a relationship that she has since enjoyed for many years. "God had genuinely put someone in my life to be the friend that I really need," Jennie said.

2. Pay attention to your imagination

When Rose (not her real name) meets new people or is introduced to them, she takes note of the movies that begin to play inside her imagination. If she sees a good movie begin to play involving both her and the person she just met, then she has learned through repeated experiences that the person is someone she can trust. If she sees a negative movie, however, she takes note of it and stays guarded until she can prove out what she just saw in her imagination. Rose is aware, however, that if she is not in a good frame of mind, she does not discern as accurately. Those movies will still play, but she will impose her own vulnerability or distrust onto someone, which is false discernment, not true discernment.

When Alli, an esthetician and graphic designer for our church, meets new people, just like Rose she sees movies play in her imagination. She has learned over time to accept this as her "heads-up" from the Holy Spirit. "It's great when it's positive," she said. "But when it's negative, it's hard to accept."

Alli explained that a movie will start with a thought and then turn into a story in her mind. She clarified that these movies in her imagination are not accurate in their details, but are how her mind processes information that she has just discerned. She once met a woman who was married, and a random thought popped into her mind: *She's not being faithful.* And then the thought turned into a movie in her mind, and Alli watched a quick movie of this woman not being faithful. Alli did not say anything about it, but she also declined all the woman's social invitations.

"Over time it all came out," Alli remarked. "She was caught red-handed, cheating on her husband."

3. Pay attention to your peace

Jesus taught His disciples a supernatural way to discern the intentions of people, in one case the intentions of strangers who offered to house them as they traveled. He told them, "If the home is deserving, let your peace rest on it; if it is not, let your peace return to you" (Matthew 10:13). His disciples, then, would know who was for them or who was against them simply by paying attention to their peace.

Peace does not always reveal what the issue is, but it does reveal when there is one. It is like an internal red light or green light that lets us know if we should move forward with someone or move away from the person. Jesus gave us His peace, and His peace leads us and rules our hearts (see Isaiah 55:12; John 14:27; Colossians 3:15).

My first job after college was in the marketing department of a large company. The manager of that department convinced the company to outsource all the marketing to him so he could start a personal business. He invited me to join his new business, which made sense since I would no longer have a job after the contract went into effect. Only I did not have a peace about it. In my excitement for this new adventure, I ignored what I felt and then regretted every moment of it. My boss turned out to be a classic narcissist, and I could not escape fast enough.

I have learned since then to be led by God's peace, and it has never failed. My first trip to China was a test of my faith and being led by peace. The Holy Spirit could not have been more clear in what He said: *Go to China!* I just could not make the right connections inside that nation. And all my Chinese missionary contacts told me not to come because it was too dangerous. To make a long story short, the Holy Spirit miraculously connected me with a young man who seemed to have all the internal connections that I was looking for. Still, it was risky because I did not know this young man at all.

Once inside the nation, we decided to minister at an orphanage located outside Beijing. My team and I, mostly young females, got into an unmarked van and drove off to who knows where. As we drove, my mind began to panic, realizing we could be kidnapped, sold or worse, and no one would be able to trace our whereabouts. I still had tremendous peace, however. That peace told me we were safe and with people we could trust.

Have you ever noticeably discerned something happening in your knower, in your imagination or through your peace before? Were you able to distinguish who was for you or against you as a result? Again, the gift of discerning of spirits comes with a learning curve, and we learn through practice to discern good from evil. My prayer is that this short list of paying attention to your knower, paying attention to your imagination and paying attention to your peace will raise your spiritual awareness enough to bring the right people into your world and keep the wrong people out.

Discerning the Enemy Within

There are still those, however, who seem to avoid detection even by the most sensitive discerners. That is because they are empowered by a demonic spirit that is an expert at disguise. This demon is known as a "religious spirit," and it sits in our churches each and every Sunday going undetected—that is, until it rears its ugly head.

Jesus asked His disciples a question: "Who do you say I am?" Simon Peter answered, "You are the Messiah, the Son of the living God" (Matthew 16:15–16). Jesus blessed Simon powerfully for his words, even using his name, Peter, which is a

Greek word for "rock," to describe the unconquerable strength of His Church: "And I tell you that you are Peter, and on this rock I will build my church, and the gates of Hades [hell] will not overcome it" (verse 18).

Afterward, Jesus gave His disciples fair warning about what to expect in the near future. He told them that He would suffer greatly in Jerusalem at the hands of the Jewish religious leaders (the Pharisees and the Sadducees), would be killed by them and then would be raised to life again.

Peter, who was previously so full of heavenly revelation, took Jesus aside and rebuked Him: "Never, Lord!" he said. "This shall never happen to you!" (verse 22).

In response, Jesus gave Peter a shocking rebuke: "Get behind me, Satan! You are a stumbling block to me . . ." (verse 23).

Was Peter really Satan? No, but his words revealed to Jesus that he was acting from self-interest. When people speak and behave from a selfish agenda, they are never in the will of God. And if Peter was standing against the will of God, like Satan, he had made himself an enemy of God, even if it was just for that moment. The well-deserved rebuke from Jesus was intended to shock him back into alignment, which meant he must deny himself, pick up his cross and follow Christ (see verse 24).

Have you ever acted in self-interest, ahead of God's interests? I believe we all have. Community and healthy accountability with other Christians should generate those needed rebukes when we go offtrack like that. Where there is no rebuke or when a rebuke goes ignored, that creates conditions for people unwittingly to be used by Satan to fight against the things they are supposed to fight for. This is what happened in Jesus' day with the religious leaders, the very leaders who crucified Him. They fought against the One they were supposed to embrace, all because of jealousy and self-interest.

The Pharisees and Sadducees demonstrated a spirit, attitude and behavior that undergird what is commonly known as a religious spirit. I believe Peter was teetering along the same line, except that Jesus rebuked him back into a right spirit. What began to happen to Peter, then, is a warning to us all. A religious spirit does a lot of evil things in the name of God, even murder, but God has nothing to do with it. It is legalistic and power seeking, and it uses religion to suppress or even kill off anyone genuinely moving in the Holy Spirit. This was the supernatural power source behind the majority of opposition we had been experiencing within our church. It was a spirit now being discerned, confronted and uprooted in order to make room for the Spirit of God.

My husband had greeted a long-standing church member, at least fifty years in attendance, just before a church service. She always sat in the same seat, and she would come early, sit down, fold her arms and frown the entire service. She habitually complained about the worship leaders, too, the new music and the music volume. When my husband greeted her, she said quite venomously, "I am praying for the worship leaders to leave!"

In true Jesus style, my husband rebuked her and said, "That is not the Spirit of Christ."

I wish it had ended right there, but I have learned over the years that those who pray are powerful, even when they pray the wrong things. This is why Jesus instructs us to bless and not curse, because we have the power to do both (see Matthew 5:44 NKJV). What ensued was a horrible sin, with a resulting divorce and the loss of two families from our fellowship, which included our worship leaders. While the people involved were ultimately responsible for the choices they made, looking back, we should have taken this woman's curse against our worship leaders more seriously. That kind of prayer can empower demonic spirits to attack people and is fueled by the spirit of religion. What happened naturally, I believe, was a reflection of the battle happening spiritually—a battle that might have been prevented if only we had understood what we were dealing with.

I know of a pastor of Middle Eastern descent who began having terrible issues with his church board and some of his ethnic congregants. Not only would they not allow him to lead as the Holy Spirit was directing him, but they also challenged his leadership at every turn, even in the middle of his sermons. Remember that a religious spirit will go so far as to murder you if it can. Because this pastor was in the United States on a work visa, his dissenters threatened to fire him and thus force him back to his native land if he did not do what they wanted. Going back to his country meant jail and death for him and his family. This is a religious spirit at its worst. Thankfully, another church intervened and took this pastor on staff to prevent the worst from happening.

Verna Brown, senior pastor of Soul Harvest Worship Center in Modesto, California, also encountered this kind of spirit in some of her congregants, one person in particular. "It's so deceptive," Verna said. "It looks like a Christian, worships like a Christian and even performs signs and wonders!"

Verna had inadvertently allowed a woman with a religious spirit to come into her church and even join her leadership team. The woman pretended submission to her leadership, but really had a hidden agenda to divide and conquer, saying it was all "Jesus." Verna admits she missed a clear point of discernment, the manifestation of a spiritual scent she described as "the smell of a dirty diaper." She thought the smell indicated a plumbing issue in her church and kept using air fresheners to try to remedy it. That smell was not the bathroom, however, but was an actual spirit attached to this person with a religious spirit. The same identifiable smell was on every person she had infected. In the end, this woman took several people out of Verna's church to herself.

The good news is that another woman showed up at Verna's church around this time, but did not have the kind of smell associated with her that the previous woman had. Actually, this time it was a taste so distinct that Verna knew she was discerning a friend and an ally in the new woman. Verna tasted honey, like candy, in her mouth. It proved to be true. This new woman and her family have become strong pillars in her church, and Verna could not be more grateful.

The gift of discerning of spirits reveals people's hidden heart motives to us, for better or worse. This gift is like a Holy Spirit security alarm that tells us when people are safe or not, or if they are somewhere in the middle. There are some spiritual conditions that are harder to discern than others since they are extremely deceptive. We learn to distinguish the "hard to discern" by studying the nature of spiritual beings, both the angels and the principalities and powers. That is my next chapter's topic.

Kingdom Principles

1. The gift of discerning of spirits will reveal people's secret heart motives, whether they are sincere and genuine or evil and deceitful.

2. When you discern a demonic assignment against you, it can be alarming within your emotions. You need wisdom and patience, not reactiveness, to handle it properly.

3. We will discern both kingdoms, not just one or the other. We don't shut our eyes to the demonic kingdom out of personal preference. We need to know what God is doing, as well as what Satan is doing, so we can respond responsibly.

4. We can begin to discern the motives of the heart by paying attention to our knower, our imagination and our peace.

5. A religious spirit can go undetected, even by the most sensitive discerners, because it is an expert in disguise.

Thoughts for Reflection

1. Have you ever overreacted to someone you have negatively discerned? What did you learn from that episode?

2. Which kingdom, God's or Satan's, do you discern more? Has God set the balance in what you discern, or do you notice tendencies to see only what you want to see?

3. Have you ever noticeably discerned something happening in your knower, your imagination or through your peace? As a result, were you able to distinguish who was for you and who was against you?

4. Many confuse reading a person's outward behavior for the gift of discerning spirits. When have you supernaturally discerned someone's motive, a motive imperceptible to the natural eye?

5. Has the behavior of someone with a religious spirit ever caught you by surprise? If so, looking back, what were some points of discernment that you missed, if any?

6

Discerning the Angels

As I sat to write this chapter, I began to study about the element of faith needed to discern the presence of angels. The Bible tells us, "The angel of the LORD encamps around those who fear Him [with awe-inspired reverence and worship Him with obedience]" (Psalm 34:7 AMP). Do you fear and reverence Him? I sure do! We know, then, that the angels are right here with us. The apostle Paul prays, "And [I pray] that the eyes of your heart [the very center and core of your being] may be enlightened [flooded with light by the Holy Spirit], so that you will know . . ." (Ephesians 1:18 AMP). This prayer was not only for the Ephesians, but was a prayer that extends to you and me. This is what the prophet Elisha prayed for his servant when their lives were threatened. He prayed that the servant's spiritual eyes would open to see the angels protecting them (see 2 Kings 6:17).

Author and minister Bobby Connor once said that we need to "invite the angels to make themselves known." I want to encourage you, then, to go ahead and ask the Lord to open your eyes to see the angels who are with you. Allow your faith to lay hold of God for this, knowing that your eyes are blessed to see (see Matthew 13:16).

This is how I prayed as I began this section of the book: I asked the Lord to allow me to see His angels, knowing from His Word that they were nearby. Almost immediately, I saw an angel standing to my right, floating up in the air. He was about six feet tall, and I could feel God's light and heat radiating off him. I even went so far as to ask him, "Why are you here?"

He replied, "I'm here to help you!"

You and I both know that was a biblical response, and I was highly encouraged, to say the least (see Hebrews 1:14).

Why is it important to see and discern the angels? There are several reasons, but the most important is that angels give us an idea of what God is doing. Angels are servants of God and of us, and they do a lot of things, such as help us, protect us, guide us, and more. Yet they function primarily as God's messengers, something I understand to mean that angels will communicate a message both verbally and even indirectly by their actions (see Psalm 104:4; Hebrews 1:7).

I once saw four angels come and stand on our church platform, and I discerned by the Holy Spirit why they had come. These were angels on assignment from God for provision. God provides for us, but it is the angels who facilitate His provision (see Genesis 24:40; 1 Kings 19:5). These angels remained motionless until after we received the Lord's tithes and gave our offerings—an offering I made sure to give to once I saw the angels. After the offering they left very quickly, I believe to cause the Lord's provision to come. When we understand the message of the messengers, often observed in their actions, then we can co-labor with God and complete what God has already initiated in heaven.

How to Discern the Angels

I have discovered that there are a few specific ways in which you will discern angels. These are that you will see them, you will feel them and you will hear them. Let's look at each of these ways in a little more detail, along with some specific examples of them taking place, so that you are more aware of how they might occur.

1. You will see them

After Elijah's victory over the prophets of Baal, his nemesis, Queen Jezebel, threatened his life, so he ran for cover. Exhausted and emotionally spent, Elijah asked God to take his life. He then fell asleep, only to be awakened by an angel—an angel he saw with his own eyes! Surprisingly, the angel made him food to eat before telling him it was time to get up and go (see 1 Kings 19:1–7). Isn't that amazing?

Over and over again, we read about angels being seen by people in both the Old and New Testaments. Angels appear in the Bible 273 times. In the New Testament, an angel appeared to Zechariah to announce the miraculous birth of his son, John, and then the same angel appeared to the virgin Mary to announce that she would become pregnant with Jesus (see Luke 1:5–31). In John 5, we read about a very special angel who "went down at a certain time into the pool and stirred up the water; then whoever stepped in first, after the stirring of the water, was made well of whatever disease he had" (verse 4 NKJV). Later, we read about the angel who woke Peter up from sleep in prison, told him to put on his clothes, sandals and coat, and then supernaturally escorted him out to freedom (see Acts 12). I believe the disciples and other converts were so accustomed to angels that when Peter showed up at Mary's home, they did not believe it at first, thinking it must be Peter's angel and not really Peter himself (see verse 15). My point is that as New Testament believers, we should think of seeing and discerning angels as normal, not weird or "out there."

Many people have seen angels as quick flashes of light in their peripheral vision. I have seen them this way as well. They look like a quick flash of small blue lights, and I will see them for a month or so and then they will stop. Other people have told me they have seen the same, only as white or gold lights and some other colors. Although there are different interpretations for the meanings of these colors, I learned from John Paul Jackson that the color blue usually means revelation and communion. When I see the blue flashes of light, then I co-labor with what God is doing and pray for deeper revelation and deeper communion, knowing the angels have been sent on assignment for this. Although this phenomenon of seeing lights peripherally might signal a possible medical issue for some people, as with many things, I believe that more often than not we have rationalized the supernatural with this explanation. The last time I posted a description of this way that we might see angels to my Facebook page, I received 155 comments, almost all from people who have seen angels just the same way, as flashes of light.

We seem to have a lot of different angelic activity in and around our church platform areas. Twice I was told about an angel with a harp standing on our downtown campus church platform. The two persons who saw this angel both told me about it the same week, but neither had talked to the other person about what he or she had seen. We do know from the Bible that angels play musical instruments; specifically, we know they play trumpets, which again fits their messenger role (see 1 Thessalonians 4:16). Although it was not perfectly clear why the angel on our platform appeared with a harp, we see in the book of Revelation that harps can be connected to intercessory worship and deliverance (see 1 Samuel 16:23; Revelation 5:8). I believe this angel came for one or both of these purposes.

During our New Year's Eve prayer service, one of our congregants saw angels coming down from heaven, carrying large baskets that were illuminated with light. She said the angels set the baskets at the front of the platform and then went back up. She peeked inside one of these illuminated baskets and saw kidneys, pancreases and fingers! She did not look in the other baskets but knew that they, too, were filled with body parts from heaven. She said, "They were there for the taking for all who had faith to receive them."

Brenda Crouch, married to Paul Crouch Jr., shared with me a powerful story about seeing an angel. Brenda was raised in a strong Christian home in Turlock, California, and had been taught well about the source of her help and protection. Growing up, Brenda had been elected by the student body as a cheerleader and was eager to fit in with the cool kids. She had been invited to a birthday party of another cheerleader and was excited to be included, although she had never attended any of their "parties" before. She assumed that a parent would be around when her parents dropped her off, but to her surprise, there were none. As the evening progressed, she learned that the single mother of this home was a practicing witch, heavily involved in the occult, and that her daughter had learned many of her mother's incantations and séance practices. There was a shift in the evening when these fellow cheerleaders began casting spells on other kids, including some of the "jocks" (athletes). Brenda witnessed these girls' eyes turning black and their odd behavior, as if they were out of their bodies, which immediately brought fear into the room. The leader of the pack called everyone to order and started a séance, lighting a single candle.

"Some kids were laughing nervously, while others played along," as Brenda described it. "I chose to abstain and sit in a chair outside the circle instead of on the ground with them."

As the leader tried to summon spirits, Brenda prayed silently, asking God to shut it down and protect her from any harm. At that moment, she felt the wings of a *huge* angel envelop her like a shield and the presence of the Lord fill her with tremendous courage.

Right then, the leader got frustrated and barked at everyone, "*Someone* is not cooperating, and the spirits won't reveal themselves!"

Brenda spoke out and told them it was the power of God against the powers of darkness, and that the demons had to flee in the name of Jesus. "Through this I was able to witness about the saving grace of Jesus to a few of my classmates," Brenda said. "I was marked as 'different' from that point on, though."

Brenda believes this was a manifestation of the Holy Spirit's power at work in her life and her call to trust in a big God!

2. You will feel them

Have you ever felt a wind blow against you, only to realize that you were indoors? It was not the air conditioner, and that windy presence was, well, impossible. That wind was most likely an angel. Angels are described in the Bible as winds or flames of fire, and they can be felt as such. "And concerning the angels He says, 'Who makes His angels winds, and His ministering servants flames of fire [to do His bidding]'" (Hebrews 1:7 AMP).

I once felt an angelic wind in a church service during an unusual time of ministry. When my husband and I stretched out our hands toward a group of people standing in the altar area of the sanctuary, we felt a strong wind come into the room. This angelic wind blew an entire section of people at the altar to the ground.

Another time, I felt two distinct winds blow through the window of my home. I am not sure how to explain this part, but I knew these angelic "winds" were from Central Asia. The following month, two women all the way from Central Asia requested to stay with us for a month. I believe their angels had gone before them to prepare the way.

I have also heard many testimonies over the years from those who have felt intense heat come upon their hands from time to time. Did an angel cause this? Most likely, again based on the Scripture stating that God makes His ministering servants flames of fire. These people also believed it was a sign to them to lay their hands on others for personal ministry and physical healing. Along this same line, Alisa Cooper, one of my interns, explained how she sometimes feels "flames of fire in the atmosphere." She has learned through repeated experiences that this feeling means someone is going to be delivered from demonic spirits.

In the past, I have felt angels tap me on the arm and shoulder in an almost playful, curious fashion. It has always happened in church, and it took me a while to catch on. When it happened, I would turn to the right and the left and ask everyone around me, "Did you touch me?" I finally figured out that what I felt was not a human touch, but that of an angel, and angels often reflect the joyfulness of heaven.

Pastor Oscar Caraballo, a pastor from Puerto Rico living in Vermont, noticed after a powerful angelic visitation how the angels kept touching the sweat on his forehead. He said, "They always make an effort to touch the sweat of God's children because it is so wonderful to them."[1]

Angels also help "lighten" heavy atmospheres. Have you ever noticed in a worship service that it might begin with a stale, sometimes heavy feeling, but then it will lift and brighten quite noticeably? Angels forever worship Jesus, and being attracted to our worship, they will join in with us. Worship leader and songwriter Angel Ladd shared with me how she navigates heavy atmospheres: "I just keep pressing through it in praise and worship. I focus on what heaven is doing and saying, and I worship and declare from that place. Where the Spirit of the Lord is, there is freedom," Angel said. "I lift high the name of Jesus and watch as the heaviness leaves the room and falls off the people."

I believe this is the working of angels, and it is very discernible. The Bible says that His yoke is easy and His burden is light (see Matthew 11:30). I am not sure how they do it, but angels help lift these yokes and burdens from us so we can worship Jesus without restraints.

Finally, angels will strengthen us noticeably. Just before His crucifixion, Jesus went out to the Mount of Olives with His disciples and began to pray deeply. As He did so, an angel appeared to Him to strengthen Him. He could then pray even more deeply, being in such great anguish that His sweat was falling like drops of blood to the ground (see Luke 22:39–44). I have discovered that this kind of angelic strengthening is something you can feel and identify. Scheduled to minister at the Shrine Auditorium in Los Angeles, California, I had become ill a month before the event. It felt like a bad flu. I could not catch a full breath for days; neither could I recover my strength. I had several people praying for me, but I was not overcoming it. As I sat on the platform, still struggling just minutes away from speaking, I felt a tangible strength enter my body. It was sudden and dramatic, and I was healed at the same time. The Bible says that God is our strength (see Psalm 118:14), and I believe what happened to me was the work of an angel He sent. You can feel it that distinctly.

3. You will hear them

We can discern angels by their distinct sounds, but when we hear them, we most often will hear a message from them. By the meaning of their name, *angel*, which is *mal'ak* in Hebrew, we understand that their main role is to act as messengers. The Hebrew word *mal'ak* comes from a root word meaning to be dispatched "as a deputy; a messenger; specifically, of God, i.e. an angel . . ."[2]

Philip heard an angel say, "Go south to the road—the desert road—that goes down from Jerusalem to Gaza" (Acts 8:26). Philip did as the angel told him, and he shared the Gospel with an important Ethiopian eunuch as a result. When Hagar had lost all hope and believed her son, Ishmael, was going to die, she heard an angel speak from heaven and say, "What is the matter, Hagar? Do not be afraid; God has heard the boy crying as he lies there. Lift the boy up and take him by the hand, for I will make him into a great nation" (Genesis 21:17–18). God then supernaturally provided for Hagar and watched over Ishmael as he grew up (see Genesis 21:19–20).

One night as I was typing away on my computer, without warning I found myself gently laid down face first into my keyboard. Then I heard the voice of an angel, and he said this to me: "It's time to connect with the South."

By the way, I did not see this angel. I only heard him. I also realize his message to me may sound very cryptic to you, but I knew exactly what it meant. It meant I needed to connect a key person in Central California with a key person in Southern California, and there is quite a long story behind it. There was only one problem. I did not personally know this key person in the South, and unless an angel went before me to prepare the way, this meeting would not take place.

I thought to myself, *Let's test this and see if I really heard the Lord or not.* So I sent a very unassuming email to the general inbox of this person I did not know and said something like, "Hi! You don't know me, but my husband and I would like to take you and your wife to dinner, and we would like to bring some friends." I named the friends, knowing we would still need divine intervention in order for the meeting to happen.

Would you believe I received an immediate and favorable response? We all went to dinner, and the South "key" said he had agreed to meet us because he "felt the presence of God" on the invitation. This all took place when I discerned the voice of an angel.

We also can discern angels by their distinct sounds. The prophet Ezekiel encountered some very unusual angels and wrote about their sounds: "When they went, I heard the noise of their wings, like the noise of many waters, like the voice of the Almighty, a tumult like the noise of an army" (Ezekiel 1:24 NKJV). Our associate pastor, Tom Hammond, would often hear wind chimes as a young child, but could never identify their source. Once he began having angelic visitations as an adult, Tom finally figured out these sounds were angels. Judy Harrill, another of our congregants, also heard the sounds of the angels upon the passing of her grandmother. She said she could hear beautiful singing and the sounds of harps playing in the hospital room.

As I said earlier, seeing and discerning angels should be common and expected for us as New Testament believers. Still, not many people can say that they have encountered angels all that much, if at all. There is an element of faith needed to discern these angelic beings. That might be one reason for it. At the same time, we will not encounter angels until we are aligned to what God is doing.

To the Angel . . .

One day I saw it in the written Word that because of the angels, a church assignment is also a city assignment, and a city assignment is also a church assignment. I will explain that more fully in a moment. In fact, Ron and I are an example of it. We were not only going to Turlock to minister at a notoriously "religious" church; we also were on assignment to transform an even more "religious" city. As a matter of fact, you and I both have a similar purpose—to transform both Church and city—but this is something we can accomplish only with the help of the angels.

In the book of Revelation, Jesus revealed to the apostle John His solemn and weighty instructions to seven different churches, each identified by their respective cities of Ephesus, Smyrna, Pergamos, Thyatira, Sardis, Philadelphia and Laodicea. Each letter of instruction also contained an unusual preface that read like this: "To the angel of the church in [city] write . . ." (Revelation 2; 3). Let's break that phrase down and look at it more carefully.

Jesus told John to write specific instructions, addressing them first "*To the angel* . . ." We know that angels are powerful created beings assigned to serve God in heaven and to help the heirs of salvation on earth—you and me (see Hebrews 1:14). Angels also have specific assignments. Just to name a few, Michael the archangel specifically protects Israel, there are angels commanded to protect us personally, and there are angels assigned to children (see Daniel 12:1; Psalm 91:11; Matthew 18:10). Here in Revelation chapters 2–3, we see that an angel is assigned to the church of a specific city and that Jesus might even communicate His instructions, at His choosing, to these angels through His designated representatives, in this case John the apostle.[3] This also shows us that angels are the spiritual administrators of the directives of God.

Jesus then added, "To the angel *of the church* . . ." The word *church* in the original Greek language is the word *ekklēsia*, which is defined as a local Christian assembly. I have heard some define the word *ekklēsia* differently, even removing the thought that it is an assembly, and a local one at that. Although the word can definitely imply the Church at large, a word study of *ekklēsia* throughout the New Testament clarifies that it most often refers to a local assembly. Regardless, the Church is people and not a building, although the Church fails to be the Church if it never gathers together.

In other words, amongst other things, these angels watched over and spiritually administered the regular gatherings of the believers as they worshiped Jesus together and ideally were equipped and released for ministry (see Ephesians 4:11–12). In these letters, Jesus addressed the churches before their respective angels, commending their strengths and righteous acts, as well as their sins and shortcomings. He also sternly warned the local *ekklēsia* of their potential removal if they did not change their ways—something the angel would facilitate if matters came to that.

Finally, He added, "To the angel of the church *in [the city]* . . ." The city, then, would be the geographical borders of influence given to the designated angel and the local church. Here is where we see the local church and city as divinely intertwined because of an angelic being, and we see how the local *ekklēsia*, both individually and corporately, is the designated catalyst for city transformation.

In a City on Purpose

Do you wonder why you live in the city or town that you live in? God is behind such matters, much more so than we think. Our heavenly Father is the original inventor of cities. You could say that the first city was the Garden of Eden, and the last city, of course, is the New Jerusalem. He places people in cities, such as He did with Adam and Eve, and even calls people out of cities, such as He did with Abraham and Lot. For that reason, I believe that God has ordered your steps and placed you in your town or city on a divine assignment. You are there to bring His Kingdom, and you are there to destroy the works of darkness.

A woman named Carol came to a recent prophetic institute at our church. She came to learn, but also to receive an anointing to see and discern the spiritual realm so she could be more effective. Carol had been divinely called out from her home in Houston, Texas, to the city of San Francisco. Her assignment? To pray for and love people and show them who Jesus is. A business owner, Carol had been visiting San Francisco when she became overwhelmed with the sound of crying and weeping while she was driving around the city. She investigated the sound but could not pinpoint it. Finally, she discerned it by the Holy Spirit. As she stood on a beach, she knew the cry was coming from the land, and it felt like an inner cry from people's hearts. When she identified it, the anointing of the Holy Spirit came tangibly upon her. "It felt like honey, very thick and sweet," she said. "And I can still feel it when I share this story."

After this experience, Carol spent a week in San Francisco to seek the Lord's direction, and then she spent another month in the city to confirm it. God gave her a specific dream and a Scripture confirming her call to a city known as the "least churchgoing metro in America," to bring His Kingdom there. Carol now engages in "friendship evangelism" and shares Jesus in the context of her many friendships with atheist and other-religion friends. She said her next assignment is to gather people to pray for San Francisco and begin the process of healing the land, as the Holy Spirit directs her.

When God called Ron and me back to Turlock, California, His plan was to transform a city by first transforming the local church. City transformation God's way would only happen through His repurposed Church, which then would reactivate the angelic assignment. God's purposes—and this includes the angels assigned to His specific purposes—will not happen past the faith of His Church on the earth. We can and often do limit God by our disobedience, which in turn restrains His angelic helpers (see Psalm 78:41 NKJV). This is true of any city. Ian Carroll, senior leader of Greater Chicago Church, shared a similar thought after he saw the "angel of Chicago." He said the angel had remained dormant for decades, but was reactivated in his assignment in 2011, in response to the fervent prayers of the local church for the city (his church, as well as others).[4] I have experienced something similar. I have seen the "angel of Turlock," and it is my belief that God reactivated this city's angel to his assignment once the local church stepped back into its purpose for our city.

I believe the absence of angels is due largely to the Church, both individually and corporately, not being aligned to its proper assignment. Angels come to help us as we obey the Lord, not as we carry out our own whims. That is a tough pill to swallow, but discernible angelic activity tells us where God is and what He is doing.

I once was in Tiānfǔ Square in Chengdu, China. (Our interpreter translated *Tiānfǔ* as "heavenly government.") The square was heavily saturated with police, and you could feel the unrest on the land. I was told that radical Buddhists had used the square as a continual place of government protest, with some setting themselves on fire to make their point. As we prayer walked the square, I became quite irritated when I discerned the lack of angelic presence. I thought to myself, *Why are there no angels?* The lack of angels was a message that something was amiss. I expressed my irritation to our host, and we began to pray for God to release His angels to that place (see Matthew 26:53). As we continued walking the area, I was amazed and surprised to see a pillar erected to the "Angel of Harmony." That was a powerful confirmation! God had already built His strategic plan into the land, even giving title and description to what He wanted established. Nevertheless, it needed the local church to come into alignment with His plan for the city if the angels were going to be released.

As an individual, you will be most effective in your purpose when you understand the city-church-angel connection and align yourself with it. In response to your alignment with your city assignment, God will release and activate the city angels to their assignment. You can discern the difference as an increase in angelic activity, just as the lack thereof also tells us where things stand. That does not mean you will not have any ministry or angelic help past your city borders. I just shared with you my own experience in Chengdu in this regard. Still, God has ordered your steps on purpose, and you are in your city for a purpose.

Test the Spirits

When my immediate family and I became Christians and officially left the LDS church, we had one relative consider making the same decision. This relative, too, was in the LDS church and was clearly being drawn away from its control by the Holy Spirit. That is, until a deceiving spirit disguised as an angel appeared to the person in the middle of the night, telling her to remain in the LDS church. Keep in mind that Mormons actively believe in angelic messengers, and they take the appearance of an angel to heart. They also don't know that they should test the spirits, nor would they know how. As a result, this relative remained in the LDS church and closed her ears to the truth from then on.

The apostle John wrote this: "Dear friends, do not believe every spirit, but test the spirits to see whether they are from God, because many false prophets have gone out into the world" (1 John 4:1). When angels appear, test them. And when someone tells you he or she has seen and heard from an angel, be prepared to put that person's words to the test. The success of the gift of discerning of spirits is not that you have just discerned something, but that you have discerned it well. You not only saw or discerned an angel, but you also tested the spirit and found that the spirit passed the test.

The apostle Paul wrote, "By this you will know the Spirit of God: Every spirit that confesses that Jesus Christ has come in the flesh is from God" (1 John 4:2 ESV). How, then, do you test the spirits? I have read some authors' very long lists of spiritual tests for such things, but my main test—actually, my only test—is to determine if the angelic experience is in agreement with the Bible. As the apostle Paul wrote, "All Scripture is God-breathed . . ." (2 Timothy 3:16). Did you read that? *All* Scripture is God-breathed; therefore, we can bank every encounter against the written Word of God to see if it holds true or not.

In Paul Cox's book *Unwrap the Gifts*, I read the story about Christina, a professing Christian who was searching spiritually after a near-death experience involving her brother. He appeared to her in a dream while he was in a coma, and when he came out of the coma, he somehow repeated the details of the dream to her. This strange spiritual experience opened Christina's heart to search out more information about such things, especially things involving near-death experiences, mediums and communication with deceased loved ones.

"I had communication with what I thought was an angel," Christina said. "The angel was a comfort. It felt caring. It came to me first with words in my spirit, speaking in my mind."[5]

Christina grew to depend on "her angel," even asking this angel for help. Soon, however, she began to be tormented, hearing evil voices and seeing ugly creatures. Repeatedly, she was physically attacked, with red marks to show for it, but nothing physical ever touched her. She sought help from some mature deliverance ministers, who figured out that the angel she was so attached to was really a demon, a demon that was eventually broken from her life.

Christina became deceived because she did not understand the Scriptures. We don't rely on angels more than we rely on God; this is what opened the door for Christina's deception and possession. We don't reach for the angels for comfort; we reach for the Comforter, the Holy Spirit.

Joseph Smith, founder of the LDS religion, was born in Sharon, Vermont, and then moved with his family to western New York, a place of religious revival during the Second Great Awakening. Smith supposedly began having visions of God, including a visitation from an ostensible angel named Moroni. The angel directed him, Smith said, to a buried set of ancient gold plates containing the Christian history of ancient America. These plates Smith translated into the Book of Mormon.[6] I believe Smith's claims could have been falsified; rather than seeing some vision he thought was from God, he might even have made up the whole angel story. But Mormons are taught this history as absolute fact. Regardless, the Bible says clearly that we are not to add to the words of Scripture (see Deuteronomy 4:2; Proverbs 30:5–6; Revelation 22:18–19). Any angel directing you to find so-called "lost" Scriptures is therefore not an angel, but a demon.

Louis (not his real name), age 21, was disillusioned with church and struggling in his marriage. He was the product of a divorce and had been raised by an emotionally unattached mother who did not demonstrate any verbal or natural affection toward him. Louis was passionate about the things of the Spirit, already showing signs of a prophetic gifting, but frustrated that he had nowhere to develop it. As his marriage was struggling, Louis began to fill his lonely places by watching dark spiritual shows on television at night and listening to dark, somewhat occult music.

"At night I began to feel a spiritual presence," Louis said. "A dark, motherly angel would come in and comfort me at night so I could sleep peacefully."

This brought Louis a comfort he had missed his entire life, but only for a season. Louis began to hear the voice of this spirit in his mind—soft words that would turn into swear words and then explosive anger. As the spirit began to take over his personality, he realized that a false angel had deceived him. He began praying with an intercession team weekly, and the spirit began to lose its grip on his mind, until he was finally delivered of it in a prayer service. "I could hear the Holy Spirit so clearly once it left," he said.

The gift of discerning of spirits allows us to discern the angels. I believe this is meant to show us what God is doing so we can more specifically co-labor with Him. The angels are servants of God who do His bidding. God is behind it when angels are present and active. He has sent those angels personally on a specific assignment, or they are there from Him to facilitate an answer to someone's prayers. God can also activate them in response to someone's prophetic decree, which is a word from Him spoken through one of His earthly representatives (see Psalm 103:20).

As much as we need to discern what the angels are doing, we also need to discern what Satan is doing. We are in a battle to advance Christ's Kingdom on earth, which ultimately leads to the displacement of satanic henchmen and strongholds. We cannot win our battles until we know what we are fighting against. We cannot distinguish or discern an enemy that we have not studied. In the next chapter, then, let's discuss the key players in Satan's army.

Kingdom Principles

1. The reason we need to discern the presence of angels is that angels give us an idea of what God is doing.

2. Angels do a lot of things, but they function primarily as God's messengers. They will communicate a message verbally, or even indirectly by means of their actions.

3. When we understand the message of the messengers, often observed in their actions, then we can co-labor with God and complete what He has already initiated in heaven.

4. You will discern angels most often by seeing them, feeling them and/or hearing them.

5. As an individual, you will be most effective in your purpose when you understand the city-church-angel connection and align yourself with it. In response to your alignment with your city assignment, God will release and activate the city angels to their assignment.

Thoughts for Reflection

1. Have you ever discerned the presence of an angel? How did you discern it?

2. Is it common for you to be aware of angelic activity, or not very common? Why do you think that is?

3. How would your awareness and obedience to your God-given assignment prompt God to activate the angels in your midst?

4. What is your purpose in your city? How might God ordain the angels to help you accomplish your purpose?

5. Why do people fear or reject the active, discernible presence of the angels?

7

Discerning the Powers and Principalities

Adam and Eve failed to discern their enemy. Do you ever wonder how that happened? Do you ever question why they missed the obvious? Satan came to them in the form of a snake. Was it that normal for snakes to talk? And then he convinced Eve, who convinced Adam, to disobey the one clear command of God: "You must not eat from the tree of the knowledge of good and evil, for when you eat from it you will certainly die" (Genesis 2:17). Neither of them could discern the truth from the lie. Consequently, the entire human race fell.

The Bible tells us that Satan works to blind our minds from the truth. "Satan, who is the god of this world, has blinded the minds of those who don't believe. They are unable to see . . ." (2 Corinthians 4:4 NLT). We have all experienced this in some form or another personally, and we have also seen the spiritual blindness of others. I am amazed at those who have witnessed the hideous acts of cruelty and extremism of ISIS and still leave everything behind to join its ranks. I have watched the Chinese make offerings and bow before ginormous statues in their temples. These idols look like nightmarish demons, by the way, yet they still worship them!

Jesus referred to the Pharisees as blind guides. "It wasn't that they would not believe, they simply could not believe," wrote Dave Williams, minister and author, in his book *Skill for Battle: The Art of Spiritual Warfare*. "The god of this world had blinded their 'spiritual' eyes and they could not see the truth."[1] Dave further explained that the blindness of the Pharisees then spread to the people. The very people Jesus taught and healed for three years suddenly turned on Him, shouting, "Crucify Him!"

Spiritual blindness can only be overcome spiritually. People will not turn to Jesus until the prayers of the Church have bound the blinding demonic spiritual powers. When the Holy Spirit fell upon the praying disciples in the Upper Room, the scene was so supernatural that it caught the attention of the entire city (see Acts 2:1–12). Peter then spoke to the crowd—the very same crowd who had condemned Jesus—and the Holy Spirit opened their eyes to the truth. They saw their sin and made a full U-turn to Jesus Christ!

When Scripture says that Satan has blinded the minds of unbelievers, understand that Satan has a rank-and-file army of dark angels who facilitate his evil wishes. In Ephesians 6:12, Paul wrote about what appears to be an organized hierarchy of beings in the demonic kingdom: "For our struggle is not against flesh and blood, but against the rulers, against the authorities, against the powers of this dark world and against the spiritual forces of evil in the heavenly realms." These spiritual beings are not Satan himself, but they serve his wicked schemes against mankind. And they are not just spirits that possess people on an individual level. They actually work in the spiritual atmosphere of a city, region or nation to blind every person under their influence.

I talked previously about the behavior and deceptive nature of a religious spirit. I also mentioned that a city will take on the personality of the demonic power that controls it; that is, until the Church overcomes it. Until then, the resident souls of those who do not yet know Christ hang in the balance. It is not that they don't want to see the truth; they actually cannot see the truth because they have been blinded by a demonic ruler.

In descending order, let's consider our discernible enemies:

1. The rulers, also translated "principalities" (Greek *archai*), are most identifiable as high-ranking spirit princes, such as the prince of Persia and the prince of Greece, who were both mentioned in the book of Daniel (see Daniel 10:13, 20).

2. The authorities (Greek *exousia*) are spirits that stand behind human authorities to oppose the work of God. Elymas the sorcerer, for example, was someone who appeared to stand under demonic authority as he attempted to oppose the work of God in order to retain control of Sergius Paulus, the governor, and the island of Patmos (see Acts 13:4–12).

3. The powers of darkness (Greek *dunamis*) work culturally and philosophically to bind people groups from seeing the Lord. Examples are false religions such as Hinduism, philosophies such as humanism, and political ideologies such as communism and all the other "isms" that deny the expression of God.

4. The spiritual forces of evil (Greek *kosmokratoras*) are the lower-ranking spirits that afflict people through infirmity, fear, rebellion, deception, divination, complacency and the like.[2]

In order to discern and overcome our spiritual enemies, we first have to study them. If we fail to recognize them, then we will come under their spell, so to speak, and be harmed. We understand this principle naturally. When I was in elementary school, for example, we were taught what behaviors to look for in strangers in order to identify them as dangerous or not. And then we were taught how to get out of danger. This instruction may have saved my life as a fourth grader, when I was walking home alone from school. A car with an older man inside began slowly circling up and down the block where I was walking. About the third circling, I identified the behavior as dangerous and quickly turned into the sheriff's home on the block. Today, I thank God that He directed me to the sheriff, and that the sheriff was home! He let me come inside, and he reported the stranger before walking me to my house.

Just as I was able to identify this stranger as evil, the Holy Spirit is also training our spiritual eyes to identify evil powers and principalities. Let's now look at some of the most common powers and principalities that afflict and deceive cities, regions and nations, as well as persecute the Church.

Belial

Belial is a spiritual power that works to make your life worthless and barren through idolatry and self-sabotaging behaviors. Its name, Belial, means exactly that—without profit, worthless, wicked, ungodly and evil. It is the antithesis of Christ and His righteousness. "What harmony is there between Christ and Belial? Or what does a believer have in common with an unbeliever?" (2 Corinthians 6:15).

Belial works to ensnare people into distinct sins so their lives are unfruitful and wasted. It partners with spiritual forces of wickedness to infect its territory with unrighteousness. It does not only entice those who don't know Jesus; it also works to entice Christians who will allow its deception. Either way, it is a reducing spirit that skillfully crafts worthlessness into the lives of its victims.

The first characteristic of Belial is idolatry. "Certain men, the children of Belial, are gone out from among you, and have withdrawn the inhabitants of their city, saying, Let us go and serve other gods, which ye have not known" (Deuteronomy 13:13 KJV). Whole cultures have come under this deception, worshiping false gods and statues, and engaging in religiously false systems. I have also encountered far too many Christians who still pray to others in addition to God, read their horoscopes, do traditional yoga and/or burn sage and other herbs to keep evil spirits away, just to name a few such practices. This is the spirit of Belial at work, enticing people into idolatry, thus shutting the door to the Holy Spirit and drawing devotion away from Christ.

The next characteristic of Belial is sexual sin. Sexual sin, which is sex in any form outside marriage, has devastated the lives of individuals and entire cultures since ancient times. The Bible says, "But among you there must not be even a hint of sexual immorality" (Ephesians 5:3). Sexual sin has crept into Christendom in the forms of tolerance and acceptance of premarital sex, homosexuality and even open marriages. The Bible makes reference to the sons of Eli the priest in this manner: "Now the sons of Eli were sons of Belial; they knew not the LORD" (1 Samuel 2:12 KJV). Why were they considered sons of Belial? If you read further in the passage, they committed unauthorized worship and routinely had sex with ungodly women in the Temple. While visiting one California city in particular, I was shocked at how many churches displayed the rainbow flag as a statement of their acceptance of the homosexual lifestyle. The Bible is clear about homosexuality, but still some churches have blatantly deviated from this truth. This is the spirit of Belial (see Judges 19:22).

Another characteristic of Belial is drunkenness. We see this connection between the spirit of Belial and drunkenness when Hannah was at the Temple, praying in deep anguish for God to give her a son. As she prayed and wept bitterly, Eli the priest observed her, and instead of consoling her, he accused her of drinking too much wine. She retorted, "Count not thine handmaid for a daughter of Belial" (1 Samuel 1:16 kjv). In other words, drunkenness can be connected to the spirit of Belial.

Finally, those under the spell of Belial have no respect for authority. Nabal, also referred to as a son of Belial, would not honor David's request for sheep, even though David and his men had voluntarily protected him and his flocks from outside harm. Nabal angrily refused David's request for help, even pretending ignorance by saying, "Who is this David?" (1 Samuel 25:10). Then later, Sheba the Benjamite, also "a man of Belial," worked to divide David's kingdom (2 Samuel 20:1 kjv). When opportunity presented itself, Sheba blew the trumpet in rebellion against David and called every Israelite to himself.

What is the penalty for Belial? You become marked for destruction! The Bible says that Nabal was struck by the Lord and died (see 1 Samuel 25:38). And Sheba's plan turned against him, forcing him to hide out in a city from Joab, the captain of David's army. When Joab put the city under siege to force him out, an old woman convinced the city to execute Sheba and thus end the siege (see 2 Samuel 20:21–22).

There was once a man I knew of who stood firmly against a new pastor's leadership in his church. This man would be a modern-day "son of Belial." As he actively campaigned against this pastor, he became afflicted with cancer. While receiving treatment, he humbly repented of his rebellion, and the cancer went into remission at the same time. As soon as he felt better, he reverted back to his divisive behavior even more forcefully.

Would it surprise you, then, that the cancer returned? At this point the Holy Spirit spoke to the pastor that if the man did not repent, he would die within three months. Sadly, he did not repent, and he died, just as the pastor was told.

Leviathan

Leviathan is a spirit principality, also known as the king of pride. Job 41 describes it in detail, starting out by asking, "Can you draw out Leviathan with a hook . . .?" and ending with "He beholds every high thing; he is king over all the children of pride" (verses 1, 34 NKJV). Pride is an attitude, but it is also a spirit. This spirit wants altitude and seeks to invade the high places. It wants to infect people in the high places because it is a glory stealer. It steals the glory that should go to Jesus Christ.

Pride comes in a lot of forms. There are proud eyes, which is a haughty look; a proud heart, which is a hard heart; a proud spirit, which is an impatient spirit; and proud speech, which is the mouth that boasts and puts other people down (see Proverbs 21:4; Ecclesiastes 7:8; 2 Peter 2:18). People infected by Leviathan will act higher, better and more superior than you. They will have a high-and-mighty attitude. They will fight unusually hard to be right at your expense. That is the nature of the spirit of Leviathan.

James 4:6 says God resists the proud, but He honors the humble. Luke 14:11 says He actually exalts the humble. God wants His humble people in the high places, not those people who are ruled by pride.

The spirit of Leviathan is often referred to as a water serpent: "You, O God . . . split the sea by your strength and smashed the heads of the sea monsters. You crushed the heads of Leviathan and let the desert animals eat him" (Psalm 74:12–14 NLT). I believe this means that this demon likes to be around the water, namely the river of the Spirit, to look for a victim. The closest word picture in the Hebrew for Leviathan is the crocodile (see Job 41:12–16). A crocodile will get you in its jaws and thrash you until you are too tired to fight. It tosses you back and forth, one way after the other, to make you give up.

When it attacks you, this spirit will also try to confuse you. How does that happen? Leviathan is described as multiheaded. That means it is divisive, it speaks out of both sides of its mouth, and it twists the truth (see Psalm 74:12–14; Isaiah 27:1). For example, you will say something and another person will hear it completely differently, resulting in strife. Or a person will change his or her story several times and then not acknowledge it when confronted.

In the first seven verses of Job 41, the Lord asks Job several questions about Leviathan, and to sum it up, I believe these questions reveal man's inability to surface and conquer pride without God's intervention. When you are dealing with Leviathan, when it attacks you, it feels as though you cannot get a grip on it to defeat it. It twists, hides and goes under the water.

I once had a ministry leader exposed for having the spirit of Leviathan. I did not catch on for a long time, but she had a trail of broken relationships and an airtight story about each one. She was always the victim in each situation, and the other people were always at fault for one reason or another. Finally, she got caught in a truth-twisting situation, and when confronted, she became demanding and reprimanding, with nonstop finger-pointing for months to try to wear down everyone involved. When that did not work, she would feign submission just long enough to make you believe she was changing her destructive patterns. And then the truth-twisting, finger-pointing behavior would start all over again.

The way to counter the spirit of Leviathan is by humbling ourselves before God. How then do we humble ourselves? We humble ourselves first by prayer and fasting. Jesus taught that there are some spirits that only go out by prayer and fasting, such as the spirit that afflicted the young boy in Mark 9:17–29. I believe the spirit of Leviathan is one such spirit. You have to have enough humility within yourself to defeat it. You cannot fight pride with pride, but humility partners with the Holy Spirit to bind this spirit and cast it out.

Mammon

"All money has a spirit on it," said Pastor Robert Morris of Gateway Church in Southlake, Texas. "It either has the Spirit of God on it or it has the spirit of Mammon on it." Morris further explained in his teaching about the spirit of Mammon that the way you get the Spirit of God on your money is to give the first 10 percent, the "tithe," to the house of God. The tithe brings God's blessing and redemption on the rest of your money and thus protects it from the spirit of Mammon. "Once you tithe, your money can't be devoured by the devourer because God's Spirit is on it," he said. "Your money is then blessed by God and has the ability to multiply."[3]

Have you ever considered that money carries a spirit with it? I have actually felt and discerned the spirit on money now and again, sensing the blessing of God on it or the filth of Mammon on it. What, then, is the spirit principality of Mammon? *Mammon* is a Chaldee or Syriac word meaning wealth or riches. It is also the name of the "god of riches."[4] The spirit of Mammon has its roots in Babylon. Babylon came into existence with the incident of the Tower of Babel, as told in Genesis 11. Here we read that all the people had one language and decided to build a tower to heaven on their own. They wanted to create their own way to heaven, which is a reflection of an arrogant spirit that denies any need for God. When the Lord saw their ambitious plans, He confused their language and caused them to scatter all over the earth. Thus *babel* means confusion, and Babylon, then, has its roots in confusion. Babylon is historically known for its pride, idolatry and cruelty, and it is prophetically known to become an economic stronghold in the earth in the end times.[5]

Although money in and of itself is not evil, the Bible instructs us that the love of money is "a root of all kinds of evil" (1 Timothy 6:10). It is the love of money that causes people to subject themselves to the evil principality of Mammon, either knowingly or unknowingly. Jesus said, "No one can serve two masters; for either he will hate the one and love the other, or else he will be loyal to the one and despise the other. You cannot serve God and mammon" (Matthew 6:24 NKJV). Mammon is looking for devotees and promises to provide identity, security, influence and power for their perfect devotion; only it forbids devotion to Jesus Christ. This spirit is also a great intimidator of Christians, telling them they cannot be generous or give to God because they don't have enough. Those who follow the dictates of Mammon, however, will eventually receive a visit from this deity. It always demands payment from its followers in one way or another and is a destroyer.

World MAP founder Reverend Ralph Mahoney has spearheaded training events and provided training resources to hundreds of thousands of indigenous pastors in pastoral leadership and evangelism around the globe. In Dave Williams's book *The Road to Radical Riches*, Mahoney shares a story about a South American town whose residents were taught how to bind their souls to the spirit of Mammon in exchange for wealth and riches. Those who made the vow to this deity quickly acquired more wealth than the average citizen and could be seen arrogantly driving around in their luxury cars and wearing fashionable clothing. In their false security of wealth, each of them became blinded to the hellish scene that eventually awaited them. Reverend Mahoney witnessed something horrific happen to each person who pledged his or her soul to Mammon. Between the ages of 40 and 45, each devotee, without exclusion, would swell up in unbearable pain. As their bodies became painfully bloated, they would shriek and scream, begging the deity for their lives. This merciless spirit gave them no reprieve before they exploded wide open, with slimy, slithering worms crawling out of their dead bodies.[6]

Mammon tries to tear down the Church by destroying its economy. Money in the hands of God's people translates into souls. It takes money to reach people with the Gospel, and for that reason this spirit works overtime to bind churches financially. You can hear this spirit talking to you whenever a church receives the tithes and offerings. It says things like, *All that preacher wants is your money.* Or, *You better not give. You won't have enough for yourself.* It also creates theological lies to convince you not to give your tithes, saying things like, *Tithing is for just the Old Testament. In the New Testament, you can give whatever you feel led to give.* Only most people rarely feel "led" to give.

Mammon also threatens pastors to do its bidding through wealth-controlling parishioners. These parishioners try to stop the move of the Holy Spirit and anything deemed "too radical" or "undignified" by threatening to withhold needed financial resources. Mammon has also gripped many pastors who have diverted the tithes and offerings to their own personal greedy use, which is robbing God. It puts them under a curse (see Malachi 3:8–9).

On one occasion, a church I know of discovered that someone was stealing from the Sunday offerings. That is always the spirit of Mammon at work. This church had a very tight system of checks and balances, but still, no one could identify the thief. As the theft continued, leadership prayed for the thief to be caught, also knowing the principle of God's Word. The Bible says in Malachi 3:8 that stealing the tithes is the same as stealing from

God, which subjects you to the curse. The leaders also knew that Mammon always comes to collect. Soon enough, one of the ushers fell under the judgment of God and the penalty of Mammon. In just a matter of months, the usher's entire household fell apart due to drugs, jail, theft, prostitution, adultery, rebellion and divorce. Through this, the church leaders were able to identify the thief, and sadly, neither the thief nor the household has ever fully recovered.

Jezebel

Years ago, there was a moral failure on our pastoral team. It was devastating, and the circumstances of the extramarital affair were hard to accept. There was also a woman who orchestrated the adulterous relationship behind the scenes. She did not have the affair, but she helped bring it together. This woman appeared very spiritual, prayerful and even prophetic, which was quite confusing at the time. I learned after some research that she fit the classic definition of a person under the influence of a Jezebel spirit. I also vilified her as an evil person in my mind for years and never considered her worthy of redemption because, after all, she was a *Jezebel*!

Much later, I wondered about the root cause of her actions and if change would ever be possible. I have dealt with others who seemed to fit much of the classic description of a Jezebel spirit, or at least parts of it. It is a spirit that is controlling, manipulative, falsely prophetic, prideful, seductive, intimidating and deceptive, with a hatred for authority. Most of the people affected are women, but not all of them. I was also frustrated that I had never successfully cast out a Jezebel spirit from a person, and neither had our deliverance teams. When we told that spirit to go, it did not go! Instead, the person had to go if the church was ever going to be rid of it.

I believe that I have finally figured out why. Notice that Jezebel is a spiritual power that received its first mention in the Bible as a human being—actually, two women with that name. Yet the behavior of those two people has become a spiritual reference point long after they are gone. It is not just that someone is acting like Jezebel, but that someone has succumbed to the spirit of Jezebel.

Jezebel is not a human spirit who has gained some type of cosmic evil power. Not at all. It is a demonic spirit that first became personified in the actions of an actual person, and has since continued its evil influence as a territorial type of demon. One of the women by the name of Jezebel in the Bible was in the Old Testament, and one was in the New Testament. There was Queen Jezebel, Baal worshiper and wife to King Ahab, and then Jezebel from the church of Thyatira, an idolater and self-proclaimed prophetess (see 1 Kings 16:29–31; Revelation 2:18–29). These are not the same woman, but two different women having similar sins and evil behaviors such as those I just described. I don't believe this is a coincidence. Then we read about a demonic principality, the "great harlot" in Revelation, and how it promotes in the nations the exact behavior we find in both Jezebels and in those we know who act like them (see Revelation 17). I believe the "great harlot" is one and the same as the spirit of Jezebel. It is an evil principality that exerts influence over people and entire nations.

Consider the deep spiritual dimensions attached to Jezebel's behavior, and then consider Jesus' remedy. Unlike with other demonic spirits that afflict people, Jesus does not say to cast out a spirit of Jezebel. Instead, He gives instructions about how to handle Jezebel, also warning her to repent or suffer serious consequences:

> Nevertheless, I have this against you: You tolerate that woman
> Jezebel, who calls herself a prophet. By her teaching she misleads

my servants into sexual immorality and the eating of food sacrificed to idols. I have given her time to repent of her immorality, but she is unwilling. So I will cast her on a bed of suffering, and I will make those who commit adultery with her suffer intensely, unless they repent of her ways.

Revelation 2:20–22

Why, then, does Jesus emphasize repentance instead of emphasizing casting the spirit out? Biblical repentance means to change your mind. When someone is under the influence of the Jezebel spirit, they are not possessed in the traditional sense. Jezebel in the Bible had to repent because the behavioral strongholds had been craftily built into her mind. She was not possessed by this demonic spirit, but had become like this spirit in her personality and behavior. This typically happens as this principality unleashes sinister and targeted circumstances into a person's life to create the needed mental strongholds that result in the patterned behaviors. These targeted attacks can be childhood sexual or physical abuse, severe neglect, painful family issues and trauma. Not everyone with a difficult upbringing comes under the influence of Jezebel, but such trauma is intended to create its effects inside a person's mind. When you encounter a person under the influence of Jezebel, realize his or her wickedness today is a deep-seated response to traumatic conditioning yesterday.

Repentance is not easy, however. Change can feel like a personal death since the behaviors are so deeply ingrained. Catherine, a woman in our church, shared her story with our congregation. "I hated my husband and verbally abused him," she said. "I finally tried to kill him and ended up in jail."

Although she was a Christian, Catherine did not fully surrender her life to Christ until she was incarcerated. The root of her behavior was childhood sexual abuse, coupled with strong family matriarchs who taught her never to trust men. "I had to learn how to stop controlling people," she explained. "It really was all about control rooted in deep emotional wounds and fear."

Today, Catherine is a medical professional and a powerful speaker, equipper and minister in our church. We have several such stories of women just like her. These are women who could not control their rage, destroyed their marriages, hated authority, lied compulsively, used sex to get their way and on and on. Every time, these were women who had been abused or traumatized in their younger years. They were set free through personal repentance, the Word of God and the power of the Holy Spirit.

If this is you, know that God loves you and has already made a way out for you. You need to be delivered in your soul, but how? The Bible instructs us to be renewed in the spirit of our mind (see Romans 12:2). To renew our mind, we meditate in God's Word. We read, speak out loud, write and memorize Bible verses that reshape our thinking and behavior. For example, "Therefore, laying aside all malice, all deceit, hypocrisy, envy, and all evil speaking, as newborn babes, desire the pure milk of the word, that you may grow thereby" (1 Peter 2:1–2 NKJV). As we review these verses over and over and others like them, we will begin to reshape from the inside out. We will change. The Bible says God's Word can divide soul and spirit, meaning it is so sharp that it has a surgical-like ability to cut things out of your soul (see Hebrews 4:12). God also promises to restore your soul (see Psalm 23:3), and restoration happens as you renew your mind with His Word.

If you live with, work with or attend church with a person under the influence of Jezebel, realize that every situation is different and you have to choose your battles. Pray specific and redemptive Scriptures for the person that counter his or her ungodly behavior. For example, if the person is seductive, then pray that he or she would not have even "a hint of sexual immorality, or of any kind of impurity" (Ephesians 5:3). If the person is controlling, then pray that he or she would have confidence in leadership and submit to their authority (see Hebrews 13:17).

Still, Jesus instructs us not to tolerate Jezebel. In other words, you have to set firm boundaries with those under this spirit's influence. Remember that people under the influence of Jezebel cannot control you, seduce you or bewitch you unless you allow it. In a church, be very diligent when such people begin tearing down leaders behind their backs. Remember, these people hate authority, but this hatred has a root cause. Show a lot of love, but confront them immediately and insist that they right their wrong with that leader. Once they know the boundaries and know they are loved, it creates enough safety for them to start changing. If they are destructive and will not repent, don't feel bad for removing them from your circle or fellowship. If you are their target, however, pray and strategically confront them. Don't be their victim.

Discern and Overcome

The Church will fail to overcome what it fails to discern. If we are going to overcome our spiritual enemies, we have to be able to identify them. Studying our spiritual enemies is not being spiritually negative or out of balance, as some have proposed. Studying our spiritual enemies and knowing who they are and how they attack is necessary, so as not to become deceived by them.

In addition to a religious spirit, Belial, Leviathan, Mammon and Jezebel will continue their sinister attacks until they are discerned and overcome by the Body of Christ. With that said, let's discuss in more depth in the next chapter what to do with the things we spiritually discern.

Kingdom Principles

1. Satan works to blind our minds from the truth (see 2 Corinthians 4:4). Spiritual blindness can only be overcome spiritually.

2. People will not turn to Jesus at the hearing of the Gospel until the prayers of the Church bind those blinding demonic spiritual powers.

3. When the Bible says that Satan has blinded people's minds from the truth, understand that Satan has a rank-and-file army of dark angels that facilitate his evil wishes (see Ephesians 6:12).

4. In order to discern and overcome our spiritual enemies, we have to first study them.

5. The most common powers and principalities that afflict and deceive cities, regions and nations, as well as persecute the Church, are Belial, Leviathan, Mammon and Jezebel.

Thoughts for Reflection

1. Does it frustrate you when people cannot see the truth and continue to ruin their lives and the lives of others through their sin? Have you ever considered it to be spiritual blindness instead of willful blindness?

2. Some believe that putting any focus or study on demons is being spiritually negative. What are your thoughts?

3. Do you recognize the characteristics of Belial, Leviathan, Mammon or Jezebel in your family?

4. Do you recognize the characteristics of Belial, Leviathan, Mammon or Jezebel in your city?

5. Have you ever failed to discern your spiritual enemy and suffered the consequences?

8

What to Do with the Things You Discern

I was on a relaxing vacation with my family when I began to discern a spiritual problem in connection with our upcoming Sunday service. My husband was ministering out of town, which meant that I would be speaking at our home church during the morning services in his absence. I felt anxious and uptight. It began as a gnawing feeling in my gut, which just grew stronger and stronger. I also kept seeing a young man in my mind's eye. This young man was new to our church and was already showing signs of trouble. He claimed to hear God and be prophetic, but he was really overly spiritual and boundaryless. I don't believe he was being led by the Holy Spirit nearly as much as he claimed. And our security team and I had already rebuked him a few times for getting out of hand. The thought that came to me over and over was, *He's going to do something*. Only I did not know what he was going to do.

That Sunday morning, I could not relax at all. I did pray about the situation, but I could not get a grip on it in my emotions. I had become consumed with the thought that this young man was coming to the service to do something disruptive. As I walked from the parking lot into the back room behind the sanctuary, I instructed our security team to be on alert and told them why. As the worship service began, I looked around, and the young man was not even there. Had I made a mistake? Was I falsely discerning something? About twenty minutes later, the young man finally appeared and made his way to the very front of the church with arms wide open, dancing wildly in exuberant worship.

This is where I began to encounter overwhelming discernment. Again, overwhelming discernment is when the feelings associated with this gift negatively control you, instead of prompting you to lead out in a mature response to whatever you have discerned. I turned to my left and spoke to our associate pastor: "I need you to take that man out of here right now!"

Keep in mind that I had nothing tangible to justify my reaction; I only had a strong, overwhelming feeling. And then things got very strange. As I spoke this to our associate pastor, again overreacting and not leading in this properly, I lit up with several hundred tiny, moving lights. These little lights moved all around me, up and down and around my person. They reminded me of the lights you would use on a Christmas tree. Our associate pastor pointed his finger at me and said, "Angels! You've got angels!"

At the same time, another young man standing in my row dramatically lifted his arms and threw his head back in worship to God, as if he had made a sudden and deep spiritual connection. He did not cause a disruption, but I believe he did this spontaneously, in response to the presence of angels.

Right when I lit up with all those lights, the young man in question, whom I had been feeling anxious about, leapt onto our platform, dancing wildly right next to our worship leader. She bravely kept leading worship while he gyrated and intermittently stared in arrogance at the congregation. My associate pastor and our security team responded instantly, escorting him off the platform and into the lobby to sort out the situation. When that happened, I stopped glowing and was able to preach and minister as if nothing had happened. The peace of God really took over.

To distinguish effectively between spirits, we have to remember that this gift is a sensory process before it is an intellectual one. "But solid food is for the mature, who because of practice have their senses trained to discern good and evil" (Hebrews 5:14 NASB). The Holy Spirit causes us to discern good and evil through our physical senses—our eyes, ears, smell, taste and touch, as well as through our emotions. Mature believers, through community and accountability, have learned through practice how to sort out accurately what they are sensing so they can respond to the information appropriately.

In hindsight, what I was discerning about the young man was accurate. My response, however, could have been better. I could tell by the activity of the angels around me that I was dealing with something very satanic that was happening with him. Still, I should not have insisted that this young man be escorted from the service without any evidence, even though he did, in my best observation, manifest demonically on the platform of our church. As disruptive as that was, there was no gun, no violence or anything else to prove that I should have had him removed from the service prematurely. This incident, at least, gave us one more window of opportunity to minister some prayers for deliverance to him, as well as to warn him sternly. What I was experiencing was overwhelming discernment, which can lead to an overreactive response. Overwhelming discernment is not wrong in itself to have, but it is our response to accurately discerned information that makes it either right or wrong. We need to learn from these situations so we can manage our responses better.

What Do I Do?

What do I do with negative information about people? This is one of the top questions I receive from those wanting to know about the gift of discerning of spirits. How do you handle negative information that you discern? The gift of discerning of spirits is a truth-telling gift and a gatekeeping gift. You will supernaturally discern both good and evil. We usually know what to do with the good, but what do we do when we discern evil in people?

The Bible gives us a remedy: "And this I pray, that your love may abound still more and more in knowledge and all discernment" (Philippians 1:9 NKJV). This verse instructs us that love needs to be balanced with discernment, and discernment needs to be balanced with love. This is where we experience true tension. When you have discerned that a deceptive or possessed person has come into your life or your church, what, then, does love look like?

1. Pray redemptively

When you discern by the Holy Spirit something negative about another person, remember that God just told you a secret. Secrets remain in the secret place—meaning between just you and God in prayer—unless God gives you permission otherwise. Remember that God loves that person, even if he or she is demonized, struggling or wicked. There will be times you are called on to deal with the situation more openly, but prayer is usually all that is required of you.

When we pray, then, we are to pray redemptively. Discerning the negative about someone can be disappointing, shocking and sometimes terrifying. To be redemptive means to save someone from error or evil. This means we don't condemn a person in prayer, but instead, we advocate for the person's salvation and deliverance. This can be difficult to do, especially when we have discerned terrible evil in someone. Instead of condemnation, we begin to call out the person's name before the Lord for salvation and/or deliverance. We bind Satan from blinding the person's eyes to the truth, and then, if he or she needs salvation, we ask God to release laborers into this person's path who will present the Gospel of Jesus Christ (see Matthew 9:38). We then continue to pray until the burden of prayer lifts.

Years ago, I was invited to teach and equip on prayer at another church. Something did not feel quite right, yet I knew the Holy Spirit was telling me to go. A week before the prayer conference, I received a call from the senior pastor there. He shared with me that his wife had been caught in a very scandalous kind of affair. At her husband's urging and to my surprise, she received my invitation for lunch to discuss the matter while I was there. When we met, she was honest and seemed repentant, but still, I discerned two hidden spiritual strongholds. They were rage and a spirit of religion. I discerned these strongholds in my emotions as distinct, lingering feelings that I knew were not mine, but hers. I had also left the door open for her to call and talk if needed, knowing by the Holy Spirit that their marriage would not make it.

I admit that I was very concerned for her soul at this point, but I just kept the matter private and in prayer. I also attempted to follow up by phone with her a few times after I returned home. When the divorce happened, I received a strange message from her husband, who insisted that I cut off communication with her. She had continued the adultery, and he was "turning her over to Satan" (see 1 Corinthians 5:5). That means he planned to exercise his spiritual authority as an apostle and remove her spiritual protection from her so she would be subjected to physical destruction. (By the way, that is a very extreme move and one of last resort. I don't know of anyone who has done it besides this man, or at least done it successfully, and I have only read of it being done just once, by the apostle Paul.) When I did not comply, he cut off communication with me, too.

I am not justifying or excusing her sin for one moment, but I did connect the dots as to the root of her rage. She was reacting to a spirit of religion that had been controlling her through her husband. Religion always tries to kill you when it cannot control you. Still, both husband and wife needed me to pray for them, and to pray redemptively, without reacting to their negative behavior and spiritual conditions.

During a ministry event, Jorge (not his real name) was praying in a side room for one of the conference speakers while the speaker ministered to the conference attendees. As he prayed, mostly in his prayer language, he encountered a sudden jolt within himself. Through this jolt he discerned that the speaker was ill, and not just with a flu or cold, but with something more serious. Jorge was then compelled to call out the speaker's name before the Lord, weeping and crying, declaring the Bible promises about healing for him. He also rebuked the spirit of infirmity several times and commanded it to leave the speaker's body (see Luke 13:10–13 NKJV).

After the conference was over, the speaker shared privately with Jorge about his physical condition. "God already knew he was struggling," Jorge said. "He allowed me to discern it through that strange jolting feeling so I could sustain him in prayer."

Jill, an accountant, encountered a problem at work when a man with an evil spirit walked into her office complex. "First, I felt the hairs on my arm go up," she said. "I knew by this physical sensation that he had an evil spirit."

Jill then described his behavior as gruff, mean and terse, and she knew that whatever business he came in for was not going to go well. Jill began to pray under her breath for the situation, asking for God's intervention.

"The man noticeably softened," she said. "I discerned the problem and then prayer fixed it. I thank God for that!"

2. Know when to address what you discern

When you discern something negative in another person, love not only considers the individual with the spiritual problem and/ or evil agenda, but also the impact of that individual on others. In these situations, you might need to do more than just pray. You might need to act on the information you have spiritually discerned. How you address such matters will depend on your level of authority in the situation, as well as the context of the situation and the relationship you have with the individual.

Many times, wives or husbands have identified by the Holy Spirit a person with an adulterous spirit who is getting too close to their spouse. Then they appropriately and privately raise the red flag to one another. Dads and moms, too, have discerned predatory friendships and romantic relationships getting too close to their underage children. Good parents pay attention to their spiritual discernment and will put up the proper boundaries when needed.

Leaders of organizations or churches will often exercise their spiritual discernment in ways that take into account the strength and maturity of those they lead. It is true that mature organizations and churches can much better navigate dealing with people who have come in with evil, demonic agendas. The mature will show more love, patience and spiritual authority when dealing with such people than the newer and less mature can show. Mature leaders also will wait for evidence to substantiate what they spiritually discern when it happens to be negative. They don't overreact, label or mistreat people because of their discernment, although they will proceed with caution. Like King Solomon, they know how to surface those hidden agendas and motives in people wisely and lovingly (see 1 Kings 3:16–28). They can lead or pastor an individual through a situation without compromising the entire organization in the process.

If you are not the leader of an organization or a church, but you have spiritually discerned something negative, don't be quick to point it out until you have truly spent time praying redemptively about it. If the matter you are discerning does not leave you or lift off you, it might be appropriate to mention it to whoever is leading, but that all depends on the mindset of that leader and the urgency of the matter you are discerning. Keep in mind that unless leaders really know and trust you spiritually, they most likely will not receive what you have "discerned" because (1) they don't agree; (2) it is the first time they have heard it and they need confirmation and tangible evidence; or (3) they already know it, but it is delicate and they cannot let on that they agree with you. For that reason, more often than not, you will just need to keep the matter in prayer and not speak into it. If you do say something, check your motives first. If you are insecure or spiritually prideful, you might be expecting personal validation from the leader for what you have discerned. Instead, you need to leave it in God's hands and not make the situation personal.

Taylor Bergthold can see and discern a spirit of fear in the people she interacts with on a friendship level, as well as in her role as a pastor's assistant at our church. A spirit of fear, by the way, is a demon and is mentioned in 2 Timothy 1:7 (NKJV): "For God has not given us a spirit of fear, but of power and of love and of a sound mind." Taylor explained how she could see this spirit at times behind people's words. "It can look like insecurity and half-truths, but it's really a spirit of fear," she said.

When this happens, Taylor prays bold prayers for such people in the privacy of her own home. She prays for their emotional healing and also casts the spirit of fear off them.

"Sometimes the Holy Spirit will then nudge me to go talk about it in a conversational, nonthreatening way," she added.

Taylor has seen noticeable change in people when she has done this.

One of our worship leaders, Joshua Vera, was leading worship at a prayer gathering when he spiritually discerned a heavy demonic presence on a young man in the room. The young man was new to their prayer gathering, having been invited by one of their regularly attending intercessors. Joshua was troubled by what he was discerning, mostly because he could not distinguish what it was.

The leaders of the prayer gathering, including Joshua, also brought the issue to one another's attention. They, too, discerned the deep spiritual issue with this person, actually distinguishing it as a homosexual spirit. They decided then to watch and wait for an opportunity to minister to him. Through the gift of discerning of spirits, Joshua and the leadership team were armed and ready to bring counsel and deliverance to the young man, if it came to that.

"We finally did get to pray for him and minister to him," Joshua said. "We only scratched the surface, though, and could not get to the real issue."

I, too, have spiritually discerned negative things about people. One instance in particular involved the theft of some equipment at our church. We had some technical equipment stolen, and the items taken were from places around the building that just happened to be "off camera." In other words, the person who stole the items knew the location of our cameras and was careful not to be seen on video. This caused us to suspect the theft was an inside job. One Saturday afternoon, I came to the church and then walked into the lobby of the sanctuary. While driving just moments prior, I had had a vision that was strong and very clear. In the vision, I saw the face of one of our employees, and this employee said to me in anger, "I'm going to get back at all of you!"

When I walked into the lobby of the church, that same employee just happened to be exiting the sanctuary, even though this person was not on the schedule to work. Here I had spiritually discerned by the Holy Spirit the secret motive of the person's heart. Now, armed with that information, I secretly texted our facility director and requested that someone check all of our equipment, doors, alarms and the like. Sure enough, there was a side door from the sanctuary to the outside that had been left ajar. And later, as you may have guessed, the employee was released from his or her position.

3. Discern the difference between a broken person and an apostate

The Bible instructs us to show hospitality to strangers because they might actually be angels and not mere men (see Hebrews 13:2). Angels can and do appear in the likeness of men. If angels can appear like men, is it possible for a demon to do the same? We already know from the Word and from testimony that a demon can masquerade as an angel of God (see 2 Corinthians 11:14), which, again, is why we need the gift of discerning of spirits and need to know how to test the spirits.

Although I have suspected it once or twice, I cannot say that I have knowingly encountered a person who was a demon in disguise. I can say that I believe I have dealt with persons who are what the Bible refers to as "twice dead" (Jude 12–13). This means they have become apostates of Christ. They have denied and disowned Jesus, and I believe they have thus forfeited their eternal home in heaven. Jude describes these individuals as "blemishes at your love feasts, eating with you without the slightest qualm" and "without fruit and uprooted" and "wandering stars, for whom blackest darkness has been reserved forever" (verses 12–13).

This is always a touchy subject for believers who have struggled in their faith and might be wondering, *Could this possibly be me?* If you have even asked that question and if you care about the answer at all, then I assure you that this is not your story. And remember the apostle Peter's dilemma. Peter denied Christ three times, but his denial was considered a crisis of faith and nothing more. Furthermore, his restoration as an apostle and preacher of the Gospel was evidence that he had never really left Christ in his heart. A twice-dead apostate, on the other hand, no longer cares. Such apostates literally have no conviction of sin, yet strangely, they still like to attach themselves to Christians and church gatherings.

My point is that most people whom we have spiritually discerned as deceptive or as having specific spirits driving them are truly broken people in need of salvation and/or deliverance. As much as I lean toward being redemptive in all situations, this gift will reveal the broken people from the apostates, so you can respond appropriately. We don't treat these two the same. One you will minister to, and the other you will need to remove from your circle or church fellowship.

Let me give you a few examples to help explain the difference. I was ministering at a church one Sunday morning, and as I began to pray before the congregation, I felt the presence of a witch in the room. What is interesting is that I had been at this church before, attending a conference, and the guest minister also sensed the presence of a witch in attendance and even addressed it. When I began to minister several months later, I had honestly forgotten that incident, but I really did discern in my spirit a person in attendance who was involved in full-on witchcraft. How, then, do you handle such a thing? It is very disturbing to most people, as you and I both know that a witch is most likely there on demonic assignment.

In that situation, I felt the leading of the Holy Spirit to say something like this: "For the person in the room who is practicing witchcraft, and you are here on assignment from Satan for this meeting today, I want you to know that Jesus loves you." I then began to reveal specific details about this person's life and past, why he or she got involved in witchcraft, and some more prophetic words that revealed the love of Jesus to the person. I also said, "I'm glad you are here! I believe God is going to meet you powerfully today."

I left it at that, knowing this witch was a broken person who really needed salvation, deliverance and personal ministry. Based on what the Holy Spirit was leading me to say, this person was not an apostate, but someone still capable of receiving conviction unto repentance.

Only once have I knowingly experienced a person—a self-proclaimed minister, actually—who I believe fit in the category of an apostate. Although I do not believe he was a demon in disguise, I do believe he was definitely an apostate fully given to Satan for his use. Within just a few months of meeting this person, I had such a rebellion in my spirit against him that I knew I was dealing with something I had never dealt with before. I even called out this person's sins prophetically by the Holy Spirit right in front of him, something I have never done to someone before or since. Remember, these are people who in their current state are unable to repent, because they no longer respond to the conviction of the Holy Spirit. They are sinful and divisive, pretending to have visions, dreams and angelic revelations, yet there is no real fruit in their lives. They also can and do carry spiritual power, performing false signs and wonders, because they have been empowered by Satan to deceive.

Sadly, this person has conducted scheme after scheme for years to steal money from his parishioners, other ministers and some very naïve ministerial organizations. There have been lawsuits but no arrests, with sinister and targeted persecution of those who have confronted him and called him out on his schemes. Because this person has wreaked havoc with far too many people and churches, he has since been removed and forbidden from many gatherings of believers. Yet he still continues his schemes wherever he finds an open door, namely in those not yet able to distinguish between a broken person and an apostate. A broken person and an apostate can look the same, but the gift of discerning of spirits will reveal the truth.

4. Learn from your mistakes

As we have seen from Hebrews 5:14, there is a connection between maturity and discerning well. I quoted this verse at the beginning of the chapter, but let's look at it again: "But solid food is for the mature, who because of practice have their senses trained to discern good and evil" (NASB). We learn to discern through practice, which implies learning by trial and error, along with a heavy dose of humility.

I have an awesome husband. He is faithful, steady, funny and always reliable. With that said, I have never been suspicious of him or his whereabouts, and I have never doubted his marital faithfulness to me. There was one day, however, when I began to struggle in this area after noticing a change on my husband's calendar. He had canceled his afternoon appointments, but could not be located at the office or at home. Within a very short time frame, I experienced overwhelming feelings of jealousy that turned to panic and then desperation. These were feelings that came out of nowhere. I was discerning something, but it had turned into overwhelming discernment, and I was losing control. I finally got the courage to send my husband a text message, just to ask him casually where he was and what he was doing.

I thought I was being calm, but my husband could tell by the tone of my text that I was upset about something. He replied, "Why?"

I explained my mysterious feelings of jealousy and then justified them with his sudden absence and canceled appointments. I know he was laughing when he did this, but he texted only a one-word explanation: "Envy."

I shot-texted back, "I know! Now where are you?"

He then sent me a picture of a receipt stamped with the date and time from the store he had just finished shopping in. Can you guess the name of the store? "Envy." I was having strong feelings of envy while my husband shopped in a store named "Envy"!

These were the moments that left me shaking my head and begging the Lord for help. I can laugh now, but it was one of many alarming experiences along this journey of learning how to walk out the gift of discerning of spirits. It is true that this gift can feel as if you have a loaded gun and you are firing it without knowing where the target is. Sometimes you don't even know you are firing the gun! When you are unfamiliar with the operation of this gift and are still learning how it flows through you, it can be quite disturbing and sometimes scary. I was receiving real information from the Holy Spirit about my husband, but I did not know how to process it. I then began walking down the road of false accusation, based on what I was feeling. On top of it, I did not realize there was something supernatural going on. Without consulting the Holy Spirit, strong feelings from nowhere began to drive my emotions, and I did not know how to pull out of it. I learned a good lesson that day about the gift of discerning of spirits. Now that I can recognize overwhelming discernment, I have learned to stop and process these extreme and sudden emotions with the Lord and with other mature Christians to get needed clarity on them. I still experience overwhelming discernment on occasion, but now I know what I am dealing with, and I have learned to wait and not overreact.

Recently, a woman was complaining to me that other people, especially leaders, were not receiving her gift of discerning of spirits as valid. She was a sincere woman, very thoughtful, and came across to me as compassionate about the plight of others. She then decided to share with me some things she was discerning. What she shared was very negative about someone in my church, as well as about a guest to our church. On top of it, she used highly spiritual, almost cryptic language to describe what she believed she was discerning.

This is a classic example of a person who still needs to practice her gift in a mature community of believers before she launches out in it. We can learn from her struggle, however. First of all, she had no investment in the persons she discerned as having deep spiritual issues. As a leader, I don't entertain such things from outsiders, largely because they have no investment and they don't carry my heart. Their "discernment" is suspect in its source for those reasons.

Secondly, using overly spiritual language does not give us credibility with others. We have to speak plainly and use words that people can understand. This woman used a lot of New Age–sounding words and made reference to some demons that most people don't ever talk about. I am actually versed in those terms and phrases, only because I work with so many who have come out of New Age and pagan communities and into Christianity. I have learned their language, so I can be a bridge to start teaching them mine. Still, we have to communicate points of discernment in plain language, which is easier said than done and takes a lot of practice.

Was anything this woman negatively discerned accurate? Yes! She had a few points of accuracy. On those points, I did lead her in prayer to close some spiritual doors to possible demonic activity. My hope for her is that she will feel safe enough to begin dialoguing through her discernment and get the coaching that she needs in it.

A Word to the Wise

As I conclude this book, I sense such a strong burden to urge you and the Body of Christ not to let this gift of discerning of spirits become diluted, misapplied and misused, or counterfeited. God is releasing this book at this time because of what He is doing in the earth. He is giving us the ability to discern through our senses like never before, because as things get darker and darker in the earth, His Church becomes more and more glorious. We cannot become that glorious Church if we continue to remain blind and deceived regarding spiritual realities. The gift of discerning of spirits is God's way of raising the standard in His Church so that we can victoriously rise above dark deception and successfully navigate what is to come.

You are going to see many books and much training on this subject in the coming days. There will be new books and training from mature and credible leaders who are road tested in this gift. There will also be a rekindling and increased demand for strong deliverance ministry, even in churches that seem more conservative. This gift will be a lead agent for making deliverance ministry more effective than ever.

You will also see a counterfeit of this gift offered to you and others by Satan himself. It will be a perversion of the gift that is more self-centered than God-centered. It will be presented as spiritually opportunistic for personal and even materialistic gain. This counterfeit will downplay the demonic and ignore our mandate to set the captives free. It will appear highly spiritual, but will arrogantly reject the truth and liberate no one. When the counterfeit comes, don't take the bait!

The gift of discerning of spirits comes with a price tag for its revelation. It requires that those who have it be selfless to the core and be co-laborers with Christ's agenda to establish His Kingdom on the earth. As much as I have struggled to walk this gift out successfully, I would not trade the results for anything. I have seen people, places and churches become powerfully liberated largely because of how this gift has operated in me and in others. Are you ready to pay the price for the powerful revelation that this gift offers? I pray that you do. It will be well worth it.

Kingdom Principles

1. We usually know what to do with the good, but what do we do when we discern evil in people?

2. When you discern by the Holy Spirit something about another person, remember that God has just told you a secret. Secrets remain in the secret place, meaning between just you and God in prayer, unless God gives you permission otherwise.

3. Philippians 1:9 instructs us that love needs to be balanced with discernment, and discernment needs to be balanced with love.

4. When you discern something negative in an individual, love not only considers the individual with the spiritual problem and/or evil agenda, but also the impact of that individual on others. A mature leader can pastor that individual through the situation without compromising an entire organization in the process.

5. Hebrews 5:14 shows us that there is a connection between maturity and discerning well. We learn to discern through practice, which implies learning by trial and error and having a heavy dose of humility.

Thoughts for Reflection

1. When you have discerned that a deceptive or possessed person has come into your life or into your church, what, then, does love look like?

2. Are you able to pray discreetly and redemptively for others, even when you have discerned something evil in them?

3. Have you ever communicated something you have discerned to a leader, only to have it rebuffed? Why do you think that happened? What could you have done differently?

4. Have you ever made a mistake in what you have discerned? What did you learn through that experience?

5. Are you practicing this gift in a faith community? Why or why not?

Appendix

Can a Christian
Be Demon Possessed?

As a new Christian, I underwent a very serious deliverance from spiritual bondage in direct connection to my occult past. As I mentioned in chapter 1, a woman at a weekly house prayer meeting I was attending saw a spirit of sorcery standing over me. As soon as she expressed that, something picked me up and threw me against the wall. Next, I went into a grand mal demonic manifestation. I wrote about this incident in more detail in my book *The Intercessors Handbook* (Chosen, 2016), but what happened to me at this prayer meeting was challenging to my pastor and to others in my church. They believed that Christians could not manifest demonically if they truly had the Holy Spirit.

I did have the Holy Spirit, but I still manifested demonically, as those areas of occultism had to be firmly addressed and dealt with. The good news is, I found my spiritual authority in Christ during that season and learned to walk out my freedom.

Since then, I have encountered Christian after Christian needing various levels of deliverance such as what I needed. After hearing my testimony of deliverance, Kyra (not her real name) came forward at the end of a church service to receive ministry from our altar team. She could barely walk forward, however, before she fell to the ground in a strong demonic manifestation. Keep in mind that Kyra is a Christian woman. She has accepted Jesus into her heart, and she has been baptized in the Holy Spirit. Still, she manifested demonically and, like me, needed deliverance from her occult past, her issues being caused by satanic ritual abuse as a child.

With that said, it is a huge myth to believe that Christians cannot be demonized. Notice, however, that I use the word *demonized* and not the word *possessed*. This is where most of our confusion has come from. We have confused *possession* with *demonization*, and they are two different things. The late Derek Prince explained his objection to the use of the description *demon possessed* in certain passages of the Bible, claiming it is a mistranslation, such as in this passage: "That evening after sunset the people brought to Jesus all the sick and demon-possessed" (Mark 1:32).

"The word possessed suggests ownership . . . by a demon," Prince said. "Now I don't believe that any born-again, sincere Christian can be owned by a demon . . . but the Greek word that's used can easily be, and should be, translated demonized."[1]

He went on to explain that many born-again Christians are still demonized. He said there are areas in their personality where the Holy Spirit is not yet in complete control because there is a demon that has to be dealt with.

John Eckhardt, overseer of Crusaders Church Chicago, wrote something similar in an article for *Charisma* magazine:

> The word "possessed" is an unfortunate translation because it connotes ownership, and we know that the devil cannot own

a Christian—that is, have complete control of him. But in the Bible, there is no real distinction between being possessed and being oppressed, digressed, suppressed, obsessed and so forth. All these terms mean that a person is, to some degree, under the influence of a demon.[2]

The question remains, then, How much of a Christian can a demon possibly possess? In examining this, we need to recognize that we are all made up of three parts: spirit, soul and body. When Jesus comes into your life, He comes into your spirit and takes up residence. Paul wrote to the Galatians, "I have been crucified with Christ and I no longer live, but Christ lives in me" (Galatians 2:20). I believe Charles H. Kraft, president and founder of Deep Healing Ministries, says it best: "A demon cannot live in the Christian's spirit—that is, the person's central core, the part that died when Adam sinned, because Jesus now lives there."[3]

So, then, how does a person know if he or she is under the influence of demons or not? I admit discussions like this can make people doubt their spiritual condition if they are not strong in the written Word and don't know who they are in Christ. It can also leave us with the impression that deliverance from demons will always be a big fight. The truth—and I hope this gives you reasonable assurance—is that demons will only do what we have allowed them to do. The disciples, too, discovered this when they ministered, and then told Jesus, "Lord, even the demons submit to us in your name" (Luke 10:17).

More often than not, I have known Christians to be delivered with minimal manifestation from spirits in their soul such as rejection, fear, self-hatred, lust, torment and so forth after they repent, renounce whatever it is, and command the spirit to go. If there is a manifestation, there might be a sigh, a cough, a shake or a twitch when the spirit leaves them, which is a signal that they are free of it. Still, there will be other believers who will have a much stronger manifestation, and we need to be prepared for that without making it a formula for deliverance. Derek Prince, for example, shared about his miraculous healing from bladder cancer. When hands were laid on him for healing, he felt a distinct spiritual battle inside himself, like two cats fighting with one another. He then let out a long, sustained "roar" and was perfectly healed from the spirit of cancer.

Does this reassure you as much as it reassures me? The truth is that you and I are possessed, in a sense, upon our confession of Christ—only not by a demon. The Holy Spirit has possessed us—the Spirit of Christ, who lives and dwells in our born-again spirit. As far as the rest of us, meaning our soul and our body, these are the areas that can come under the influence of demons that have to be expelled. Still, I am confident in the power of God to overcome any such negative influence, should it come, knowing that the greater One lives and dwells inside us (see 1 John 4:4). We will always have a sure remedy in the Holy Spirit.

Notes

Chapter 1: Seeing Both Sides of the Supernatural

1. *MOUNCE Concise Greek-English Dictionary of the New Testament*, s.v. "*symphērō*," BibleGateway, https://www.biblegateway.com/passage/?search=i+cor +12%3A7&version=MOUNCE.

Chapter 2: The Gift of Discerning of Spirits

1. For more on this spirit's identity as a python spirit, see Bible Hub's online commentaries on Acts 16:16, http://biblehub.com/commentaries/acts/16-16.htm.

2. Francis Frangipane, *Discerning of Spirits* (Cedar Rapids, Iowa: Arrow Publications, 2011), Kindle edition, chapter 1.

Chapter 3: The Fundamentals of Distinguishing between Spirits

1. James and Michal Ann Goll, *Angelic Encounters: Engaging Help from Heaven* (Lake Mary, Fla.: Charisma House, 2007), Kindle edition, chapter 9.

2. *Frisbee: Life and Death of a Hippie Preacher*, directed by David Di Sabatino (Passion River, 2008), DVD.

Chapter 4: Discerning Spiritual Atmospheres

1. Dictionary.com definitions, s.v. "atmosphere," http://www.dictionary.com /browse/atmosphere.

2. Helen Calder, *Unlocking the Gift of Discernment* (Victoria, Australia: David McCracken Ministries, 2011), Google Play ebook, chapter 1.

3. Blue Letter Bible Lexicon: Strong's H8104, s.v. "*shamar*," https://www .blueletterbible.org/lang/Lexicon/Lexicon.cfm?strongs=H8104&t=KJV.

4. Cindy Jacobs, *Possessing the Gates of the Enemy: A Training Manual for Militant Intercession* (Grand Rapids, Mich.: Chosen Books, 1994), 223.

5. Botho Molosankwe, "Sign Language 'Fake' Blames Illness," *IOL News* online, December 12, 2013, http://www.iol.co.za/news/south-africa/gauteng/sign -language-fake-blames-illness-1621044#.UqmmlCfuxy8.

6. Greg Myre, "Mandela Sign Language Interpreter Says He Had Schizophrenic Episode," *The Two-Way: Breaking News from NPR*, December 12, 2013, http://www.npr.org/sections/thetwo-way/2013/12/12/250409375/mandela -sign-language-interpreter-says-he-had-schizophrenic-episode.

7. Perry Stone, "5 Steps to Change the Spiritual Atmosphere in Your Home," *Charisma* online, December 4, 2014, http://www.charismamag.com/spirit /spiritual-warfare/21558-how-to-change-the-atmosphere-in-your-home.

8. As told in Jacobs, *Possessing the Gates*, 175–76.

Chapter 6: Discerning the Angels

1. James and Michal Ann Goll, *Angelic Encounters: Engaging Help from Heaven* (Lake Mary, Fla.: Charisma House, 2007), Kindle edition, chapter 4.

2. Blue Letter Bible Lexicon: Strong's 4397, s.v. "*mal'ak*," https://www.blueletter bible.org/lang/lexicon/lexicon.cfm?t=kjv&strongs=h4397.

3. I give a very thorough explanation of this concept and its parameters in chapter 6 of my other book, *The Intercessors Handbook: How to Pray with Boldness, Authority and Supernatural Power* (Chosen, 2016).

4. Ian Carroll, *As It Is in Heaven: Seven Core Values of a Revival Culture* (Oak Park, Ill.: Ian Carroll Ministries, 2016), 78.

5. Paul Cox, *Unwrap the Gifts: Receive Your Spiritual Inheritance Through Prayer Ministry* (Lake Mary, Fla.: Creation House, 2008), Kindle edition, chapter 1.

6. For more on this, visit https://en.wikipedia.org/wiki/Joseph_Smith.

Chapter 7: Discerning the Powers and Principalities

1. Dave Williams, *Skill for Battle: The Art of Spiritual Warfare* (Lansing, Mich.: Decapolis, 2011), Kindle edition, chapter 9.

2. I mention these in more detail in my book *The Intercessors Handbook: How to Pray with Boldness, Authority and Supernatural Power* (Chosen, 2016), but my source for the Greek was Tom White, *The Believer's Guide to Spiritual Warfare* (Minneapolis: Chosen, 2011), 55.

3. "Robert Morris: Breaking the Spirit of Mammon," The Blessed Life video, January 5, 2017, http://www.theblessedlife.com/series/blessed-life/episode/breaking -spirit-mammon.

4. Bible Study Tools Dictionary, s.v. "Mammon," http://www.biblestudytools .com/dictionary/mammon/.

5. Ibid., s.v. "Babylon," http://www.biblestudytools.com/dictionary/babylon/.

6. Dave Williams, *The Road to Radical Riches: You Are Destined for Outrageous Wealth* (Lansing, Mich.: Decapolis, 2000), 65–66.

Appendix: Can a Christian Be Demon Possessed?

1. "Derek Prince: War on Earth," YouTube video, 10:10, posted by Filip Peoski, September 8, 2008. https://www.youtube.com/watch?v=3fUeDuPtrz4.

2. John Eckhardt, "Can a Christian Have a Demon?", *Charisma* online, August 22, 2015 (originally appearing in the March 2003 issue of the magazine), http://www.charismamag.com/anniversary/pages-from-our-past/24188-john-eckhardt-can-a-christian-have-a-demon.

3. Charles H. Kraft, *Defeating Dark Angels: Breaking Demonic Oppression in the Believer's Life* (Minneapolis: Chosen, 2016), Kindle edition, chapter 2 (Myth 1).

Jennifer Eivaz is a minister and international conference speaker who carries the wisdom and fire of the Holy Spirit. She presently serves as an executive pastor with Harvest Christian Center (HCC) in Turlock, California, and is passionate about teaching and activating the Body of Christ for intercession and hearing the voice of God. Jennifer's teaching style is authentic and aimed at the heart. She believes it is time for a balanced, biblical teaching on the gift of discerning of spirits, including how the gift is to be used and not used, and how it is profitable not only in the person's life who is gifted, but in the lives of those around that person, and in cities and nations. Jennifer is a graduate of Oral Roberts University in Tulsa, Oklahoma. She is married to HCC's senior pastor, Ron Eivaz, and they have two children.

To find out more about Jennifer and her ministry, you can visit her online:

Website: www.jennifereivaz.com
Blog: www.jennifereivazblog.com
Facebook: www.facebook.com/jennifereivaz/
Twitter, Periscope and Instagram: @PrayingProphet

Harvest Christian Center
225 Fourth St.
Turlock, CA 95380
www.harvestturlock.org

More from Jennifer Eivaz!

Visit jennifereivaz.com for a full list of her books.

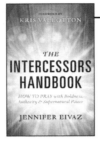

Using biblical principles and her own experiences of spiritual breakthrough, Jennifer Eivaz offers a practical guide to effective supernatural prayer. You'll discover how to shift your practical needs to the spiritual realm, take hold of your authority and pray in a way that makes a difference. Take your prayers to the places where the real battle is happening—and experience the victory and results you've been seeking.

The Intercessors Handbook

"A challenging and practical book that is much needed for the Church. It is a map of how to pray, igniting within us a passion to embrace the journey of prayer that is the privilege and responsibility of every believer."
—*Banning Liebscher, founder and pastor,*
Jesus Culture

"What Jennifer explains is easy to grasp, yet profound when put into application."
—*Steve Shultz, founder,* The Elijah List

✓Chosen

 Stay up to date on your favorite books and authors with our free e-newsletters. Sign up today at chosenbooks.com.

 Find us on Facebook. facebook.com/chosenbooks

 Follow us on Twitter. @Chosen_Books